Best of the Best

MOUNTAIN WEST

Cookbook

Selected Recipes from the
Favorite Cookbooks of
COLORADO, UTAH, and NEVADA

K. LEE, WIKIPEDIA.ORG

Rocky Mountain National Park encompasses approximately 265,770 acres in Colorado's northern Front Range of the Rockies. Located northwest of Boulder, the park contains 359 miles of trails, 150 lakes, and 450 miles of streams, and over 60 named peaks higher than 12,000 feet. The Continental Divide and the headwaters of the Colorado River are also located in the park.

Best of the Best from the

MOUNTAIN WEST

Cookbook

Selected Recipes from the
Favorite Cookbooks of
COLORADO, UTAH, and NEVADA

EDITED BY

Gwen McKee

AND

Barbara Moseley

QUAIL RIDGE PRESS

Preserving America's Food Heritage

Library of Congress Cataloging-in-Publication Data
Best of the best from the Mountain West cookbook : selected recipes from
   the favorite cookbooks of Colorado, Utah, and Nevada / edited by
   Gwen McKee and Barbara Moseley. — 1st ed.
      p. cm.
   ISBN-13: 978-1-934193-37-2
   ISBN-10: 1-934193-37-2
      1. Cookery, American. 2. Cookery–Rocky Mountains. I. McKee,
   Gwen II. Moseley, Barbara.
   TX715.B4856166 2011
   641.5978–dc22   2010022152

ISBN-13: 978–1-934193-37-2 • ISBN-10: 1-934193-37-2
Book design by Cyndi Clark
Cover photo by Greg Campbell • Illustrated by Tupper England

Printed in Canada
First edition, January 2011

On the cover: Marinated Grilled Flank Steak, page 141 and
Cattlemen's Club Twice-Baked Potatoes, page 106

QUAIL RIDGE PRESS
P. O. Box 123 • Brandon, MS 39043
info@quailridge.com • www.quailridge.com

Contents

PHOTO BY JAN MARIE ALBERT

Named after the Mormon pioneer Ebenezer Bryce, Bryce Canyon in southwestern Utah became a national park in 1928. An 18-mile scenic drive culminates at Rainbow Point, the highest part of the park at 9,105 feet, offering panoramic views approaching 200 miles of visibility.

Quest for the Best Regional Cooking

The Mountain West states of Colorado, Utah, and Nevada have so many fascinating places and facts and history that it was absolutely an adventure finding out about the territory as well as their cooking. "America the Beautiful" was written atop one of Colorado's most famous mountains, Pikes Peak. In Salt Lake City, you can be sweltering by the Great Salt Lake in June, and forty minutes later be in snow at Snowbird Resort in the Wasatch Range of the Rocky Mountains. In Nevada, Las Vegas doesn't hold all the glitter—there's silver and gold in them thar hills, and turquoise and opals, too. And for sure, you can also rustle up some mighty good meals everywhere you go.

Chuck wagon food of sourdough biscuits and beef stews, Dutch oven fare, and miners' pasties are historical to this region and still enjoyed. Basque sheep herders from the Pyrenees Mountains of Spain and France migrated to Nevada, and brought their food culture and cooking methods for beef, lamb, chorizo, soup, beans, bread, flan, etc. The recipe titles let you know you are in for a treat: Spicy Bean and Beef Bake, Sloppy Joe Biscuit Bake, Silver State Beef Short Ribs, Dancing Palomino Spice Cake, etc. There are also recipes from restaurants and notables that are so exceptional you will want to get out the white tablecloth.

Traveling to every state in the United States in search of the best cookbooks and recipes took Barbara and me the better part of 27 years. What started in our home state of Mississippi with one cookbook, grew to include our neighboring states, then as each one neared completion, we reached out farther and farther away from home to explore the cuisines of states far and wide. The experience has been one that has enabled us to bring home each new state's recipes to become ours forever.

But nothing seems so special and dear as when you share it with others who you know will enjoy it as much as you do. Our BEST OF THE BEST STATE COOKBOOKS feature chosen favorite recipes that we are proud to have brought from each state home to you, wherever you are. I wish we could introduce you to the many people we have met

in every state who were proud of their cooking heritage and eager to show us just how good their recipes were, and are! Sometimes it was a particular local ingredient, or the way they kneaded the dough, or browned the flour, or marinated the meat, or maybe a secret method they used to make something particularly unique to their way of cooking. It has truly been a delicious experience!

From Rocky Mountain Blueberry French Toast to Prospector's Gold Nuggets to Gabby's No-Peek Prime Ribber, we know you'll discover a treasure lode of delicious Mountain West recipes.

Gwen McKee

Gwen McKee and Barbara Moseley, editors of the
BEST OF THE BEST STATE COOKBOOK SERIES

Beverages and Appetizers

Hoover Dam is a hydroelectric generating station located 30 miles southeast of Las Vegas, Nevada, on the Colorado River. Lake Mead, formed by water impounded by Hoover Dam, is the largest reservoir in the United States.

Hot Apricot Buttered Rum

¼ cup packed brown sugar
2½ cups water
½ stick unsalted butter,
  cut in bits
½ tablespoon cinnamon
¼ tablespoon freshly grated
  nutmeg

3 whole cloves
½ cup dark rum
¼ cup apricot-flavored
  brandy
Fresh lemon juice
4 sticks cinnamon

In a saucepan, stir together brown sugar, water, butter, cinnamon, nutmeg, and cloves. Simmer for 5 minutes, stirring occasionally. Stir in rum, brandy, and lemon juice. Divide among 4 heated mugs and insert cinnamon stick. Makes 4 servings.

What's Cookin' in Melon Country (Colorado)

Gluhwein

This hot spiced wine is a favorite after-skiing drink. One cup boiling water to which add a thick slice of lemon, 4 cloves, and 2 cinnamon sticks—boil 5 minutes. Then add 2 cups of any heavy red wine (Marca Petri is good), and sugar to taste. Reheat, but do not boil.

Aspen Potpourri (Colorado)

The Continental Divide of the Americas, or Great Divide, is the principal, and largely mountainous, hydrological divide of the Americas that separates the watersheds that drain into the Pacific Ocean from those river systems that drain into the Atlantic Ocean (including the Gulf of Mexico). The Great Divide follows along the main ranges of the Rocky Mountains.

Chocolate Nog

1 quart eggnog
1 (5½-ounce) can
  chocolate syrup

¼ cup crème de cacao
1 cup whipping cream
Chocolate curls (optional)

Combine eggnog, chocolate syrup, and crème de cacao; cover and chill. Before serving, beat whipping cream to soft peaks. Reserve ½ cup of the whipped cream for garnish. Fold the remaining whipped cream into the eggnog mixture. Pour into serving glasses. Dollop with reserved whipped cream. Garnish with chocolate curls. Makes 12 (4-ounce) servings.

Sharing Our Best (Colorado)

Irish Coffee

According to the Irish, this drink will "keepeth and preserveth the head from whirling, the eyes from dazeling, the toong from lisping, the mouth from maffling, the teeth from chattering, and the throte from rattling."

8 warm coffee cups (or Irish
  coffee glasses)
16 teaspoons superfine sugar
8 cups freshly brewed strong
  stiff coffee

6–8 ounces Irish whiskey
1 cup heavy cream, whipped

Heat cups or glasses by rinsing with very hot water, or let them sit near or on a warm stove. Fill each glass with 2 teaspoons superfine sugar. Fill each glass ¾ full with strong, hot coffee. Stir until sugar is dissolved. Add ¾–1 ounce of Irish whiskey to each glass and stir well. Top each serving with a dollop of whipped cream. Serve immediately. Do not mix the cream through the coffee. The hot, whiskey-laced coffee is to be sipped through the velvety cream. Serves 8.

Traditional Treasures (Nevada)

Lime Slush

2 cups sugar
8 cups water
1 (12-ounce) can frozen
   limeade

5 fresh limes, juiced
2 (12-ounce) cans lemon-lime
   soda

Combine sugar and water in a large saucepan and heat slightly until sugar is dissolved. Add frozen limeade and juice of 5 limes. Mix and pour into shallow pan. Freeze. Remove from freezer about an hour before serving and break up into slush. Pour into punch bowl and add lemon-lime soda. Makes 18 (4-ounce) servings.

Lion House Weddings (Utah)

Cowboy Cider

1 cup sugar
3 cups water
12 whole cloves
4 allspice berries
2 or 3 sticks cinnamon

½ teaspoon ground ginger
3 cups orange juice
8 cups apple cider
2 cups lemon juice

Boil sugar and water for 10 minutes. Add cloves, allspice berries, cinnamon, and ginger. Cover and let stand for 1 hour. Strain, then add orange juice, apple cider, and lemon juice. Bring to a light boil and serve.

The Cowboy Chuck Wagon Cookbook (Utah)

Thirty Second Dynamite Dinner

You can add different fruits to this basic smoothie to fit your mood. It's great for a snack before or after dinner, and it's packed with protein.

1 cup milk	**Dash of nutmeg**
1 cup sliced peaches	**Dash of cinnamon**
2 tablespoons wheat germ	**1½ cups ice**

Pour milk into smoothie container. Add peaches, wheat germ, and spices, then ice. If using stir stick, place in hole in top. Press the mix button and let run for 30 seconds, rotating stir stick counterclockwise while mixing. Press down the smooth button and let run for 45 seconds, continuing to rotate stir stick. Press mix button and press thumb tab on spout to pour.

Smoothies & Ice Treats (Utah)

Strawberry Cheesecake Smoothie

You can never go wrong with cheesecake. Now you can have it anytime with only half the guilt. This smoothie version of the classic dessert is lower in calories and fat, but high in taste!

1 (14-ounce) can sweetened condensed milk	**1 banana, sliced**
2 tablespoons lemon juice concentrate	**1 cup strawberries (fresh or frozen)**
1 (8-ounce) can crushed pineapple, undrained	**1 cup ice**
1 (3-ounce) package cream cheese, softened	**Fresh strawberries for garnish**

Pour condensed milk, lemon juice, and crushed pineapple with juice into smoothie container. Add cream cheese, banana, strawberries, and ice. Insert stir stick in top and press mix button. Mix for 30 seconds while rotating stir stick counterclockwise. Press smooth button and let run for 45 seconds, continuing to rotate stir stick. Press mix button and pour into glass from spout. Garnish with strawberries, if desired.

Smoothies & Ice Treats (Utah)

Spicy Black Bean and Corn Salsa

A delightfully colorful change to traditional salsa.

16 ounces cooked black beans

16 ounces fresh or frozen corn kernels

½ cup chopped fresh cilantro

¼ cup chopped green onion

¼ cup chopped red onion

⅓ cup fresh lime juice

3 tablespoons vegetable oil

1 tablespoon ground cumin

Salt and freshly ground black pepper

½ cup chopped ripe tomatoes, drained

In large bowl, combine beans, corn, cilantro, green onion, red onion, lime juice, oil, and cumin. Season with salt and pepper to taste. Cover and chill at least 2 hours or up to overnight. Just before serving, stir in tomatoes. Serve with blue and white corn chips. Makes 4–6 cups.

Colorado Collage (Colorado)

Nevada Ranchers' Cactus Salsa

2 cups chopped ripe tomatoes

1 cup chopped red onion

1 cup nopalitos (cactus meat)*, drained and rinsed

½ cup chopped fresh cilantro

¼ cup diced serrano chiles

½ teaspoon coarse salt

⅓ cup fresh lime juice

Combine all ingredients. Chill at least one hour before serving. Serves 4 rough-riding cowgirls or 6 city gals with sports cars.

*If you can't find nopalitos, substitute mild green chiles.

Authentic Cowboy Cookery Then & Now (Nevada)

Mango Salsa

Great served over grilled fish.

1 red pepper, diced
1 small red onion, diced
1 mango (firm, not overripe), diced
½ cup chopped cilantro
2 tablespoons fresh lime juice
1 tablespoon olive oil
1 tablespoon seasoned rice vinegar
1 garlic clove, minced
¼ teaspoon cayenne pepper

Mix together red pepper, red onion, diced mango, and cilantro. Whisk together lime juice, olive oil, rice vinegar, garlic, and cayenne. Toss ingredients with dressing. Chill until ready to serve. Best if prepared a few hours ahead of serving time.

Lake Tahoe Cooks! (Nevada)

Cowboy Caviar

2 tablespoons red wine vinegar
1½ teaspoons oil
1½–2 teaspoons hot sauce
1 clove garlic, minced
⅛ teaspoon pepper
1 firm ripe avocado
1 (15-ounce) can black-eyed peas
1 (11-ounce) can corn, or kernels from 2 ears of fresh corn, blanched
⅔ cup chopped cilantro
⅔ cup thinly sliced green onions
8 ounces Roma tomatoes, coarsely chopped
Salt to taste

Mix vinegar, oil, hot sauce, garlic, and pepper in a bowl. Cut avocado into ½-inch cubes and add to the vinegar mixture, mixing gently. Drain and rinse the peas and corn. Add to the vinegar mixture with cilantro, green onions, and tomatoes; mix gently. Add salt to taste. Serve with tortilla chips. Serves 10–12.

Always in Season (Utah)

Hot Artichoke Dip

½ cup chopped frozen
  spinach
½ cup mayonnaise
½ cup sour cream
½ cup grated Parmesan
  cheese
¾ cup grated Cheddar
  cheese

1 (8-ounce) can diced green
  chiles
1 (14-ounce) can chopped
  artichoke hearts, drained
1 teaspoon minced garlic

Thaw and drain spinach and mix together with all ingredients. Pour into glass 9x13-inch casserole dish and bake at 350° until hot and bubbly. Serve hot with bread or crackers.

The Fruit of the Spirit (Nevada)

Creamy Spinach Dip

Healthy as well as delicious.

1 (10-ounce) package frozen
  chopped spinach, thawed
  and well drained
1 cup salad dressing (Miracle
  Whip)

1 cup sour cream
½ cup chopped parsley
½ cup chopped green onions
1 teaspoon dill weed
½ teaspoon lemon or lime juice

Combine ingredients in a 1-quart bowl. Mix well with a wooden spoon. This dip will store for one week in the refrigerator in a plastic container. Serve with assorted vegetables and crackers. Makes 2½ cups.

Vacation Cooking: Good Food! Good Fun! (Utah)

Glen Canyon Dip

3 ripe avocados
2 teaspoons lemon juice
1 cup sour cream
1 cup mayonnaise
1 package taco seasoning
2 (9-ounce) cans bean dip

1 bunch green onions, chopped
3 medium tomatoes, chopped
1 (6-ounce) can pitted olives, sliced
8 ounces Cheddar cheese, grated

Peel and mash avocados in a bowl, add lemon juice and set aside. Combine sour cream, mayonnaise, and taco seasoning in another bowl and set aside. Spread bean dip on a serving plate, spread avocado mixture over bean dip and then layer with sour cream mixture. Top with onions, tomatoes, and olives, and sprinkle all with cheese. Serve with your favorite chips or crackers.

Utah Cook Book (Utah)

CHRISTIAN MEHLFÜHRER, WIKIPEDIA.ORG

Utah's Glen Canyon was carved from the Colorado River over an estimated 5 million years. Lake Powell, created by the Glen Canyon Dam is the second largest man-made reservoir in the United States (behind Lake Mead, Nevada). Glen Canyon National Recreation Area encompasses the area around Lake Powell in southeastern and south central Utah and northwestern Arizona, covering 1,254,429 acres of mostly desert.

Ham Spread

1 (8-ounce) tub soft-style
  cream cheese with chives
  and onion
½ teaspoon Dijon mustard
1 tablespoon mayonnaise
⅓ cup finely chopped, fully
  cooked ham

¼ cup shredded Cheddar
  cheese
Crackers, bread, or celery
  sticks

In a small mixing bowl, stir together cream cheese, mustard, and mayonnaise. Stir in ham and Cheddar cheese. Cover and chill. Spread on crackers, bread, or celery sticks. Cover and store leftover spread in the refrigerator for up to 5 days. Makes enough spread for 6 slices of bread.

Variations: To make roast beef spread, substitute cooked roast beef for the ham, and Swiss cheese for the Cheddar. To make turkey spread, substitute cooked turkey for the ham, and mozzarella cheese for the Cheddar.

Lion House Entertaining (Utah)

Baked Brie with Caramelized Apple Topping

A perfect paring of flavors and textures.

1 large Granny Smith
  apple, peeled, cored
  and coarsely chopped
  (about 2 cups)
½ cup pecan pieces

⅓ cup (packed) brown
  sugar
2 tablespoons Kahlúa
1 (about 2-pound) wheel
  Brie, rind left on

Mix apple with pecans, brown sugar, and Kahlúa. Set aside. Place Brie in shallow, oven-proof dish; top with apple mixture. Bake at 325° 10–15 minutes, or until topping is bubbly and cheese is softened. Serve with lavosh or water crackers. Makes 16–20 servings.

Palates (Colorado)

Pizza Fondue

1 (26- to 28-ounce) jar
  spaghetti sauce with meat
2 teaspoons Italian seasoning
1 tablespoon cornstarch or
  instant tapioca

½ cup sliced pepperoni
1 cup grated mozzarella cheese

Combine all ingredients except mozzarella cheese in greased 2- to 3½-quart slow cooker. Cover and cook on low heat for 2–3 hours. Add cheese the last hour of cooking. Serve with bread sticks, pita bread, or chunks of crusty Italian bread for dippers. Makes 8–10 servings.

101 Things To Do With a Slow Cooker (Utah)

Summer Pizza

Use your imagination with this one!

2 packages crescent rolls
2 (8-ounce) packages cream
  cheese, room temperature
⅔ cup mayonnaise
1 teaspoon cayenne pepper
  or Tabasco to taste
1 teaspoon onion salt

1 teaspoon garlic salt
¾ teaspoon dill
¼ cup chives, finely chopped
Toppings (see below)
Monterey Jack or Cheddar
  cheese

Unroll crescent rolls and lay in a 13x9-inch baking dish with flat sides touching. Bake at 350° for 18–20 minutes or until golden. Combine cream cheese, mayonnaise, spices, and chives. Spread onto cooled crescent rolls. Top with desired toppings; top with cheese, if desired. Cut into 2x2-inch squares and serve.

TOPPINGS:
Raw vegetables such as chopped broccoli, cauliflower, mushrooms, green pepper, etc.; small canned shrimp, sliced black olives, cocktail onions, or sliced cherry tomatoes.

Steamboat Entertains (Colorado)

Hot & Spicy Ribbon Chips

6 medium Colorado russet
  variety potatoes
1 tablespoon + 1 teaspoon
  salt
Oil for frying

1 tablespoon chili powder
1 teaspoon garlic salt
¼–½ teaspoon cayenne
  pepper

With a vegetable peeler, peel thin strips of potatoes lengthwise to make ribbons, or with a knife, cut potatoes into very thin lengthwise slices. Place in 1-quart ice water mixed with 1 table-spoon salt. Heat oil in a deep-fat fryer or heavy pan to 365°. Combine chili powder, remaining 1 teaspoon salt, garlic salt, and cayenne pepper; set aside. Drain potatoes and pat dry with paper towels. Fry potatoes in batches until golden and crisp; remove to paper towels. Season with chili mixture. Makes 8–12 servings.

Colorado Potato Favorite Recipes (Colorado)

Here's to the USA Crostini

12 slices Italian crusty bread
2½ tablespoons olive oil,
  divided
2 (6-ounce) jars marinated
  artichoke hearts, rinsed and
  drained

2 tablespoons heavy cream
Salt and black pepper to taste
½ cup sliced greek olives
¼ cup chopped red onion

Preheat broiler. Arrange bread slices on a baking sheet and brush tops with 2 tablespoons olive oil. Broil 5 inches from heat until golden, about 30 seconds. Turn toasts over and broil until golden. Transfer to a rack to cool.

  Combine artichokes and cream in a food processor. Transfer to a bowl and season with salt and pepper to taste. Combine olives, onion, and remaining oil in a bowl. Spread toasts even-ly with artichoke cream and top with olive mixture. Drizzle with a little more olive oil before serving. Makes 12 hors d'oeuvres.

All American Meals Cookbook (Nevada)

Prospector's Gold Nuggets

½ cup soft butter
2 cups Cheddar cheese
  grated
1 tablespoon canned green
  chiles, or jalapeños
  minced

½ teaspoon dry mustard
1 teaspoon Worcestershire
3–4 drops Tabasco
Pinch cayenne pepper
½ teaspoon onion salt
1¼ cups flour

Blend together butter, cheese, chiles, mustard, Worcestershire, Tabasco, cayenne, and onion salt until well-mixed. Add flour to make a stiff dough. Roll into balls. Place on ungreased cookie sheet and press lightly with tines of a fork. Bake at 350° about 15 minutes until lightly browned. Serve hot. Yields 3½ dozen.

Colorado Foods and More. . . (Colorado)

NATIONAL ARCHIVE

The Pike's Peak Gold Rush of 1858–1861 was the boom in gold prospecting and mining in the Pike's Peak Country of the Southern Rocky Mountains (what is now the state of Colorado). In July 1860, Clark, Gruber & Company began minting gold coins in Denver, bearing the phrase "Pikes Peak Gold" and an artist's rendering of the peak on the obverse. As the artist had never actually seen the peak, it looks nothing like it. This was the last gold-mining region in the United States where it was still legal for private individuals to mint pioneer gold coins of their own design. In 1863 the U.S. Treasury purchased their minting equipment for $25,000 to open the Denver Mint. Today, the Denver Mint is the single largest producer of coins in the world.

Hot Mushroom Turnovers

FILLING:

3 tablespoons butter or margarine
½ pound mushrooms, minced
1 large onion, minced
¼ cup sour cream

1 teaspoon salt
¼ teaspoon chopped thyme leaves
2 tablespoons flour

In 10-inch skillet over medium heat in 3 tablespoons hot butter or margarine, cook mushrooms and onion until tender, stirring occasionally. Stir in sour cream, salt, thyme, and flour; set aside.

DOUGH:

1 (8-ounce) package cream cheese, softened
1½ cups all-purpose flour

½ cup butter or margarine, softened
1 egg, beaten

In large bowl with mixer at medium speed, beat cream cheese, flour, and butter or margarine until smooth; shape into ball. Wrap and refrigerate for 1 hour.

On floured surface with floured rolling pin, roll ½ of dough ⅛ inch thick. With floured 2½-inch-round cookie cutter, cut out as many circles as possible. Repeat.

Preheat oven to 450°. Onto ½ of each Dough circle, place a teaspoon of mushroom mixture. Brush edges of circle with egg; fold Dough over Filling. With fork, firmly press edges together to seal. Prick top. Place turnovers on ungreased cookie sheet; brush with remaining egg. Bake for 12–14 minutes until golden.

Virginia City Alumni Association Cookbook (Nevada)

Crab-Stuffed Mushrooms

⅓ cup minced green pepper
⅓ cup chopped red bell
  pepper
¼ cup minced onion
2 cloves garlic, minced
½ cup unsalted butter,
  divided

1 egg, beaten
¼ cup freshly grated
  Parmesan cheese
⅓ cup lump crabmeat
⅛ teaspoon cayenne pepper
½ cup bread crumbs
24 firm white mushrooms

Sauté peppers, onion, and garlic in ¼ cup butter until soft. Remove from heat and add egg, cheese, crabmeat, cayenne, and bread crumbs. Remove stems from mushroom caps. Melt remaining butter and dip each cap in melted butter. Stuff with crabmeat stuffing. At this point, can be refrigerated up to 3 days. Bake at 400° until lightly browned on top. Serve immediately. Makes 2 dozen.

Steamboat Entertains (Colorado)

Crab Rangoon

1 (8-ounce) package cream
  cheese
1 can chopped crabmeat
1 garlic clove, mashed
¼ teaspoon Worcestershire

3 drops Tabasco
½ teaspoon salt
½ teaspoon white pepper
Won ton skins

Mix all ingredients together except skins until smooth and fluffy. Put 1½ teaspoons mixture in center of won ton skin. Wet edges with water and press edges together. Deep-fry until golden brown.

Mountain Cooking and Adventure (Colorado)

Miniature Crab Cakes

1 pound crabmeat
¼ cup finely diced onion
¼ cup finely diced red bell
  pepper
3 cups fresh bread crumbs,
  divided
½ cup mayonnaise
¼ cup cream cheese,
  softened

1 tablespoon Dijon mustard
1 egg
Pinch of cayenne pepper
⅛ teaspoon paprika
¼ teaspoon salt
1 tablespoon finely chopped
  parsley

In a medium bowl, mix crabmeat, onion, bell pepper, 1 cup bread crumbs, mayonnaise, cream cheese, mustard, egg, cayenne, paprika, salt, and parsley. Refrigerate for 1 hour. Place remaining bread crumbs in a shallow bowl. Using a tablespoon, form a crab cake about 1 inch in diameter. Coat both sides with bread crumbs and place on baking sheet which has been sprayed with vegetable or olive oil spray. Continue until all crabmeat mixture is used. This can be done a day ahead, covered with plastic wrap, then refrigerated until ready to use.

Bake at 375° for 10–12 minutes or until golden brown. Serve warm with a dollop of Chipotle Mayonnaise on top. Makes about 24 mini crab cakes or 12 large crab cakes.

CHIPOTLE MAYONNAISE:

2 whole chipotle chiles
  (canned smoked jalapeño
  peppers)
1 cup mayonnaise

1 tablespoon minced garlic
½ cup chopped fresh parsley
¼ teaspoon salt

Place all ingredients in blender or processor and blend until smooth. This can be made a day ahead. Makes about 1 cup.

Savor the Memories (Utah)

Shrimp Cocktail "Martini Style"

10 cups chopped, very ripe seedless watermelon, divided
4 cups superfine sugar
¼ cup light corn syrup
Juice of 1 lemon
2 cups peeled, seeded, finely chopped red tomatoes
1 tablespoon finely chopped seeded fresh jalapeño chiles
3 scallions
1 tablespoon chopped fresh cilantro
1 tablespoon each Tabasco and fresh lime juice
2 tablespoons olive oil blend (do not use extra virgin olive oil)
Salt and pepper to taste
2 heads frisée lettuce or chicory
16 large cooked shrimp, peeled, deveined, chilled
8 each red and yellow teardrop tomatoes, halved
Sprigs of fresh cilantro

Purée 8 cups watermelon in batches in a food processor. Pour into a bowl. Add sugar, corn syrup, and lemon juice. Stir until sugar dissolves. Pour mixture into a freezer container. Freeze overnight. Process frozen mixture in a food processor until slushy. Return to freezer container and freeze for 2 hours.

Mix chopped tomatoes, remaining 2 cups watermelon and jalapeño chiles in a bowl. Cut the green part off the scallions and reserve for garnish. Chop remaining white part finely; add to the tomato mixture. Add chopped cilantro, Tabasco, lime juice, and olive oil. Season with salt and pepper and toss to mix well. Cover and chill until serving time.

Rinse lettuce in cold water. Separate leaves and pat dry. Place lettuce leaves in bottom of 4 frozen martini glasses. Top with 1 tablespoon scoop of tomato mixture and 1 tablespoon scoop of watermelon sorbet. Place 4 shrimp around the rim of each glass. Garnish each with tomato halves, green part of scallions, and cilantro sprigs. Yields 4 servings.

Recipe by James Perillo, Executive Chef, Caesar's Palace Hotel and Casino
Las Vegas Glitter to Gourmet (Nevada)

Lemon Garlic Shrimp

2 pounds large shrimp
  (21–26 per pound) peeled,
  deveined, and cooked,
  tails on
¼ cup olive oil
2 lemons, zest and juice

¼ cup chopped fresh parsley
1 tablespoon minced garlic
1 tablespoon chopped fresh
  dill, or 1 teaspoon dried dill
½ teaspoon salt
Pinch of red pepper flakes

In a bowl, combine all ingredients. Stir well. Taste for seasoning. Cover; refrigerate until ready to use. Serve with lemon slices and parsley sprigs. Can be made hours ahead. Serves 8–10, allowing 5–6 shrimp per person.

Savor the Memories (Utah)

Shrimp in Jackets

1 pound frozen, medium,
  shelled shrimp, thawed
1 teaspoon garlic salt

1 pound bacon (about 15
  slices)

Sprinkle shrimp with garlic salt; wrap each in ⅓ slice of bacon. Arrange on broiler rack. Broil 3–4 inches from heat just until bacon is crisp and browned, 8–10 minutes, turning occasionally. Makes about 40 servings.

The Best of Down-Home Cooking (Nevada)

All American Buffalo Chicken Wings

BLUE CHEESE DRESSING:

4 tablespoons minced yellow onion

2 garlic cloves, minced

¼ cup minced parsley

2 cups mayonnaise

1 cup sour cream

2 tablespoons fresh lemon juice

2 tablespoons white vinegar

¾ cup crumbled blue cheese

½ teaspoon black pepper

¼ teaspoon cayenne pepper

Combine all ingredients in bowl; cover and chill.

CHICKEN WINGS:

40 chicken wings

2–4 cups vegetable oil for deep-frying

1 stick butter

1 small bottle hot sauce

40 celery sticks

Disjoint wings at elbow and discard tips. Heat oil in deep-fryer to 375°. Fry wings until crisp and golden, about 8–10 minutes. Drain on paper towels. Melt butter in a saucepan and blend in the bottle of hot sauce. Place chicken wings in large bowl and pour hot butter sauce over wings. Toss well to coat. Arrange wings on platter and serve with celery sticks and the bowl of Blue Cheese Dressing for dipping. Serves 8–12.

All American Meals Cookbook (Nevada)

"Oh, give me a home where the buffalo roam. . . ." These lyrics to an 1873 cowboy ballad still hold true in Utah. Antelope Island, the largest island in the Great Salt Lake, holds populations of pronghorn antelope, porcupine, badger, coyote, bobcat, bighorn sheep, American bison, and millions of waterfowl. The bison were introduced to the island in 1893. The remote Henry Mountains in southeastern Utah is also home to a large herd of bison.

Smoked Chicken Pesto Quesadillas

If you really want to dazzle your friends, make this as an appetizer. The flavors meld beautifully. Be sure to make enough because it goes quickly.

8 ounces pesto, homemade
  or good quality brand
8 (8-inch) flour tortillas
1 (8–10-ounce) smoked
  chicken breast, (or turkey),
  pulled into thin shreds

¾ pound provolone, or
  combine provolone and
  mozzarella, grated
Mazola oil

Spread 3 heaping tablespoons of pesto on each tortilla. Divide the chicken breast shreds over the pesto on each tortilla. Sprinkle ⅓–½ cup of cheese over the chicken. Place another tortilla on top. Heat ⅛ inch of oil in a black iron frying pan and heat each side until golden brown and the cheese is melted. Serves 8–12 as an appetizer or can be used as a main course.

Lighter Tastes of Aspen (Colorado)

Cocktail Meatballs with Madeira Sauce

6 tablespoons finely chopped
  onion
4 tablespoons butter
⅔ cup fine bread crumbs
2 cups half-and-half
2 pounds lean ground beef
2 eggs

3 teaspoons salt
½ teaspoon pepper
¼ teaspoon nutmeg
1 chicken bouillon cube
1 cup water
¼ cup Madeira wine
Parsley

Sauté onion in butter until brown. Soak crumbs in half-and-half. Combine beef, eggs, salt, pepper, and nutmeg; mix until smooth. Chill for 2 hours.

    Shape into balls. Fry in butter to brown evenly. Place in glass chafing dish. Combine bouillon cube, water, and wine. Heat and dissolve cube completely. Pour over meatballs and warm before serving. Garnish with parsley.

Kitchen Chatter (Nevada)

Miniature Reubens

2 (8-ounce) packages cocktail rye bread
Mustard
½ pound thinly sliced corned beef
1 (8-ounce) can sauerkraut, drained
1 (8-ounce) package thinly sliced Swiss cheese
½ pound (2 sticks) margarine, divided

Spread half the bread slices with mustard. Top with a folded piece of corned beef, covering the bread completely but not extending over the edge. Spread about 1 teaspoon sauerkraut oven the meat. Place 2 thin slices of Swiss cheese over sauerkraut; trim edges even with bread. Top with remaining bread.

In large skillet, melt 4 tablespoons margarine. Sauté sandwiches over moderate heat a batch at a time; do not crowd. When underside is golden, turn and brown other side. Add additional margarine as needed; serve warm.

If not serving immediately, place on baking sheet and freeze. When almost frozen, remove from freezer and cut each sandwich in half. Sandwiches are easier to cut when partially frozen. May be frozen for up to 3 months. Reheat frozen. Before serving, bake at 400° for 10–15 minutes until heated through and bubbling.

Recipes from Sunset Garden Club (Nevada)

 With mostly mountainous and desert terrain, altitudes vary in Nevada from above 13,000 feet to below 1,000 feet.

Twilight in the Rockies Cocktail Kebabs

½ cup oil
½ cup soy sauce
1 tablespoon sherry
5 tablespoons brown sugar
1 teaspoon prepared
 mustard
1 garlic clove, finely minced

1–1½ teaspoons red chili
 pepper, crushed
2 pounds elk, deer or beef
 steaks, sliced across the
 grain diagonally into
 paper-thin strips
 (4x1x¼ inches)

Blend all ingredients, except steak, for marinade. In shallow pan, place meat strips and cover with marinade. Marinate steaks 20 minutes, turning to coat. Thread strips of meat on pre-soaked bamboo skewers (to prevent burning). Brush with marinade. Broil quickly on hibachi or grill over hot coals until done, approximately 5 minutes, turning and basting. Yields 18–20 appetizers.

Colorado Foods and More. . . (Colorado)

Bread and Breakfast

SHAWN McKEE

Editor Gwen McKee with husband Barney, son Brian, and daughter-in-law Betsy, skiing Breckenridge, Colorado. Breckenridge is a popular ski resort during the winter months, servicing multi-difficulty ski slopes on the Rocky Mountains.

Onion Cracker Bread

This low-fat, delicious cracker bread is a great alternative to bread with a meal.

DOUGH:

1 tablespoon yeast	**1 teaspoon salt**
1⅓ cups water	**1 tablespoon vegetable oil**
1¾ tablespoons sugar	**3½ cups all-purpose flour**

Dissolve the yeast in the water. Add the remaining ingredients and knead until a smooth dough is formed—knead either by hand or in a food processor. Cover the dough and set aside to rise for 45 minutes. Preheat the oven to 450°. (Recipe prepared for high altitude cooking.) While the dough rises, prepare the topping.

TOPPING:

2 medium onions, diced	**Coarse kosher salt**
1 tablespoon vegetable oil	**1 egg white, beaten with**
1 tablespoon poppy seeds	**1 tablespoon water**
3 green onions, finely chopped	

Sauté onions in the oil until soft. Remove from heat and stir in poppy seeds and chopped green onions. In a small bowl, whisk egg white with water.

Divide dough into 3 pieces. Pat or roll into rectangles about ⅓-inch thick. Rest the dough for 10 minutes (to relax gluten in flour and to make dough easier to stretch). Grease 3 large cookie sheets, about 11x17 inches. If you only have one pan, just stretch and bake one at a time. Stretch each piece of dough to cover the bottom of the pans. Stretch gently with the flat palm of your hand under the dough. Don't worry about the dough being absolutely even, the irregularities are part of its charm; creating soft and crispy pieces of cracker where the dough is thick or thin.

Brush the dough with egg white. Distribute the onion-poppy seed topping evenly over dough. Sprinkle very lightly with salt. Bake until golden, about 10–15 minutes. Cool and break into pieces for serving. Serves 6–8.

Lighter Tastes of Aspen (Colorado)

Easy Onion Rolls

2 cups flour	½ cup milk
½ teaspoon salt	2 tablespoons butter
1 tablespoon baking powder	1 small red onion, chopped
½ cup butter or butter-flavored vegetable shortening	1 small white onion, chopped
	½ teaspoon ground thyme
½ cup sour cream	1 teaspoon rosemary leaves

Preheat oven to 425°. Lightly grease or spray cookie sheet. In a large mixing bowl, blend dry ingredients. Cut in butter until mixture resembles coarse meal. Add sour cream and stir until barely mixed. Add milk, and mix or knead until a rich elastic dough forms. Set aside.

In a heavy skillet over medium heat, melt butter and sauté chopped onions with spices until soft and transparent. Cool slightly. Roll out dough in a large rectangle, approximately ¼ inch thick. Spread onion mixture over dough, and roll into a tight log. Cut into 1-inch slices and place approximately ½ inch apart on cookie sheet. Bake for 15 minutes.

How to Win a Cowboy's Heart (Utah)

No Knead Hot Rolls

1 package dry yeast	2½ cups flour, divided
1 tablespoon sugar	1 egg
1 teaspoon salt	2 tablespoons soft butter
1 cup warm water	

Dissolve yeast, sugar, and salt in warm water. Add 1¼ cups flour and stir. Add egg, butter, and remaining 1¼ cups flour and stir. Cover and let rise for 45 minutes. Turn out on floured board and work just until dough will roll out. Butter dough and shape into rolls. Place into greased pans and let rise for 45 minutes. Bake for 20 minutes in 400° oven.

The Best of Down-Home Cooking (Nevada)

Popovers

1 cup flour, sifted
¼ teaspoon salt
1 teaspoon sugar

1 tablespoon oil
1 cup skim milk
2 eggs

Preheat oven to 400°. In a small bowl, mix flour with salt and sugar. Combine oil, milk, and eggs in blender; process until very smooth. Add to the blender the flour mixture. Process at high speed for about 1 minute. Fill greased muffin pans half full with the batter. Bake for about 40 minutes or until brown. Keep oven door closed while baking to prevent popovers from collapsing. Serves 12. Serve immediately.

Sharing Our Diabetics Best Recipes (Nevada)

Dill Bread

While I was working in a doctor's office in Carson City in the '80s, a patient came in with a basket of dill bread still warm from the oven, along with some nice, soft butter. We sat down and had a feast on what seemed like the most delicious bread I had ever eaten. It remains a real treat at our family gatherings.

2 tablespoons dill seed
   (ground up)
1 tablespoon dried onion
4 tablespoons sugar or honey
½ teaspoon baking soda
2 teaspoons salt

2 eggs
2 tablespoons butter
1 pint cottage cheese
2 packages yeast, dissolved in
   1 cup very warm water
5 cups flour, maybe 6

Mix dill seed, dried onion, sugar, baking soda, and salt. Add eggs, butter, cottage cheese, and yeast; mix thoroughly. Add flour, 1 cup at a time; knead at least 8 minutes, adding flour until stiff. Put in a greased bowl in a warm place and let rise until double in size, about 1 hour. Remove; knead again. Place in greased loaf pan(s); let rise until double, about 20 minutes. Bake at 350° for 30–45 minutes, depending on the size of the pan.

God, That's Good! (Nevada)

Cowboy Cheese Bread

2½ cups flour
2 teaspoons baking powder
¾ teaspoon salt
¼ teaspoon garlic powder
2 tablespoons dried parsley
1½ teaspoons dried onion
1 tablespoon sugar
½ cup butter, divided

¼ cup butter-flavored
 shortening
2 eggs
½ cup milk
1 cup grated Cheddar cheese
¼ cup grated Parmesan
 cheese

Mix all dry ingredients and seasonings together. (Do not mix in either cheese at this time.) Cut ¼ cup butter and shortening into dry ingredients; mix until it resembles coarse meal. Mix eggs and milk together, then add to flour mixture, and mix again. Add both cheeses, and knead until the cheese is worked through. Roll dough out into a 12-inch circle, then cut with a pizza cutter into pie-shaped wedges. Place wedges the way they were cut into an oiled Dutch oven, then melt remaining butter and drizzle over wedges. Cover and cook with 16–22 coals (400°), with a ratio of 1 (bottom)/3 (top), for 20–30 minutes or until no longer doughy inside. Serves 8–10.

The Beginner's Guide to Dutch Oven Cooking (Utah)

Let Freedom Ring Buttermilk Drop Biscuits

3 cups all-purpose flour
2 tablespoons sugar
4 teaspoons baking powder
1 teaspoon salt

1 teaspoon baking soda
1½ sticks chilled unsalted
 butter, cut into ¼-inch pats
1 cup buttermilk

Preheat oven to 425°. Whisk together flour, sugar, baking powder, salt, and baking soda. Using fingers or dough cutter, cut butter into dry ingredients until mixture resembles coarse meal. Add buttermilk and stir until moistened. Drop biscuits (about ¼ cup dough per biscuit) onto baking sheet about 2 inches apart. Bake until biscuits are golden, about 15 minutes. Serve warm. Serves 12.

All American Meals Cookbook (Nevada)

Back at the Ranch Spicy Cheese Biscuits

7 cups all-purpose flour
4 tablespoons baking powder
2 tablespoons sugar
4 teaspoons cayenne pepper
1 teaspoon salt
2 cups grated sharp Cheddar
  cheese
1 cup grated sharp Romano
  cheese
1 cup cold shortening, cut into
  pieces
2½ cups cold buttermilk

Preheat oven to 450°. Grease a large baking sheet. Sift first 5 ingredients into a bowl. Mix in cheeses. Add shortening and mix with your fingers until mixture resembles coarse meal. Add buttermilk, stirring until dough begins to form. Turn dough onto floured surface and knead gently until smooth, about 8 turns. Roll out dough to about 1 inch thick. Use a biscuit cutter to cut out biscuits. Gather dough scraps and repeat roll out. Cut out biscuits. Put biscuits on baking sheet and bake until golden, about 15 minutes. Serve hot with butter and honey. Serves 4 cowboys on a Friday night or 10 ranch guests on Monday morning.

Authentic Cowboy Cookery Then & Now (Nevada)

Sky-High Biscuits

2 cups all-purpose flour plus
  1 cup whole-wheat flour
  (or 3 cups all-purpose flour)
4½ teaspoons baking powder
2 tablespoons sugar
½ teaspoon salt
¾ teaspoon cream of tartar
¾ cup butter or margarine
1 egg, beaten
1 cup milk

In a bowl, combine flour, baking powder, sugar, salt, and cream of tartar. Cut in butter or margarine until mixture resembles coarse cornmeal. Add egg and milk, stirring quickly and briefly. Knead lightly on floured surface. Roll or pat gently to 1-inch thickness. Cut into 1- to 2-inch biscuits. Place in a 12- to 14-inch Dutch oven. Bake over a 450° fire for 10–12 minutes. Makes about 12 biscuits.

Dutch Oven Secrets (Utah)

American Indian-Style Chipotle Cornbread

1 cup yellow cornmeal
1 cup all-purpose flour
¼ cup sugar
2 teaspoons baking powder
1 teaspoon baking soda
1 teaspoon salt
1 cup grated sharp Cheddar
  cheese
1 cup buttermilk
3 large eggs
6 tablespoons (¾ stick)
  unsalted butter, melted,
  cooled
2 tablespoons canned chipotle
  chiles, seeded and minced

Preheat oven to 375°. Grease a 9x5x2-inch metal loaf pan. Combine first 6 ingredients. Fold in cheese. Whisk together buttermilk, eggs, melted butter, and chiles. Add buttermilk mixture to dry ingredients and stir until blended. Pour batter into loaf pan. Bake until tester inserted into center comes out clean, about 35 minutes. Cool in pan 15 minutes. Turn bread out. Let cool completely before slicing. Makes 1 loaf.

All American Meals Cookbook (Nevada)

Cornbread Spanish-Style

1 cup cornmeal
¼ cup sugar
1 teaspoon salt
1 cup sifted flour
3 teaspoons baking
  powder
1 egg
1 cup milk
¼ cup shortening
1 (16-ounce) can cream-style
  corn
1 cup cottage cheese

Combine dry ingredients; add egg, milk, shortening, corn, and cottage cheese. Stir lightly. Pour half of batter in greased 9-inch square pan. Sprinkle with half the Filling. Add remaining batter; top with remaining Filling. Bake at 400° for 45 minutes.

FILLING:

1½ cups grated longhorn or
  Cheddar cheese
1 (4-ounce) can green chiles,
  chopped

Mix both ingredients.

Southwestern Foods et cetera (Colorado)

Dried Cherry Buttermilk Scones

The tartness of the cherries complements the sweetness of the biscuit. If you have never tried scones, you must try these!

2 cups all-purpose flour
⅓ cup sugar
1½ teaspoons baking powder
½ teaspoon baking soda
6 tablespoons butter, chilled

½ cup buttermilk
1 large egg
1½ teaspoons vanilla
⅔ cup dried sour cherries

Preheat oven to 400°. In a large bowl, sift together the dry ingredients. Cut butter into ½-inch cubes and distribute over flour mixture. With a pastry blender, cut in the butter until the mixture resembles coarse crumbs. Stir together the buttermilk, egg, and vanilla. Add to the flour mixture. Stir in the cherries. With lightly-floured hands, pat the dough into an 8-inch diameter circle on an ungreased cookie sheet. With a serrated knife, cut into 8 separate wedges. Bake 18–20 minutes, or until a cake tester inserted into the center comes out clean. Cool for 5 minutes. Serve warm. Makes 8 scones.

Recipe from Posada de Sol y Sombra, LaVeta
Colorado Bed & Breakfast Cookbook (Colorado)

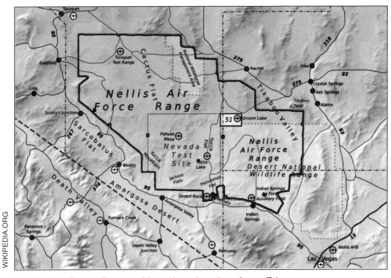

Nellis Air Force Range, Nevada, showing Area 51

Drop Scones

2 cups all-purpose flour
1 tablespoon baking powder
¼ cup granulated sugar
Pinch of salt
½ cup cold butter, cut into
    small pieces

2 eggs, beaten
½ cup whipping cream
½ cup raisins or dried
    cranberries or other dried
    fruit and nuts

Preheat oven to 400°. Mix flour, baking powder, sugar, salt, and butter together. Using pastry blender or 2 knives, cut in flour mixture, then mix briefly with a fork until dough resembles coarse meal.

In separate bowl, combine eggs and cream, and beat together. Pour egg mixture into flour mixture and blend until dry ingredients are just moistened. Add dried fruit and nuts, and mix briefly. Drop batter in 3-ounce rounds (about half the size of a tennis ball) onto well-greased cookie pan. Bake until tops are golden brown, about 18–20 minutes. Makes 10–12 scones.

Note: With cranberries add ½ cup walnuts and 2 teaspoons orange zest; with apricots add ½ cup slivered almonds and 1 teaspoon almond extract. You can use chocolate chunks with roasted hazelnuts, also.

Soup for Our Souls (Nevada)

The Nellis Air Force Range (formerly Nevada Test and Training Range) is a training facility of the United States Air Force located in the desert of southern Nevada. It is the largest of its kind in the United States, encompassing 4,687 square miles. Area 51, a large secretive military airfield, is located within the range, situated on the shore of a dry lake bed, Groom Lake. The base's primary purpose is to support development and testing of experimental aircraft and weapons systems. This installation was once so secret, its existence was denied by the government agencies and contractors that had connections there.

Cinnamon Surprise

This is a light change from heavy pastries and cinnamon rolls.

2 (8-count) packages refrigerator crescent roll dough	1 teaspoon sugar
	1 teaspoon cinnamon
	16 marshmallows
2 tablespoons brown sugar	2 tablespoons melted butter

Separate roll dough on lightly floured surface. Mix brown sugar, sugar, and cinnamon in small bowl. Dip marshmallows one at a time in melted butter; roll in sugar mixture, coating well. Place on triangle of roll dough. Bring up edges to enclose marshmallow, sealing well. Place 2 inches apart on baking sheet. Brush lightly with remaining melted butter. Bake at 375° for 10–13 minutes or until marshmallows melt, leaving rolls with hollow, sweet-coated centers. Yields 16 servings.

Beyond Oats (Colorado)

All-In-One Cinnamon Rolls

2 packages dry yeast	½ cup dried chopped currants
2½ cups milk, scalded	½ cup chopped nuts
½ cup packed brown sugar	1 teaspoon cinnamon
1 tablespoon salt	Oil
5 tablespoons margarine, softened	1 pound powdered sugar
6–7 cups flour, divided	Milk

Dissolve yeast in warm milk. In a bowl, mix well the sugar, salt, and margarine. Add 3 cups flour and yeast mixture; beat well. Mix in currants and nuts. Continue adding flour a little at a time until a soft dough forms. Add cinnamon and knead well. Place in lightly oiled bowl and let double in size.

Form dough into balls and place into a lightly oiled 12-inch Dutch oven; let rise double again. Bake at 400° for 30–35 minutes (8–10 coals on bottom, 18–20 coals on top). When done, remove from oven. Mix powdered sugar and just enough milk to make a thin glaze. Drizzle over rolls. Makes 1 dozen large rolls. Enjoy.

Dutch Oven Gold (Utah)

Balloon Buns

2 tablespoons yeast
⅔ cup warm water
½ cup shortening
4 cups hot water
6+ cups flour
½+ cup sugar

2 teaspoons salt
2 eggs
Large marshmallows
Melted butter
Cinnamon sugar

Dissolve yeast in warm water. Add shortening to the hot water and let it sit until melted and cooled to lukewarm. Add flour, sugar, and salt to yeast mixture. Add eggs (and a little more sugar, if you like your bread sweeter). Add more flour until dough is thick but moist. Turn dough out onto a floured surface and knead until smooth and bubbly. Let rise until double; punch down and let rise again.

Break pieces off one at a time. Flatten dough. Roll a large marshmallow in melted butter, then cinnamon sugar mixture, and put in the center of the dough piece. Fold dough around it and seal together. Put sealed-side-down in a greased 16-inch Dutch oven after dipping top in melted butter. Let rise about one hour. Bake at 350° for 15–20 minutes or until golden brown. Makes about 24 Balloon Buns.

Dutch Oven Secrets (Utah)

Perhaps the greatest influence on Utah's topography is ancient Lake Bonneville. Fossilized shoreline evidence of the great lake that once covered most of Utah and portions of Idaho and Nevada can still be found, including the remains of mammoth, musk ox, ancestral camel, horse, deer, and mountain sheep that once roamed the area. Geologists believe the lake originated during the last ice age. At its crest, Lake Bonneville was over 5,200 feet in elevation and 1,050 feet deep, 145 miles wide and 346 miles long. Today's Great Salt Lake, Utah Lake, and Sevier Lake are the largest remnants of Lake Bonneville.

Spudnuts

2 cups milk
1 package yeast
½ cup warm water
½ cup white sugar, divided
7 cups white flour, divided
3 eggs

1 cup mashed potatoes
 (instant works fine)
½ cup shortening, melted
1 tablespoon salt
2 teaspoons cinnamon

Scald milk. Dissolve yeast in warm water. Add 1 tablespoon white sugar to water and yeast and let stand for 15 minutes. When milk has cooled to lukewarm, add 2 cups of the flour. Beat to a smooth batter and add the yeast. Let this rise for 20 minutes. Add eggs to mashed potatoes; add melted shortening and whip until very smooth. Potato mixture must be warm. Add to the batter and mix well.

Add remaining flour to which salt and cinnamon have been added. Mix and knead to a smooth dough. Let rise once and knead down. The second time it rises, roll out to ½-inch thickness and cut as for doughnuts. Let rise and drop into hot grease (350°) and cook for 3–4 minutes or until light golden brown. Drain on paper towels. Coat with remaining sugar, or when cool, dip one side in a thin icing of powdered sugar and milk.

A Century of Mormon Cookery, Volume 2 (Utah)

DAVID ILIFF, WIKIPEDIA.ORG

Beginning on July 24, 1847, construction of Salt Lake Temple took 40 years to complete. Granite used at the site was quarried in Little Cottonwood Canyon, 20 miles southeast of the site, and transported to the site by teams of oxen. Four days of travel was required for each wagonload to reach the temple site. The Salt Lake Temple is the largest (of more than 130 around the world) and best-known temple of The Church of Jesus Christ of Latter-day Saints. The Salt Lake Temple is the centerpiece of the ten-acre Temple Square in Salt Lake City, Utah. Although there are no public tours inside the temple, the temple grounds are open to the public and are a popular tourist attraction.

Cinnamon Breakfast Squares

1 cup peeled, seeded, and
   shredded zucchini
¼ cup oil
1 teaspoon vanilla
1 egg
¼ cup brown sugar
¼ cup white sugar
1 cup flour
1 teaspoon baking soda
½ teaspoon salt
½ teaspoon cinnamon
1 tablespoon grated orange
   rind (optional)

Combine zucchini with oil and vanilla. Stir in unbeaten egg. Add sugars and blend. Sift dry ingredients together and add to mixture. Stir until well mixed (do not beat). Blend in orange peel. Spread into a greased 8x8-inch pan. Bake at 350° for 30 minutes. Cool 10 minutes. Cut into squares and break open like muffins; spread with honey butter.

How to Enjoy Zucchini (Utah)

Walnut Streusel Muffins

Georgie's favorite! Muffins get top honors for texture, appearance and flavor.

1½ cups brown sugar, packed
3 cups all-purpose flour,
   divided
¾ cup butter or margarine
1 cup chopped walnuts,
   divided
2 teaspoons baking powder
1 teaspoon nutmeg
1 teaspoon ginger
½ teaspoon baking soda
½ teaspoon salt
1 cup buttermilk or sour milk
2 eggs, beaten

Preheat oven to 350°. Grease muffin cups. In medium bowl, combine sugar and 2 cups flour. Cut in butter to make fine crumbs. In small bowl, combine ¾ cup of the crumbs and ¼ cup of the walnuts; set aside. Into remaining crumb mixture, stir in remaining 1 cup flour, baking powder, spices, baking soda, salt, and remaining ¾ cup walnuts. In another small bowl, combine buttermilk and eggs; stir into dry ingredients just to moisten. Fill muffin cups ⅔ full. Top each with a generous spoonful of reserved crumb-nut mixture. Bake at 350° for 20–25 minutes or until springy to the touch. Makes 18 muffins.

Nothin' but Muffins (Colorado)

Saucy Blueberry Lemon Muffins

These wonderfully tart creations melt in your mouth.

½ cup butter or margarine
½ cup sugar
2 eggs
2 cups flour
3 teaspoons baking powder

¼ teaspoon salt (optional)
⅓ cup milk
1 cup blueberries, canned or
   frozen, thawed and drained
Rind of 1 lemon, grated fine

Preheat oven to 350°. Grease muffin cups. Cream butter, sugar, and eggs in a small bowl. In large bowl, combine flour, baking powder, and salt. Add creamed mixture alternately with milk, stirring only until mixed. Fold in blueberries and lemon rind. Fill muffin cups ⅔ full. Bake at 350° for 25–30 minutes.

SAUCE:

¼ cup fresh lemon juice   ⅓ cup sugar

Combine lemon juice and sugar in small pan and bring to boiling. Pour Sauce evenly over top of baked muffins. Bakes 12 muffins.

Nothin' but Muffins (Colorado)

Backpack Muesli

Hearty, warm breakfast for the back country.

1 cup regular oats, uncooked
1 cup shredded whole-wheat
   cereal, crushed
¼ cup raisins
¼ cup coconut

¼ cup dried apples, chopped
¼ cup nuts or seeds
⅔ cup nonfat dry milk powder
1 teaspoon cinnamon
3 cups water

Mix dry ingredients in a plastic bag for camping. In the evening, add 3 cups of water, cover mixture and soak all night. In the morning, heat to boiling over the fire. Add more nonfat dry milk if desired. Yields 4 servings.

Simply Colorado (Colorado)

Colorado Coffee Cake

4½ cups flour	1½ cups sour cream
1½ cups sugar	½ teaspoon salt
1½ cups butter or solid vegetable shortening	1 teaspoon baking powder
	1 teaspoon baking soda
2 eggs, beaten	2 teaspoons almond extract

Preheat oven to 350°. Grease two 9- or 10-inch springform or deep round foil pans. Combine flour and sugar. Cut in butter or shortening. Reserve 2 cups of this crumb mixture. To remaining crumb mixture, add eggs, sour cream, salt, baking powder, baking soda, and almond extract. Mix well. Spread mixture over bottom and up sides of pans.

FILLING:

1 pound cream cheese, softened	2 eggs, beaten
¼ teaspoon vanilla	¼ cup sugar

Combine cream cheese, vanilla, beaten eggs, and sugar. Spread half of this mixture over the batter in each pan.

TOPPING:

1 cup raspberry preserves, divided	1⅓ cups almonds, chopped

On top of the cream cheese mixture on each cake, spread ½ cup of the raspberry preserves. Whirl almonds in processor until chunky. Combine with reserved crumb mixture and sprinkle over preserves on each cake. Bake cakes for 45–55 minutes until a toothpick inserted in center of cake comes out clean. Cool the cake at least ½ hour before serving. Yields 2 (10-inch) round cakes.

Hint: This recipe is better to make ahead and refrigerate.

West of the Rockies (Colorado)

Braided Cream Cheese Bread

1 (8-ounce) carton sour cream, scalded	1 teaspoon salt
½ cup sugar	2 packages dry yeast
½ cup butter or margarine, melted	½ cup warm water (105°–115°)
	2 eggs, beaten
	4 cups all-purpose flour

Combine scalded sour cream, sugar, butter, and salt; mix well and let cool to lukewarm. Dissolve yeast in warm water in a large mixing bowl; stir in sour cream mixture and eggs. Gradually stir in flour; dough will be soft. Cover tightly and chill overnight.

FILLING:

2 (8-ounce) packages cream cheese, softened	1 egg, beaten
¾ cup sugar	⅛ teaspoon salt
	2 teaspoons vanilla extract

Divide chilled dough into 4 equal parts. Turn each out onto a heavily floured surface and knead 4 or 5 times. Roll each into a 12x18-inch rectangle. Spread ¼ of filling over each rectangle, leaving a ½-inch margin around edges. Carefully roll up jelly-roll-style, beginning at long side. Firmly pinch edge and ends to seal. Place rolls seam side down on greased baking sheets. Make 6 equally x-shaped cuts across the top of each loaf. Cover and let rise in a warm place for one hour or until doubled in size. Bake at 375° for 15–20 minutes.

GLAZE:

2 cups sifted powdered sugar	¼ cup milk
	2 teaspoons vanilla extract

Spread loaves with Glaze while warm.

Four Square Meals a Day (Colorado)

Savory Gruyère Cheesecake

This savory cheesecake is a fabulous choice for brunch or lunch. Beautiful to serve and scrumptious!

1⅓ cups fine toasted
  bread crumbs
5 tablespoons unsalted
  butter, melted
24 ounces cream cheese,
  softened
¼ cup heavy cream
½ teaspoon salt
¼ teaspoon ground nutmeg
¼ teaspoon cayenne pepper
4 eggs
1 cup shredded Gruyère
  cheese

1 (10-ounce) package frozen
  chopped spinach, thawed
  and squeezed dry
2½ tablespoons minced
  green onions
3 tablespoons unsalted butter
½ pound mushrooms, finely
  chopped
Salt and freshly ground black
  pepper to taste
Marinara Sauce

In small bowl, combine bread crumbs and melted butter. Butter a 9-inch springform pan. Press crumbs onto bottom and sides of pan. Bake at 350° for 8–10 minutes; set aside to cool.

In large bowl, beat cream cheese, cream, salt, nutmeg, and cayenne pepper together until smooth. Beat in eggs, one at a time. Divide cheese mixture between 2 bowls. Stir Gruyère cheese into one. Stir spinach and green onions into the other. Pour spinach filling into cooled crust.

In medium skillet, melt 3 tablespoons butter and sauté mushrooms over medium-high heat until all moisture evaporates, stirring frequently. Season to taste with salt and pepper. Spoon mushrooms over spinach filling. Carefully pour Gruyère filling over mushrooms. Set pan on baking sheet. Bake at 325° for 1¼ hours. Turn oven off and cool cheesecake for one hour with door ajar, then cool on rack until room temperature. Serve in wedges topped with warm marinara sauce. Makes 12 servings.

Crème de Colorado (Colorado)

Utah Valley Applesauce Bread

Applesauce bread can be made a month in advance and frozen for holiday giving. It stays very moist because of the applesauce and slices easily.

4 cups flour	½ teaspoon nutmeg
2 tablespoons cornstarch	½ teaspoon salt
2 cups sugar	1 cup vegetable oil
4 teaspoons baking soda	3 cups applesauce
1 teaspoon cinnamon	1 cup raisins
½ teaspoon cloves	½ cup chopped pecans
½ teaspoon allspice	

Mix the first 9 (dry) ingredients in a bowl. In another bowl, combine the remaining ingredients. Combine both mixtures and mix well. Spoon batter into 2 greased 5x9-inch loaf pans. Bake at 350° for one hour. Cool in pans for several minutes; remove to wire racks to cool completely.

Utah Cook Book (Utah)

Ham Quiche Biscuit Cups

1 (8-ounce) package cream cheese, softened	2 tablespoons chopped green onions
2 tablespoons milk	1 (10-count) can refrigerated flaky biscuits
2 eggs	
½ cup shredded Swiss cheese	½ cup finely chopped ham

Preheat oven to 375°. Grease 10 muffin cups. Beat cream cheese, milk, and eggs until smooth. Stir in Swiss cheese and green onions. Separate dough into 10 biscuits. Place one biscuit in each cup. Firmly press in bottom and up sides, forming a ¼-inch rim. Place half of ham in bottom of dough cups. Spoon about 2 tablespoons cheese and egg mixture over ham. Top with remaining ham and bake for about 25 minutes or until filling is set and edges of biscuits are golden brown. Remove from pan. Serve immediately. Serves 10.

Recipe from Meadow Creek Bed and Breakfast, Pine
Colorado Bed & Breakfast Cookbook (Colorado)

Breakfast Sausage Bread

2 (1-pound) loaves frozen
  white bread dough,
  thawed
½ pound mild pork sausage
½ pound hot pork sausage
1½ cups sliced fresh
  mushrooms
½ cup chopped onions
3 eggs

2½ cups shredded mozzarella
  cheese
1 teaspoon dried basil
1 teaspoon dried parsley
  flakes
1 teaspoon crushed dried
  rosemary
1 teaspoon garlic powder

Allow dough to rise until nearly doubled. Meanwhile, in a skillet over medium heat, cook and crumble sausage. Add mushrooms and onions. Cook and stir until sausage is browned and vegetables are tender; drain. Cool. Beat 1 egg, set aside. To sausage mixture, add remaining eggs, cheese and seasonings; mix well.

Roll each loaf of dough into a 16x12-inch rectangle. Spread half sausage mixture on each loaf to within one inch of edges. Roll jellyroll-style, starting at a narrow end; seal edges. Place on greased baking sheet. Bake at 350° for 25 minutes; brush with beaten egg. Bake 5–10 minutes more or until golden brown. Slice and serve warm. Yields 2 loaves.

Country Classics II (Colorado)

Potato Cheese Muffins

2 cups all-purpose flour
8 packets sugar substitute
4 teaspoons baking powder
1 teaspoon salt
2 eggs
1½ cups 2% milk
½ cup cooked mashed
  potatoes
¾ cup grated light Cheddar
  cheese
⅓ cup margarine, melted

Preheat oven to 400°. Line muffin tins with paper cups or spray with vegetable oil spray. In a large mixing bowl, combine flour, sugar substitute, baking powder, and salt. In a medium-size mixing bowl, beat eggs well with an electric mixer or a wooden spoon. Stir in milk, mashed potatoes, grated cheese, and melted margarine. Mix well. Add egg mixture to flour mixture and stir just until mixed. Spoon batter into paper lined cups and bake 25 minutes or until firm and lightly browned. Makes 10 servings.

Sharing Our Diabetics Best Recipes (Nevada)

Frittatas

The Frittata is like an omelet but easier to make—you don't have to try and fold it over with all the goodies in the middle. Everything is cooked inside the Frittata.

2 eggs
¼ cup diced ham
2 tablespoons chopped onion
Oregano to taste
Salt and pepper to taste
Parmesan cheese
1–2 tablespoons olive oil

Whisk eggs in a medium-size bowl. Add diced ham and onion. Add seasonings to taste. Sprinkle with Parmesan cheese to taste. Heat olive oil in bottom of sauté pan. Pour in frittata mixture and cook until one side is done. Flip and cook the other side until golden brown. Drain on paper towels. Serve for breakfast.

Note: Substitute other veggies and cooked meats, if desired.

Cherished Recipes (Utah)

Johnny Cakes

6 eggs
1 (8.5-ounce) package corn
  muffin mix
1 (8-ounce) can whole-kernel
  corn, drained
1 cup Filling
1 teaspoon cooking oil
1 cup sour cream
1 cup salsa

In a small mixing bowl, beat eggs until foamy, then add unprepared muffin mix until thoroughly blended. Add corn and desired Fillings, blending well. In a large frying pan on medium, heat oil. Spoon about ¼ cup of batter for each cake into hot pan. When bubbles appear at edges, turn over and cook until lightly browned. Serve with sour cream and salsa. Serves 4.

FILLING SUGGESTIONS:

Chopped ham
Diced cooked bacon
Thinly sliced green onions
Mushrooms
Red or green pepper, chopped
Or a combination of several

Recipes for Roughing It Easy (Utah)

Quick Yeast Raised Pancakes

If you like homemade bread, you will truly enjoy these fragrant pancakes.

2 cups milk
2 eggs, slightly beaten
2 tablespoons vegetable oil
2 tablespoons honey
2 cups unbleached flour
3 tablespoons dry active yeast
1 teaspoon salt

In small saucepan, heat milk, eggs, oil, and honey to 120°. Meanwhile, in large mixing bowl, mix flour, yeast, and salt. Pour liquids over flour mixture and whisk for 1–2 minutes until smooth. Set bowl in a warm spot for about 5 minutes. The batter will rise during this time. Heat griddle to medium-high and oil. Stir down batter and ladle ¼ cup of batter onto lightly greased griddle. Cook 2–3 minutes, turn and cook 1–2 minutes longer. They should rise nicely and turn golden brown. Serve with whipped butter and warm maple or fruit syrup. Serves 4–6.

Good Morning, Goldie! (Colorado)

Upside-Down Apple French Toast

Prepare the night before or at least three hours in advance.

½ cup (1 stick) butter
1¼ cups packed brown sugar
1 tablespoon water
3 Granny Smith apples
Cinnamon, to taste
½ cup raisins (optional)
1 loaf French bread, sliced
  1½ inches thick

1½ cups milk
6 eggs
1 teaspoon vanilla
Nutmeg, to taste
Crème Topping
Sliced almonds, for garnish

Combine butter, brown sugar, and water in saucepan. Heat on medium until bubbling, stirring frequently. Place in a 9x13-inch pan and allow to cool for 20–30 minutes. Peel, core and slice the apples. Place the slices in rows, close together (overlapping), on top of the sauce in pan. Sprinkle with cinnamon and raisins. Place the slices of bread on top of the apples. Mix together the milk, eggs, and vanilla. Pour over bread. Sprinkle with a little nutmeg. Cover and refrigerate. Bake at 350° for approximately 60 minutes, or until golden brown and crispy on top. Serve upside-down. Spoon the sauce in the pan over the French toast. Serve with Crème Topping and garnish with almonds. Serves 6.

CRÈME TOPPING:

½ cup whipping cream
½ cup sour cream

¼ cup sugar
½ teaspoon almond extract

Whip on high until thickened. Place 2 tablespoons of topping on top of French toast.

Recipe from The Manor, Ouray
Colorado Bed & Breakfast Cookbook (Colorado)

Rocky Mountain Blueberry French Toast

12 slices stale French bread
cut into 1-inch cubes
16 ounces cream cheese,
chilled and cut into
1-inch cubes

1 cup fresh blueberries, rinsed
and drained
12 large eggs
⅓ cup maple syrup
2 cups milk

Generously grease 8 au gratin dishes. Place ½ of the bread cubes in the dishes. Scatter the cream cheese over the bread and sprinkle with one cup of the berries. Arrange the remaining bread cubes over the berries. In a large bowl combine the eggs, syrup, and milk. Mix and pour evenly over the bread-cheese mixture. Spray the undersides of 8 pieces of foil generously with a vegetable spray and cover each au gratin dish. Refrigerate overnight.

In the morning, set the dishes out to bring them to room temperature. Bake in a 350° oven, covered, for 25 minutes. Uncover and bake an additional 15 minutes or until puffed and golden. Serve with Blueberry Syrup.

BLUEBERRY SYRUP:

1 cup sugar
2 tablespoons cornstarch
1 cup water

1 cup fresh blueberries, rinsed
and drained
1 tablespoon unsalted butter

Combine the sugar, cornstarch, and water over medium-high heat. Cook for 5 minutes or until thickened. Stir occasionally. Stir in the blueberries and simmer for 10 minutes or until the blueberries burst. Add the butter. Stir until melted. Drizzle over French toast. Makes 8 servings.

Recipe from Cattail Creek Bed and Breakfast Inn, Loveland
Distinctly Delicious (Colorado)

Fabulous French Toast

5 eggs
⅔ cup half-and-half
2 tablespoons orange juice
  concentrate
2 tablespoons sugar
Grated zest of orange

2 teaspoons cinnamon
6 stale plain croissants, cut
6 tablespoons butter
Powdered sugar or orange
  marmalade

Beat eggs and cream together. Add orange juice, sugar, zest, and cinnamon, and whisk until blended. Pour into shallow pan. Dip each croissant half in egg mixture. Melt a few tablespoons butter in skillet over medium heat. Fry croissants until golden. Sprinkle sugar or marmalade over croissants and serve. Serves 6.

Recipes from Sunset Garden Club (Nevada)

Stuffed French Toast with Strawberries

8 slices white or wheat bread,
  cut 1 inch thick
1 (8-ounce) package cream
  cheese, softened
6 tablespoons strawberry
  preserves
1⅓ cups milk

4 eggs
2 teaspoons granulated sugar
2 teaspoons vanilla
1 teaspoon cinnamon
4 cups sliced strawberries
4 tablespoons powdered sugar

Cut each bread slice in half crosswise. With a sharp knife, cut a horizontal slit in each half slice to make a pocket. In a medium bowl, combine cream cheese and preserves. Spread $\frac{1}{16}$ of the mixture inside each bread pocket. Pinch edges of bread together to hold filling. In a shallow bowl, whisk together milk, eggs, sugar, vanilla, and cinnamon. Dip filled bread slices in egg mixture to coat. Cook about 6 minutes or until golden brown, turning once. Top with strawberries and sprinkle with powdered sugar.

Pleasures from the Good Earth (Utah)

Fried Apples

Our mom used to serve these with fried quail, biscuits and gravy for breakfast when we were kids. They are also excellent served with pork.

¼ cup margarine
6 medium tart apples,
  unpeeled and sliced*

½ cup sugar
1 teaspoon cinnamon
¼ cup water (more if needed)

In a skillet, heat margarine; add apples, sugar, cinnamon, and water. Cover. Simmer for about 20 minutes or until apples are tender. (If apple mixture starts to thicken before apples are tender, add a little more water.)

*Jonathan apples are best for this recipe.

Country Classics (Colorado)

Stacey's Western Baked Omelette

⅓ cup sliced green onions
1 tablespoon butter or
  margarine
1½ cups cooked rice
1 cup shredded Cheddar
  cheese
1 medium tomato, chopped

1 can diced green chiles,
  drained
6 eggs, beaten
⅓ cup milk
1 teaspoon Worcestershire
½ teaspoon salt
Picante sauce (optional)

In small skillet over medium heat, cook onions in butter until tender but not brown. Combine rice, cheese, tomato, and chiles in large bowl; add cooked onions. Combine eggs, milk, Worcestershire, and milk in small bowl. Stir into rice mixture. Pour into buttered 9-inch quiche dish or pie pan. Bake at 350° for 30–35 minutes. Serve with picante sauce, if desired. Makes 4 servings.

Recipe from The Painted Lady Bed & Breakfast Inn, Colorado Springs
Pure Gold—Colorado Treasures (Colorado)

Roughcut Cactus and Egg Omelet

2 tablespoons butter	8 large eggs
1 (8-ounce) can nopalitos (cactus), drained and rinsed	⅓ cup milk
	¼ teaspoon salt
⅛ cup chopped yellow onion	¼ teaspoon black pepper

Melt butter in a skillet and sauté nopalitos and onion until tender. In a bowl, beat together eggs, milk, salt, and pepper. Pour egg mixture over nopalitos and onions and cook over low heat until eggs set. Fold eggs over with a spatula. Continue cooking about 3–5 minutes to desired doneness. Serve hot. Serves 1 hungry cowboy or 2 ranch guests.

Authentic Cowboy Cookery Then & Now (Nevada)

Khemosabi Quiche

This is a quiche that real men will eat.

½ cup butter	1 cup shredded Monterey Jack cheese
2 large brown onions	
8 ounces mushrooms	2 unbaked pie shells
½ ounce dry vermouth	6 eggs
2 tablespoons minced garlic	1 cup whipping cream
1 cup shredded Cheddar cheese	1 tablespoon Worcestershire

Melt butter in skillet. Chop onions and slice mushrooms. Add vermouth and garlic to skillet. Add onions and mushrooms. Sauté until golden. Reserve 2 tablespoons of each cheese. Alternate layers of remaining cheeses and mushroom mixture in 9-inch pie shells until all ingredients are used. Combine eggs, cream and Worcestershire in bowl; mix with wire whisk. Pour over layers in pie shells. Top with reserved cheeses. Bake at 350° for 45 minutes. Serve warm or cold. May reheat in microwave, if desired. Yields 12 servings.

Beyond Oats (Colorado)

Shorty's Scramble

6 eggs
½ cup cooked sausage,
   ham, or bacon pieces
½ bell pepper, chopped

½ onion, chopped
1 tomato, chopped
½ cup grated cheese
Salsa

Scramble eggs in mixing bowl and pour into greased frying pan. Cook over medium heat for 1½ minutes, until eggs start to thicken. Add meat, pepper, onion, tomato, and cheese. Mix and cook until eggs are cooked all the way. Top with salsa to taste.

The Cowboy Chuck Wagon Cookbook (Utah)

Brunch Casserole

This is wonderful to serve to guests for a mid-morning brunch.

6 slices white bread
2 cups shredded Jack cheese
2 cups shredded Cheddar
   cheese
1 pound link sausage, cooked
1 (4-ounce) can mild diced
   chiles
6 eggs

2 cups milk
1 teaspoon salt
½ teaspoon pepper
1 tablespoon oregano
¼ teaspoon dried mustard
¼ teaspoon garlic powder
½ teaspoon paprika

Cut crust from bread. Butter one side and place buttered-side-down in 9x13-inch pan. Layer ½ cheeses, chopped sausage, remaining ½ cheeses, then chiles. Beat together eggs, milk, and spices. Pour over ingredients in pan. Cover and chill overnight.

   Bake uncovered at 325° for 50 minutes. Serves 6–8. Serve with fresh fruit.

Home Cooking (Nevada)

A One-Pot Breakfast

1–1½ pounds ground sausage
1 medium to large onion, chopped
1 (4-ounce) can sliced mushrooms (or fresh)
1 green pepper, chopped

1 (28-ounce) package cubed hash brown potatoes
¼ cup milk
8–10 eggs, beaten
½ pound Cheddar cheese, grated

In a large (12-inch) Dutch oven, heating just from below for now, brown the sausage, keeping it broken up in small pieces. Just before it is thoroughly browned, add onion, mushrooms, and green pepper. Once the vegetables are semicooked, add hash browns, mix, and cook for about 10 minutes.

Mix milk with eggs and pour over hash brown mixture. Stir, cover, and cook (adding coals to the top of the oven) at 325°–350° for about 20 minutes or until eggs are firm. Be careful not to burn the bottom at this stage. In the last 5 minutes of cooking, sprinkle cheese over top of egg mixture, cover once again, and cook until cheese has melted. Serve with your favorite salsa for a delicious one-pot breakfast.

Backyard Dutch Oven (Utah)

Chile Relleno Eggs with Stewed-Tomato Sauce

2 (4-ounce) cans whole green chiles, or 8 fresh roasted
2 cups grated Monterey Jack cheese, divided
6 eggs
1 tablespoon flour
2 cups milk
½ teaspoon nutmeg
1½ tablespoons butter

Preheat oven to 325°. Slit each chile down one side and fill loosely with grated cheese, using one cup of cheese for all the chiles. Lay filled chiles in lightly buttered, oven-proof casserole dish or shallow bowl.

In separate bowl, beat eggs and flour, then mix in milk and nutmeg. When blended well, fold in remaining grated cheese. Pour egg mixture over filled chiles, dot with butter, and bake for 45 minutes to 1 hour, until top is bubbly and knife inserted near center comes out clean. To serve, spoon Stewed-Tomato Sauce over eggs.

STEWED-TOMATO SAUCE:

2 (16-ounce) cans stewed tomatoes
1 teaspoon garlic powder
1 teaspoon basil flakes
1 tablespoon parsley flakes
½ teaspoon onion powder
½ teaspoon salt
¼ teaspoon black pepper
¼ teaspoon allspice
2 tablespoons butter

Combine all ingredients in a medium saucepan. Simmer over medium heat for 15–20 minutes, until heated through.

How to Win a Cowboy's Heart (Utah)

Sundance Chicken Hash

Foods served in the Foundry Grill at Sundance Resort represent the best of fresh American home-style cooking, often created over a wood-fire grill with fresh ingredients from Sundance's own gardens and local purveyors. This is Chef Trey Foshee's version of comfort food.

2 tablespoons clarified butter or vegetable oil

3 cups peeled, cubed potatoes (½ inch)

¾ cup red onion pieces (½ inch)

¾ cup peeled, roasted red bell pepper pieces (½ inch)

1 cup shredded roasted chicken

¼ cup minced scallions

1 tablespoon chopped parsley

Salt and pepper to taste

6 large eggs, cooked as you like

Heat a large nonstick sauté pan over high heat. Add clarified butter and potatoes. Cook until well browned, tossing occasionally. Reduce heat to medium and add onion. Sauté for 3–4 minutes or until tender. Add bell pepper and chicken and cook until heated through. Add scallions, parsley, salt and pepper. Mound onto 6 serving plates. Top each serving with an egg. Serves 6.

Always in Season (Utah)

Sundance Resort is a ski resort located 13 miles northeast of Provo, Utah, on Mount Timpanogos in Utah's Wasatch Range. Skiing began on the site in 1944. Actor Robert Redford acquired the area in 1969, and established a year-round resort that would later spawn an independent film festival and a nonprofit institute of the same name. The resort is named after the role he played in the 1969 film, *Butch Cassidy and the Sundance Kid.* (The resort of Sundance is not to be confused with the town of Sundance, Wyoming, the location from where the Sundance Kid received his name.) The Sundance Film Festival, held 30 miles north in Park City, is a competition for independent film makers that has become extremely popular in the film industry and media. It is the largest independent film festival in the United States, and also one of the largest in the world.

Breakfast Potato Boats

8 left-over or freshly baked potatoes
¼ cup chopped onion
½ cup butter
½ teaspoon salt
¼ teaspoon pepper
2 teaspoons seasoned salt, divided
1 teaspoon paprika
2 cups grated cheese
2 cups cooked and crumbled bacon

Make a cut in the top of the potatoes and scoop out all the insides, reserving shells. Or make 8 boats out of tin foil and use mashed potatoes. Mix potatoes, onion, butter, and seasonings (reserve 1 teaspoon seasoned salt). Spoon mixture back into potato shell and bake in a 12-inch Dutch oven that has been warmed and lightly oiled. Bake 30 minutes on 10–12 briquettes in your Volcano, or 10 briquettes on the bottom and 15 on top for outdoor cooking; on a propane fire, cook very low with 10 briquettes on top. Remove lid and put reserved seasoning, grated cheese, and bacon bits on top. Serve with bacon, hot rolls, or pancakes.

Log Cabin Campfire Cookn' (Utah)

Marco Polos

These are real quick whole-meal sandwiches that are great for drop-in guests.

6 English muffin halves
1 pound thinly sliced ham
1 pound thinly sliced turkey
½ onion, sliced thin

1 tomato, sliced
1 or 2 (10-ounce) packages
 broccoli, cooked and
 drained

Butter each muffin half and arrange on a cookie sheet. Broil to toast. On each muffin, arrange ham slice, turkey, onion, tomato, and 1–2 stalks broccoli.

CHEESE SAUCE:

3 tablespoons butter
3 tablespoons flour
2 cups milk, or
 half-and-half

1–1½ cups grated Cheddar
 cheese
½ teaspoon salt
Paprika

Melt butter in saucepan; stir in flour, then milk, stirring until thickened. Add Cheddar cheese and salt; stir until melted. Pour hot Cheese Sauce over warmed sandwiches (warm 10 minutes in a covered pan at 325°), then sprinkle with paprika.

Note: Sandwiches can also be heated in the microwave after the cheese sauce has been poured over them.

Kitchen Keepsakes (Colorado)

Molly Brown

This was probably the most popular item in the restaurant I once owned. We also did a version with roast beef, turkey, and Cheddar cheese we called the Horace Tabor.

1 wide-size loaf sour-dough bread, unsliced	**1 teaspoon Worcestershire**
⅓ cup mayonnaise	**¼ teaspoon white pepper**
2 teaspoons Dijon-style mustard	**6 ounces thinly sliced ham**
1 teaspoon lemon juice	**6 ounces thinly sliced turkey**
	6 slices Swiss cheese
	Melted butter

Slice bread lengthwise; trim crust from the slices. (Save top and bottom pieces; they are great for garlic toast or croutons.) Flatten each slice with rolling pin. Combine mayonnaise, mustard, lemon juice, Worcestershire, and pepper. Spread mayonnaise mixture on each slice of bread. Layer ham, turkey, and cheese on each slice. (Use amounts of ham, turkey, and cheese as needed, not necessarily the amounts mentioned.) Roll-up sandwich; secure with toothpick. Brush with melted butter and place on baking sheet. Bake in preheated oven at 375° for 12–15 minutes or until golden brown. Serves 5–6.

Mystic Mountain Memories (Colorado)

The Molly Brown House Museum in Denver, Colorado, chronicles the life of Margaret Tobin Brown (July 18, 1867–October 26, 1932). An American socialite, philanthropist, and activist, Molly became famous in the 1912 sinking of the *RMS Titanic* after getting lifeboat 6 to return to look for survivors. She became known after her death as The Unsinkable Molly Brown. Margaret and J.J. Brown purchased the home in 1894 after making their fortune in gold mining. It was in Margaret "Molly" Brown's possession until her death.

The city of Leadville, Colorado, was founded near silver deposits in 1877 by mine owners Horace Austin Warner Tabor and August Meyer, setting off the Colorado Silver Boom. By 1880, Leadville was one of the world's largest silver camps, with a population of over 40,000.

Italian Hero Loaf

3¼ cups flour, divided
1 tablespoon sugar
1 teaspoon salt
1 package quick-rising yeast
1 cup hot water (125°–130°)
1 tablespoon margarine,
  softened
8 ounces sliced cooked ham
4 ounces sliced provolone
  cheese

4 ounces sliced salami
1 (2-ounce) jar sliced
  pimentos, drained
½ cup pitted ripe olives,
  drained
1 egg white, beaten
Sesame seeds
Creamy Italian dressing
  (optional)

Set aside one cup flour. In large bowl of mixer, mix remaining flour, sugar, salt, and yeast. Stir in hot water and margarine. Mix in only enough reserved flour to make soft dough. Allow mixer to knead dough an additional 4 minutes.

On greased baking sheet, roll dough into 10x14-inch rectangle. Layer ham, provolone, and salami over center third of dough length; top with pimentos and olives. Make cuts from filling to dough edges at 1-inch intervals along sides of filling. Alternating sides, fold strips at an angle across filling; cover. Place large shallow pan on counter; half fill with boiling water. Place baking sheet over pan; let dough rise 15 minutes. Brush loaf with egg white; sprinkle with sesame seed. Bake at 400° for 25 minutes or till done. Cool slightly; serve warm with Italian dressing, if desired. Refrigerate leftovers; reheat to serve.

More Goodies and Guess-Whats (Colorado)

Soups, Chilis, and Stews

PHOTO © FRANK JENSEN, STATE OF UTAH DIVISION OF TRAVEL DEVELOPMENT

A 1.5-mile hike brings visitors to Delicate Arch, one of more than 2,000 sand-stone arches found in Utah's Arches National Park. It is the most widely-recognized landmark in the park, but was not within the original boundaries when the area became a U.S. National Monument in 1929. It was added in 1938.

Light and Healthy Bean Soup

1 (16-ounce) can seasoned
 tomatoes
1 (14-ounce) can chicken
 broth
1 cup salsa
2 cups water
1 (8-ounce) can corn
1 (16-ounce) can garbanzo
 beans, rinsed and
 drained
1 (16-ounce) can kidney
 beans, rinsed and drained

1 (15-ounce) can black beans,
 rinsed and drained
1 large onion, chopped
1 clove garlic, minced
1 medium green pepper,
 chopped
½ teaspoon ground thyme
½ teaspoon oregano leaves
¼ teaspoon basil leaves,
 crushed slightly
¼ cup cilantro, chopped
½ cup uncooked white rice

Put all ingredients into slow cooker. Stir. Cover and cook on low 6–8 hours. Serve with warmed tortillas or fresh, crusty bread. Serves 8–10.

Quick Crockery (Colorado)

Green Chili and Bean Soup

1 (16-ounce) package dried
 pinto beans
1 (3-pound) pot roast
2 cloves garlic
2 tablespoons oregano
2 tablespoons chili
 powder

1 (4-ounce) can green chiles,
 drained, chopped
1 tablespoon salt
1 medium onion, chopped
2 (28-ounce) cans tomatoes,
 mashed
3 cups water

Soak beans in water to cover overnight. Combine beans, pot roast, garlic, oregano, chili powder, green chiles, salt, onion, tomatoes, and water in slow cooker. Cook on medium for 6 hours. Remove roast. Discard fat and bones; shred meat. Place shredded meat in slow cooker. Cook for one hour longer. Serve over tortillas or corn chips, topped with shredded cheese, chopped onion, chopped tomatoes, sour cream, or avocado slices. Yields 12 servings.

The Flavor of Colorado (Colorado)

Boulder Black Bean Soup

The perfect supper after an awesome day of skiing!

2 teaspoons olive oil
1 medium onion, chopped
3 cloves garlic, minced
1 teaspoon dried whole
  oregano
½ teaspoon dried thyme
½ teaspoon cumin
¼ teaspoon cayenne pepper
3 cups canned black beans,
  rinsed and drained

3 cups low-sodium chicken
  broth
2 tomatoes, chopped
½ cup chopped onion
  (optional)
½ cup shredded reduced-fat
  Monterey Jack cheese
  (optional)

Heat oil in a large saucepan over medium heat. Sauté onion and garlic until tender (about 5 minutes). Stir in oregano, thyme, cumin, and cayenne pepper; cook one minute longer. Place half of beans in a blender and purée until smooth, adding chicken broth as needed to make a smooth purée. Add purée, remaining whole beans and broth to saucepan. Bring to a boil over medium heat then simmer uncovered for 20–30 minutes. Serve garnished with diced tomatoes and, if desired, onion and shredded cheese. Yields 8 servings.

Simply Colorado (Colorado)

The City of Boulder, Colorado, is in Boulder Valley where the Rocky Mountains meet the Great Plains, 35 miles northwest of Denver. Just west of the city are imposing rock formations of sedimentary stone along the east slope of Green Mountain, known as the Flatirons. The Flatirons are a widely recognized symbol of Boulder.

Basque Vegetable Soup

1 pound white pea beans
½ pound dried peas
Meaty ham knuckle
3 bay leaves, divided
1 onion, stuck with 2 whole
  cloves
3 quarts water
6 potatoes, cut small
4 carrots, sliced

4 turnips, diced
5 leeks, cut up
6 garlic cloves, chopped
1 teaspoon thyme
1 small cabbage, shredded
12 sausages
Grated cheese
French bread

Soak pea beans and dried peas overnight in water (unless they are the quick-cooking type).

   Next day, drain and put them into a deep kettle with a meaty ham knuckle, 2 bay leaves, onion with cloves, and 3 quarts water. Cook 1 hour and taste for salt (if ham is salty, salt will not need to be added.) Cook until beans are tender, and drain, reserving liquid. In bean liquid, cook potatoes, carrots, turnips, leeks, garlic, thyme, and remaining 1 bay leaf. When tender, add shredded cabbage, the beans and peas, meat from ham bone, and sausages. Cook until cabbage is just tender and soup very thick. Serve with grated cheese on top and French bread. Serves 6–8.

The Great Nevada Cookbook (Nevada)

The silver rush of the 1850s brought Basque people from their European mountain homeland to the Mountain West area of the United States. After the boom went bust, they went back to their heritage as sheep ranchers. In 1959, the first national Basque festival was held in Sparks, Nevada, with nearly 6,000 Basque-Americans in attendance.

Onion Soup Basquaise

Using cooked bread as a basic ingredient makes this soup very Basque.

2 small French bread rolls,
    thinly sliced
⅓ cup cooking oil or olive oil
4 medium onions, cut in
    ½-inch-thick slices

½ pound Swiss cheese, grated
    (4 cups)
3 (10¾-ounce) cans beef
    consommé
3 cans water

Place bread slices on a cookie sheet and bake at 250° for about 40 minutes. While the bread is baking, heat oil in a frying pan and sauté onions until they are limp. Remove bread slices from oven; increase temperature to 350°.

In a 3- to 4-quart casserole, layer half the toasted bread slices; top with half the onions, then half the Swiss cheese. Repeat layers.

In a separate pan, mix consommé and water and heat to boiling on the stove. Gently pour hot consommé over layers in casserole. Bake casserole, uncovered, at 350° for 30 minutes. Yields 8–10 servings.

Note: The soup puffs up as it bakes, so do not fill casserole too full. Leave at least 2 inches between soup and top of casserole.

Chorizos in an Iron Skillet (Nevada)

Broccoli-Cauliflower-Cheese Soup

3 chicken bouillon cubes
3 cups water
½ cup diced celery
½ cup diced carrots
¼ cup diced onion
1 cup chopped broccoli

1 cup chopped cauliflower
6 cups milk
½ cup butter, melted
2 tablespoons flour
½ pound Velveeta cheese,
    cubed

Dissolve bouillon cubes in water in a large pot. Add vegetables and cook until tender. Add milk. Cream the melted butter and flour until smooth, add to soup mixture and stir. Simmer. Add cheese; stir until cheese is melted.

Recipes from the Heart (Nevada)

Mushroom and Barley Soup

1½ pounds boneless beef
  chuck, cut into ¾-inch
  cubes
1 tablespoon cooking oil
1½ cups chopped onions
1 cup diced carrots
1 cup sliced celery
1 pound fresh mushrooms,
  sliced
2 garlic cloves, minced
½ teaspoon dried thyme

1 (14½-ounce) can beef broth
1 (14½-ounce) can chicken
  broth
2 cups water
½ cup medium pearl barley
1 teaspoon salt (optional)
½ teaspoon pepper
3 tablespoons chopped fresh
  parsley

In a Dutch oven or soup kettle, brown meat in oil. Remove meat with a slotted spoon and set aside. Sauté onions, carrots, and celery in drippings over medium heat until tender, about 5 minutes. Add mushrooms, garlic, and thyme; cook and stir for 3 minutes. Add broths, water, barley, salt and pepper. Return meat to pan and bring to a boil. Reduce heat, cover and simmer for 1½–2 hours or until barley and meat are tender. Add parsley. Serves 10.

Country Classics II (Colorado)

Cream of Corn Soup

2 strips bacon, finely chopped
2 tablespoons finely chopped
  onion
2 cups frozen or fresh corn
2 tablespoons butter

2 tablespoons flour
2 cups milk
1 teaspoon salt
½ teaspoon pepper
2 cups light cream

Fry diced bacon until crisp; put aside and sauté onion in drippings until soft. Put corn through chopper; add to bacon and onion. Add butter and then the flour; cook slowly for 3 minutes. Add milk, salt and pepper and cook until thickened, then add cream and heat until smooth.

The Best of Friends (Colorado)

Chinese Chicken Corn Soup

This soup is served as a first course in Chinese restaurants but also makes a good meal.

5–6 chicken thighs	**Chicken broth or water to**
1–2 chicken breast halves	**cover**

Cook the chicken in canned chicken broth or water. If using water, add 1 chopped onion and 1 sliced rib of celery with leaves, and salt and pepper to taste. You may also roast the chicken, but be careful not to dry out the meat. Discard skin and separate meat from bones. Cut into bite-size pieces or shred and set aside.

BROTH:

1 tablespoon minced garlic	**¼ pound mushrooms, sautéed**
1 tablespoon minced ginger	**in a little butter or oil**
2 teaspoons vegetable oil	**½ cup peas, fresh or frozen**
1 quart chicken broth	**Soy sauce to taste**
1 (15-ounce) can sweet	**Sugar to taste**
whole-kernel corn (or fresh)	**Salt and pepper to taste**
1 (15-ounce) can creamed	**2 egg whites**
corn	**Chopped cilantro (optional)**

Sauté garlic and ginger in soup pot in a small amount of oil until flavor is released, 1–2 minutes. Add broth, cooked chicken, corn, mushrooms, soy sauce, and sugar. Simmer for 20–30 minutes. Add peas and simmer until they are tender. Adjust seasoning with soy sauce, sugar, salt and pepper, if necessary. Just before serving, scramble the egg whites. Add egg whites to broth in a slow steady stream while stirring broth. Serve with chopped cilantro, if desired.

Note: If using fresh corn, add with the peas so they're not overcooked. Frozen corn also works well in this recipe.

Soup for Our Souls (Nevada)

Gayle's Chicken Tortilla Soup

2 (14-ounce) cans chicken
  broth
2 cups diced, cooked chicken
1 (4-ounce) can mild diced
  green chiles
1 (15-ounce) can corn, drained
1 (10¾-ounce) can fat-free
  cream of chicken soup

½ teaspoon ground cumin
Fresh chopped cilantro to taste
Fresh lime juice (optional)
Condiments: shredded cheese,
  crushed tortilla chips, diced
  tomatoes, diced avocado,
  sliced green onions, sliced
  black olives, sour cream

Bring broth to a boil and add remaining ingredients, except condiments. Simmer for a few minutes to blend flavors, then ladle into bowls. Top immediately with desired condiments and serve.

Note: You can place condiments in bowl first and pour soup on top.

Only the Best (Utah)

Mexican Chicken Chile Pepper-Tortilla Soup

1 large onion, cut into
  medium dice
3 tablespoons olive oil
8 cups chicken stock
4 roasted Anaheim or
  California green peppers,
  peeled, stemmed, seeded,
  and diced
2½ cups finely chopped
  chicken

2 teaspoons dried oregano
6 corn tortillas, halved and cut
  into ½-inch-wide strips
Salt and pepper to taste
1 large tomato, cored and
  diced
1 avocado, diced
¾ cup chopped fresh cilantro

In heavy-bottomed, 4-quart saucepan, cook onion in olive oil over moderate heat for 10 minutes, stirring frequently. Add stock, chiles, chicken, and oregano; bring to boil over high heat. Reduce heat to moderate and simmer for 15 minutes or until chicken is cooked through. Add tortillas and cook 5 minutes. Season with salt and pepper. Garnish each portion with tomato, avocado, and cilantro before serving.

Lake Tahoe Cooks! (Nevada)

Homemade Chicken Noodle Soup over Mashed Potatoes

When I ask the men in my family what they want for their birthday dinner, this is their request.

1 large chicken
1 onion, quartered
2 carrots, chopped
2 stalks celery
2 cloves garlic, minced
1 tablespoon chicken bouillon
  granules

2 carrots, grated
¼ cup minced fresh parsley
1 package fresh linguine
  noodles, cut into 2-inch
  pieces
1½ cups frozen petite peas
Mashed potatoes

Place chicken in large pot and cover with water. Add onion, chopped carrots, and celery stalks. Bring to a boil; simmer gently about 2 hours or until tender.

Remove chicken from stock, and let cool; remove meat from bones. Cut up chicken and store in the refrigerator until ready for use. Strain broth and chill. Remove fat from top of cooled broth.

About 30 minutes before serving, place broth in pot, adding garlic, bouillon, grated carrots, and minced parsley. Add more water as needed to make enough broth. Bring to a boil, then add chicken pieces, linguine noodle pieces, and peas. Cook until noodles are done. Serve over mashed potatoes in bowls. Serves 8–10.

Recipe by Bruce and Christine Olsen
Five-Star Recipes from Well-Known Latter Day Saints (Utah)

FLICKREVIEWR@WIKIPEDIA.COM

The Mormon Tabernacle Choir is a 360-member, all-volunteer choir. The choir is sponsored by The Church of Jesus Christ of Latter-day Saints. However, the choir is completely self-funded, traveling and producing albums to support the organization. Since its establishment more than 150 years ago, the choir has performed and recorded extensively, not only in the United States but around the world. Since its first recording in 1910, the choir has earned five gold albums and two platinum albums.

Split Pea Soup with Ham

2 pounds cooked ham
1 (16-ounce) package (2 cups)
  dried split peas
1 teaspoon salt
½ teaspoon basil leaves

1 large onion, chopped
¼ teaspoon pepper
8 cups water
4–5 celery stalks, sliced
5–6 carrots, peeled and sliced

Cut ham into ½- to 1-inch cubes. In a 12-inch Dutch oven, combine all ingredients except celery and carrots. Simmer, covered, at about 325°–350°, for one hour. (Heat from bottom only). Stir in celery and carrots. Continue simmering, covered, for ½–1 hour, or until peas are tender and soup thickens.

Backyard Dutch Oven (Utah)

The Alpine Village Chicken Supreme Soup

ROUX:

½ cup oil

1 cup flour

Heat oil until smoking; add flour and stir constantly with wire whisk. It should be the consistency of mashed potatoes. Remove from heat when slightly browned.

SOUP:

2½ quarts water
1 pound ground, cooked
  chicken
2 teaspoons Kitchen Bouquet
2 teaspoons celery salt

1 medium onion, ground
¼ teaspoon pepper
2–3 carrots, ground
2 teaspoons chicken bouillon

Boil all Soup ingredients together for about 30 minutes. Add Roux to Soup and use whisk to blend. Enjoy.

Feeding the Flock (Nevada)

Baked Tortellini Soup

1½ pounds sausage links
1 cup chopped onion
1 teaspoon minced garlic
¼ teaspoon black pepper
2 tablespoons olive oil
4 cups beef broth
2 cups water
1½ teaspoons Italian
  seasoning
1½ cups peeled and thinly
  sliced carrots

1 (16-ounce) can whole
  tomatoes
1 (16-ounce) can kidney beans,
  drained and rinsed
1 (6-ounce) can pitted, sliced
  black olives, drained
2 cups diced zucchini
16 ounces cheese tortellini
Freshly grated Parmesan
  cheese for garnish

Preheat oven to 400°. In roasting pan, combine sausage, onion, garlic, and pepper. Add olive oil and toss to coat. Roast, uncovered, stirring occasionally, 20–30 minutes, until sausage is brown. Remove from oven. Reduce oven temperature to 325°. Drain any grease from sausage and cut into ¼-inch slices. Return to roasting pan. Add broth, water, seasoning, and carrots. Bake 30 minutes, until sausage is tender. Remove from oven.

Squeeze tomatoes by hand to break up, then stir tomatoes with juice, beans, olives, and zucchini into roasting pan with sausage. Bake 15–20 minutes. Add tortellini and bake 5 minutes longer. Ladle into bowls and garnish with Parmesan cheese. Great served with garlic bread.

Note: This soup may be cooked on the stovetop, also.

CASA Cooks (Nevada)

Nevada is the driest state in the nation, with an average annual rainfall of only about 7 inches. Much of the state is uninhabited, sagebrush-covered desert. The wettest part of the state receives about 40 inches of precipitation per year, while the driest spot has less than four inches per year.

Chuckwagon Soup

1 pound hamburger meat
1 medium onion, chopped
3 stalks celery, chopped
3 carrots, sliced
4 potatoes, peeled and cubed
  (or rice, barley, or noodles)
1 (10-ounce) package frozen
  mixed vegetables (or add
  corn, peas, beans, or any
  other vegetable to taste)

1 (16-ounce) can tomatoes
  (or tomato sauce)
Water to cover
4 beef bouillon cubes
¼ teaspoon black pepper
1½ teaspoons salt
¼ teaspoon garlic powder
Cheddar cheese, grated
Flour and water mixture to
  thicken

In a large saucepan, brown the hamburger with the onion. Drain fat. Add celery, carrots, potatoes, frozen mixed vegetables, and tomatoes. Add water, bouillon cubes, and seasonings. Bring to a boil, reduce heat and simmer until vegetables are tender. Thicken as necessary with flour mixture. Ladle into bowls and top each generously with grated cheese.

As with any soup, this is better the second day as flavors have blended. This is also a good soup to make when there are little dabs of leftover vegetables to use, and it's definitely one you can make your own with dashes of your favorite seasonings. Serves 6–8.

More Kitchen Keepsakes (Colorado)

Portuguese Sopas

1 (5-pound) chuck roast
1 (8-ounce) can tomato sauce
½ medium onion, finely
  chopped
½ teaspoon black pepper
1 teaspoon salt
1 cup burgundy wine or
  ¼ cup vinegar
1 cup water
¼ cup ketchup

¼ teaspoon garlic salt
½ teaspoon whole cloves
¼ teaspoon whole cumin seed
½ teaspoon whole allspice
3 or 4 bay leaves
1 stick cinnamon
Sprigs of mint
French bread
Dill pickles

Put roast in heavy roaster (one with a lid) and place tomato sauce, onion, pepper, salt, wine, water, ketchup, and garlic salt around the roast. Put remaining spices in a tea strainer or wrap in cheesecloth. Put container with spices down into the juice. Cover roaster and cook for 3–3½ hours at 350°.

When cooked, remove pan from heat and let cool so that all fat will come to the top of the pan. Remove fat, then add 1½–2 quarts water (to suite taste). Simmer with meat for 30 minutes or so. Pour juice over mint and sliced French bread. Serve meat in separate bowl. Do not forget to serve with dill pickles.

The Great Nevada Food Festival Cookbook (Nevada)

Spicy Southwestern Chowder

2 slices uncooked bacon, chopped
1 medium onion, chopped
1 cup shredded carrots (about 2medium)
1–2 jalapeño peppers, seeded and minced
2 cloves garlic, minced
1½ teaspoons chili powder
½ teaspoon ground cumin
3 cups low-fat milk

2 cups reduced-sodium chicken broth
3 cups cooked brown rice
1 (16-ounce) package frozen corn or 1 (17-ounce) can corn, drained
6 large sourdough round rolls, hollowed out, leaving ½-inch walls
Green onions for garnish

Cook bacon in Dutch oven over medium-high heat 5–7 minutes, stirring until bacon is crisp. Drain all but 1 tablespoon fat. Add onion, carrots, jalapeños, garlic, chili powder, and cumin. Cook 3–5 minutes, stirring constantly until onion is tender. Reduce heat to medium. Add milk, broth, rice, and corn. Cook, stirring, 10–12 minutes until mixture boils. Cook 1 minute more; remove from heat. Ladle into bread rounds. Garnish with green onions. Makes 6 servings.

30 Days to a Healthier Family (Utah)

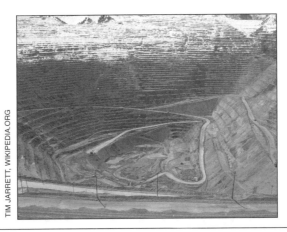

TIM JARRETT, WIKIPEDIA.ORG

Bingham Canyon Mine, the world's largest man-made excavation and first open-pit mine, is located twenty-eight miles southwest of Salt Lake City, Utah. The mine is two and one-half miles across, and three-quarters of a mile deep. In production since 1906, ore from the mine has yielded more than 17 million tons of copper, 23 million ounces of gold, and 190 million ounces of silver. Cumulatively, Bingham Canyon has produced more copper than any other mine in the United States, and is the second in the world after Chuquicamata in Chile.

Hearty Potato-Ham Chowder

3 cups peeled, cubed
  Colorado potatoes
1 cup water
⅔ cup finely chopped onion
1 teaspoon crushed dried
  marjoram
½ teaspoon dry mustard
2 teaspoons instant chicken
  bouillon granules
¼ teaspoon pepper
3 cups milk, divided
¼ cup all-purpose flour
¾ cup shredded Swiss cheese
1 cup chopped reduced-sodium
  ham
2 tablespoons snipped parsley

In a large saucepan, combine the potatoes, water, onion, marjoram, mustard, bouillon granules, and pepper. Bring to boiling; reduce heat. Cover and simmer about 20 minutes or until potatoes are tender. Mash potatoes slightly; do not drain. Combine one cup of the milk and flour, whisk to blend well. Add to hot mixture along with remaining milk and cheese. Cook and stir until slightly thickened and bubbly. Cook and stir one minute more. Stir in ham and parsley; heat through. Makes 4–6 servings.

Colorado Potato Favorite Recipes (Colorado)

Potato Bisque

2 medium onions, diced
1½ cups diced celery
2–3 tablespoons margarine
8–10 potatoes, diced ½ inch
2 cups water
4 chicken bouillon cubes
3 cups milk, divided
4–6 tablespoons cornstarch
2 tablespoons salt, or to taste
Sprinkle of chopped parsley

Fry onions and celery in margarine. Add potatoes, water, and bouillon cubes; cover and cook 15–20 minutes until potatoes are tender. Add 2½ cups milk and bring to a boil. Mix ½ cup milk with cornstarch. Pour into pot, add salt, and stir well. Cook 3–5 minutes more to thicken. Sprinkle with parsley.

Championship Dutch Oven Cookbook (Utah)

A Cowboy's "Real Chili Got No Beans in It, Ma'am" Chili

1 cup diced yellow onions
3 cloves garlic, minced
2 tablespoons oil
2 pounds beef sirloin, cubed into ¼-inch squares
2 cups chopped, peeled ripe tomatoes
1 cup tomato sauce
1 (12-ounce) bottle beer
1 cup strong brewed coffee
2 (6-ounce) cans tomato paste
½ cup low-salt beef broth
½ cup packed brown sugar
3 tablespoons chili powder
1 teaspoon cumin
1 teaspoon unsweetened cocoa powder
1 teaspoon dried oregano
1 teaspoon ground cayenne pepper
1 teaspoon salt
½ teaspoon black pepper
4 fresh jalapeño chile peppers, seeded and chopped

Sauté onions and garlic in oil. Add sirloin and lightly brown in oil for about 8–10 minutes. Mix tomatoes, tomato sauce, beer, coffee, tomato paste, beef broth, brown sugar, chili powder, cumin, cocoa powder, oregano, cayenne pepper, salt, and black pepper. Reduce heat to low and simmer for about 1½ hours. Stir in jalapeños and simmer for another 30 minutes. Authentic chili should not be thick. Serves 2 cowboys or about 6 tenderfoot sissies.

A Cowboy Cookin' Every Night (Nevada)

Rocky Mountain Campfire Chili

2 pounds ground beef, elk, or deer (or mixed)

2 medium yellow onions, chopped

3 cloves garlic, minced

Oil

1 (16-ounce) can tomatoes, broken up

4 tablespoons tomato paste

4 ounces diced green chiles

2 pickled jalapeño peppers, chopped (optional)

3 tablespoons chili powder

1 teaspoon salt

1 teaspoon cumin

1 tablespoon oregano

2 (14½-ounce) cans beef broth

5 cups water

1 (15-ounce) can pinto beans

Brown meat with onions and garlic in oil. Add tomatoes, tomato paste, chiles, jalapeños, seasonings, beef broth, and water. Bring mixture to a boil. Reduce heat to low and cook 4–5 hours, stirring occasionally. Adjust seasonings, if necessary. Add beans during last 30 minutes of cooking. Serve hot in bowls with an assortment of condiments such as grated cheeses, sliced olives, Pico de Gallo, chopped onions, etc. Yields 3 quarts.

Colorado Foods and More. . . (Colorado)

The largest mountain chain in North America is the Rocky Mountains. The length of the system is about 3,300 miles; the width is as much as 400 miles. They extend from northern New Mexico to the Arctic Ocean in northwestern Alaska, crossing parts of Colorado, Wyoming, Utah, Idaho, Montana, and Washington in the United States and parts of Alberta, British Columbia, the Yukon Territory, and the Northwest Territories in Canada. The Rockies are often divided into four sections—Southern, Middle, Northern, and Arctic Rockies. The Southern Rockies are sometimes referred to as the Colorado Rockies since the 30 highest summits of the Rocky Mountains all lie within the state of Colorado.

Baked Chili

CHILI:

1 pound ground beef
1 large onion, chopped
1 large green pepper, chopped
1 (16-ounce) can kidney beans, rinsed and drained
1 (15¼-ounce) can whole-kernel corn, drained
1 (15-ounce) can tomato sauce

1 (14½-ounce) can diced tomatoes
1 (4-ounce) can diced green chiles
2 teaspoons chili powder
½ teaspoon sugar
1 teaspoon salt
1 teaspoon ground cumin
½ teaspoon garlic powder

In a Dutch oven or large 4-quart pan, cook beef, onion, and green pepper over medium heat until meat is cooked through. Drain. Rinse and drain kidney beans; add to meat mixture. Add drained corn, tomato sauce, tomatoes, green chiles, chili powder, sugar, salt, cumin, and garlic powder. Bring to a boil, stirring occasionally. Reduce heat; cover and simmer for 10 minutes.

CORNBREAD BISCUITS:

1 cup all-purpose flour
1 cup cornmeal
2 teaspoons baking powder
⅛ teaspoon salt

1 egg
½ cup milk
½ cup sour cream

Combine flour, cornmeal, baking powder, and salt in a medium bowl. In a separate bowl, beat egg, milk, and sour cream until smooth; stir into dry ingredients just until moistened. Set aside.

Transfer Chili to an ungreased 9x13-inch baking dish. Drop biscuit batter by heaping teaspoonfuls onto hot Chili. Bake uncovered at 400° for 15–17 minutes or until biscuits are lightly browned. Makes 8 servings.

Lion House Entertaining (Utah)

Chili

4 large onions, chopped
1 large green pepper, seeded, chopped
3 tablespoons olive oil
1 tablespoon mustard seeds
2 tablespoons chili powder
2 teaspoons cumin seeds (optional)
2 teaspoons unsweetened cocoa

½ teaspoon ground cinnamon
3 (16-ounce) cans kidney beans, with juice
1 (6-ounce) can tomato paste
1 cup water
1 (16-ounce) can whole tomatoes
1 pound firm tofu, diced

In a large kettle, sauté onions and pepper in oil over medium-high heat until onions are golden. Add mustard seeds, and cook, stirring, for another minute. Add chili powder, cumin, cocoa, cinnamon, beans and their juice, tomato paste, and water. Pour in the liquid from the can of tomatoes, then chop tomatoes and add to the pot (or pulse the tomatoes and their liquid in a blender). Add tofu, and stir. Reduce heat and simmer for 40 minutes, stirring often.

After 20 minutes, check the consistency of your chili. If the chili is runnier than you like, simmer uncovered. If the chili is thicker than you like, add more water and simmer covered. If the chili is just right, simmer covered. In any case, stir frequently to prevent scorching. Salt to taste. Serve with relishes of grated Cheddar cheese, diced green onions, chopped tomatoes, diced green chiles, or peeled and diced cucumber. For vegans and non-dairy vegetarians, you can get a soy cheese (a non-dairy product found in the dairy section at health food stores), if you want. Serves 4–6.

How to Feed a Vegetarian (Colorado)

Beef Stew with Potato Dumplings

This is a very hearty stew. In pioneer days, they probably would have used only a few of the vegetables listed below. They used vegetables that were in season or what they had stored for the winter.

STEW:

1 pound beef stew meat
Oil, lard, or bacon grease for frying
1 large onion, diced
2 tablespoons flour
3–4 cups beef broth or water
2 stalks celery, sliced
3 large carrots, sliced
Salt and pepper to taste
1 cup fresh or frozen peas
1 cup fresh, frozen, or canned corn
2 cups chopped cabbage

Brown meat in a small amount of oil in Dutch oven. Add onion and cook until tender. Sprinkle meat and onion with flour and let cook a few minutes more. Add beef broth or water, celery, carrots, and salt and pepper to taste. Cover and cook on stove-top at low heat until meat is very tender, about 45 minutes to 1 hour, stirring occasionally. Then add rest of ingredients and cook until all vegetables are tender. Add more broth if needed. After vegetables are tender, drop Potato Dumplings by spoonful into the boiling stew. Cover, reduce heat, and cook for 20–30 minutes until dumplings are done. Add more broth if needed. You may also thicken stew (after dumplings are done) with a water-flour mixture, if a thicker broth is desired.

POTATO DUMPLINGS:

1 egg
¾ cup bread crumbs
1 tablespoon diced onion
1 tablespoon flour
½ teaspoon salt
Dash or 2 of pepper
2 cups shredded potatoes
Additional flour for coating

Combine egg and bread crumbs and mix well to soften bread crumbs. Add onion, flour, salt, and pepper; mix again. Stir in potatoes, then form into small balls (about golf-ball size) and roll in a small amount of flour. Cook in stew as directed above.

Favorite Utah Pioneer Recipes (Utah)

Cowboy Stew

STEW:

1 cup dried beans

2 ounces side pork (3 strips bacon)

Flour

1 pound stew meat

1 cup tomatoes or juice

1 onion, finely chopped

½ cup chopped celery

Salt and pepper to taste

Be sure to wash and soak beans overnight—this will help shorten cooking time. Cook pork until fat is fried out and pork is crisp. Remove pork from pan. Lightly flour chunks of meat (buffalo, elk, deer, beef, bear, etc.) and fry until brown. Add beans, tomatoes, onion, celery, and seasoning. Be sure to put pork back in stew. Cover and cook for 2–3 hours. If you add ½ cup water, dumplings can be put on top 20 minutes before serving.

NEVER FAIL DUMPLINGS:

2 cups sifted flour

½ teaspoon salt

4 level teaspoons baking powder

1 egg

Enough milk to fill cup with beaten egg

Sift together dry ingredients. Break egg into measuring cup. Beat lightly with fork and fill cup to top with milk. Pour into mixing bowl, add dry ingredients, and mix enough to moisten dry ingredients. Let stand for 5 minutes to rise. Drop batter by spoonfuls onto stew. Cover and cook for 20 minutes. These are just as good warmed the next day.

Log Cabin Grub Cookbook (Utah)

Basque Stew

1 pound oxtails
2 pounds beef stew meat
Oil for braising
2 medium carrots, sliced
1 medium onion, sliced
2 stalks celery, chopped

2 tablespoons flour
2 quarts water
½ head white cabbage, in chunks
3 zucchini, sliced
Salt and pepper to taste

Preheat oven to 450°. Cut oxtails at the joints. Place in oven roasting pan with beef stew meat and a little oil. Place pan in oven and brown meat, stirring often. It will cook fast. When meat has browned, remove and turn off oven. Add carrots, onion, and celery to pan and return to hot oven for about 10 minutes to allow the vegetables to brown slightly. Remove from oven.

Stir in flour. Add water to pan and simmer on top of stove, covered for about 2 hours or until oxtail joints and meat are tender. Add cabbage and zucchini. Check for seasoning and add salt and pepper if necessary. Cook another 20–25 minutes or until done. Serve with side dishes of carrots, potatoes, and peas. Yields 8 servings.

Easy Cookin' in Nevada (Nevada)

Salads

Lake Tahoe, located in both California and Nevada, is nestled in the Sierra Nevada Mountains west of Carson City, Nevada. At 22 miles long, 11 miles wide, and an average depth of 989 feet, it is the largest alpine lake in North America. Nevada lays claim to 30 percent of Lake Tahoe, some 31,700 acres.

PHOTO © NEVADA COMMISSION ON TOURISM

Spinach Salad with Black Pepper Dressing

BLACK PEPPER DRESSING:

⅓ cup low-fat mayonnaise
2 tablespoons honey
1 tablespoon rice or white
  wine vinegar
½ teaspoon freshly ground
  black pepper

¼ teaspoon garlic powder
¼ teaspoon salt
1 tablespoon water

Whisk ingredients together. Set aside.

SALAD:

¾ pound fresh spinach
2 tomatoes, cut in thin
  wedges
¼ pound mushrooms, thinly
  sliced

2 hard-boiled eggs, diced
2 avocados, cubed
3 thin slices red onion
¼ cup bacon bits
1 cup croutons

Wash spinach in cold water to remove dirt, and dry in a salad spinner. Discard stems; tear spinach leaves into bite-size pieces. Place in large bowl with other Salad ingredients except croutons.

Keep Salad, croutons, and Dressing separate until serving time. At serving time, toss Salad and croutons with Dressing.

Lake Tahoe Cooks! (Nevada)

Strawberry-Spinach Salad with Honey Pecan Dressing

HONEY PECAN DRESSING:

⅓ cup light salad oil
3 tablespoons honey
1 tablespoon lemon juice
2 teaspoons vinegar
1 teaspoon soy sauce

1 teaspoon dill (optional)
⅓–½ cup pecans
2 tablespoons warm water
Grated lemon rind
2 cloves garlic

In a blender, mix all the ingredients until smooth. Chill thoroughly. This dressing can be made ahead and kept under refrigeration for up to 2 weeks.

SALAD:

Spinach leaves
Fresh strawberries

Fresh mushrooms
Slices of bacon, cooked crisp

Wash and vein the spinach leaves. Place sliced, fresh strawberries and mushrooms on top. Crumble some cooked, crisp bacon on top. Arrange on a plate and spoon Honey Pecan Dressing over the top.

Recipe from Heartstone Inn, Colorado Springs
Distinctly Delicious (Colorado)

In mountaineering terminology, a fourteener is a mountain that exceeds 14,000 feet above mean sea level. There are only 68 such peaks in the continental United States—and 54 of them are in Colorado. Mount Elbert near Leadville is the highest point in Colorado at 14,433 feet.

Caesar Salad

Large head romaine
1 egg
½ tube anchovy paste
3 cloves garlic, crushed
1 splash Worcestershire
1 splash Tabasco
1 heaping tablespoon Dijon
  mustard

1 cup olive oil
1 splash lemon juice
1 splash wine vinegar
1 cup freshly grated Parmesan
  cheese
½ cup toasted croutons

Wash lettuce and tear in bite-size pieces. Boil egg for 30 seconds and cool immediately with cold water. Mix together anchovy paste, crushed garlic, Worcestershire, Tabasco, mustard, and egg. Whisk well. Add olive oil to mixture along with lemon juice and wine vinegar. Blend well. Toss salad with dressing right before you are ready to eat, adding the grated cheese and croutons last.

The Fruit of the Spirit (Nevada)

Craisin Salad

DRESSING:
½ cup chopped onion
1 cup sugar
1½ teaspoons salt

2 teaspoons dry mustard
½ cup red wine vinegar
1 cup oil

Mix ingredients in blender; set aside.

SALAD:
1 head red leaf lettuce
1 head green leaf lettuce
1 head iceberg lettuce
1 (8-ounce) package shredded
  mozzarella cheese
1 (8-ounce) package shredded
  Parmesan cheese

1 pound bacon, cooked and
  crumbled
1 bag craisins
1 package sliced almonds,
  toasted
4–8 cooked and cut-up chicken
  breasts (optional)

Combine all Salad ingredients and toss with Dressing right before you serve. For a main meal salad, add cut-up chicken breasts. Serves 12.

Making Magic (Utah)

India Slaw Salad

1 small head cabbage
1 cup chunk pineapple, drained
1 (2-ounce) jar diced pimento, drained
1 cup golden raisins

1 (11-ounce) can Mandarin oranges, drained
⅔ cup sliced pitted black olives, drained
1 cup honey roasted peanuts

Chop cabbage medium-fine, put in colander, and rinse. Drain well. Cut pineapple chunks in half. Mix all ingredients together, except nuts.

DRESSING:

½ cup mayonnaise
1 tablespoon dill weed
1½ teaspoons curry
½ teaspoon ginger

1 tablespoon sugar
1 tablespoon vinegar
1 teaspoon dry mustard
1 tablespoon mustard

Mix ingredients well and pour over salad. Mix well. Add nuts to salad just before serving. Serves 4–6.

Timbreline's Cookbook (Nevada)

MARY E. EATON, WIKIPEDIA.ORG

The sego lily was declared to be the official state flower of Utah on March 18, 1911. Blooming in early summer, the sego lily has white, lilac, or yellow flowers and grows on open grass and sage rangelands in the Great Basin in Utah. The flower has historic significance as well as natural beauty. The soft, bulbous root of the sego lily was collected and eaten in the mid 1800's during a crop-devouring plague of crickets in Utah.

Slimscrumptious
Chinese Chicken Salad

2 chicken breasts, skinned
  and boned
2 slices fresh ginger
1½ cups water or chicken
  broth
3 cups shredded romaine
  lettuce
3 cups shredded cabbage
1 cup bean sprouts
½ cup chopped cucumber

½ cup pea pods, stringed
  and cut into strips
¼ cup chopped celery
¼ cup chopped green onions
½ cup shredded carrot
½ of 1 package ramen
  noodles, broken up
1 tablespoon shredded
  beni shoga (pickled ginger)

Place chicken breasts in skillet with fresh ginger pieces and water or chicken broth. Bring to a boil. Reduce heat to low, simmer and cook partially covered for 10–15 minutes or just until chicken is done. Drain chicken. Cool and cut into very thin slices. Arrange lettuce on 3 dinner plates. Then arrange cabbage, chicken, and vegetables over salad. Sprinkle uncooked ramen noodles over top.

DRESSING:

3 tablespoons rice or regular
  vinegar
¼ cup water
1 tablespoon sesame oil

1 tablespoon soy sauce
2 teaspoons sugar
⅛ teaspoon salt

Shake Dressing ingredients together in a covered jar, pour over salad and toss very well. Serve at once.

Bless This Food (Nevada)

Chicken Salad Cassidy

David Cassidy is a visible force in Las Vegas, both in the showrooms and in the community. His high-energy performances have been witnessed by many in EFX at the MGM Grand and At the Copa at the Rio. He has also served as Grand Marshal in the Henderson Industrial Days Parade. He organized a celebrity charity golf tournament to give back to the community that he and his family call home—Las Vegas.

2 tablespoons Dijon mustard
⅓ cup tamari
Splash of balsamic vinegar
2 whole chicken breasts,
   cut into small strips
1 teaspoon butter
1 teaspoon olive oil
Salt to taste
1–2 heads romaine lettuce
Assorted mixed greens
1 green onion, chopped

Raisins (optional)
Sunflower seed kernels
   (optional)
Sliced beets (optional)
1 hard-cooked egg, sliced
   (optional)
Equal parts olive oil, Dijon
   mustard, and tarragon
   vinegar
½ teaspoon (or less) salt

Mix mustard, tamari, and balsamic vinegar in a medium bowl. Add chicken strips and stir to coat. Let marinate for 15 minutes. Melt butter with 1 teaspoon olive oil in a skillet. Season with salt to taste. Heat until hot and add the chicken and marinade mixture. Cook until chicken is browned and cooked through. Set aside and keep warm.

Combine the romaine lettuce, mixed greens, green onion, raisins, and sunflower seeds. Top with sliced beets and sliced egg. Cover with chicken and pan juices. Whisk the olive oil, mustard, tarragon vinegar, and ½ teaspoon salt in a small bowl until creamy. Pour over salad and toss to coat. Yields 2–4 servings.

Las Vegas Glitter to Gourmet (Nevada)

Spicy Southwestern Taco Salad

⅔ cup chopped yellow onion
1 pound boneless, skinless
   chicken breast, cut into
   1-inch cubes
1 cup black beans, drained
¾ teaspoon turmeric
¼ teaspoon cayenne pepper
¼ teaspoon black pepper

½ cup diced red bell pepper
4 scallions, diced, divided
4 cups shredded iceberg
   lettuce
4 tablespoons no-oil salsa
4 tablespoons nonfat sour
   cream

Spray a nonstick skillet with nonfat cooking spray. Sauté onion 5–7 minutes or until golden. Add chicken and sauté 3–4 minutes or until chicken is browned. Stir in black beans, turmeric, cayenne, and pepper, and sauté 3–4 minutes. Reduce heat to medium low. Stir in half the scallions. Sauté 2–3 minutes until scallions are softened. Serve hot taco salad over lettuce. Top with remaining scallions, salsa, and sour cream.

The Protein Edge (Nevada)

AMATERIA1121, WIKIPEDIA.ORG

The Joshua tree is an unusual tree-like species found in high elevations (around 4,000 feet) of the desert Southwest, principally in parts of California, Arizona, Nevada, and Utah. Archaeological evidence indicates that the species dates back some two million years. Native Americans knew the Joshua Tree as a source of food and fiber, but early European settlers often thought it as grotesque and misshapen. However, the Mormons, trying to find their way back from California to Utah, used the Joshua Tree as a guide. They gave the plant its name in the early 19th century, because it reminded them of the biblical prophet Joshua, with his arms upraised in prayer. They saw this plant as a spiritual sign of welcome into the Promised Land.

Tarragon Beefsteak Salad

2 pounds beef sirloin, cut
  ¾–1 inch thick
1 cup salad oil (part olive oil,
  if desired)
⅓ cup red wine vinegar
1 tablespoon tarragon leaves
1 teaspoon salt
¾ teaspoon sugar
½ teaspoon dry mustard
½ teaspoon freshly cracked
  pepper
¼ teaspoon garlic powder
2 large red onions, sliced and
  separated into rings
½ pound fresh mushrooms,
  sliced (optional)
Romaine or other lettuce
  leaves
½ cup chopped fresh parsley
2 tablespoons capers

Grill sirloin (on BBQ or under broiler) for 3–4 minutes on each side. Cook just to rare. Cool slightly for handling. Using a very sharp knife, carve steak into very thin strips, 2–3 inches long. Combine oil, vinegar, tarragon, salt, sugar, mustard, pepper, and garlic powder in large bowl. Add beef strips, onion rings, and mushrooms, tossing lightly to combine. Cover and refrigerate at least 2 hours or overnight, if desired.

  To serve, arrange lettuce leaves on large platter or in salad bowl. Place steak salad on leaves. Sprinkle with parsley and capers.

A Gathering of Recipes (Nevada)

Pasta Salad with Roasted Asparagus

1½ pounds asparagus, trimmed and cut diagonally into 1-inch pieces
1 red or yellow bell pepper, cored, seeded, and cut into 1-inch strips
3 tablespoons olive oil, divided
Coarse salt
½ pound pasta, spirals, or twists

1 tablespoon lemon juice
1–2 tablespoons chopped fresh herbs (basil, oregano, or thyme), chopped
Freshly ground black pepper to taste
¼ cup toasted pine nuts or sprigs of fresh herbs for garnish (optional)

Preheat oven to 500° and begin heating large pot of boiling salted water for pasta. Combine asparagus and peppers in large mixing bowl. Toss with 2 tablespoons olive oil. Spread on baking sheet and sprinkle with coarse salt. Roast for about 7 minutes, until asparagus is tender when pierced with fork. Return to bowl. Stir to cool.

Cook pasta until done. Drain and rinse thoroughly to cool. Toss with vegetables, remaining 1 tablespoon olive oil, lemon juice, and fresh herbs. Season to taste with pepper and additional salt or herbs, if needed. Garnish with pine nuts or fresh herbs, if desired. Serve at once. Serves 4–6.

JLO Art of Cooking (Utah)

Spicy Avocado Salad

1 teaspoon salt
1 clove garlic, minced
1 teaspoon Worcestershire
½ teaspoon Tabasco
Juice of ⅓ lemon
3 tablespoons olive oil
3 ripe tomatoes, diced
2 ripe avocados, diced
Freshly ground pepper
    to taste

1 green chile, seeded, minced
3 tablespoons minced cilantro
3 tablespoons (heaping)
    diced Monterey Jack cheese
3 tablespoons (heaping)
    crumbled crisp-fried bacon
2 tablespoons (heaping)
    minced onion
½ green bell pepper, diced

Mash salt and garlic in bowl with fork until smooth paste forms. Whisk in Worcestershire, Tabasco, lemon juice, and olive oil until well blended. Pour over mixture of tomatoes, avocados, pepper, green chile, cilantro, cheese, bacon, onion, and green pepper in bowl; mix well. Marinate in refrigerator for 30 minutes. Serve on bed of mixed salad greens. Yields 4 servings.

Best Bets (Nevada)

Calico Corn Salad

2 (16-ounce) packages
    frozen corn, thawed
4 small zucchini, diced
1 large sweet red pepper,
    diced
2 (4-ounce) cans green
    chiles, chopped
5 green onions, chopped

⅔ cup olive oil
¼ cup fresh lime juice
2 tablespoons cider vinegar
2–2½ teaspoons ground
    cumin
1½ teaspoons salt
1 teaspoon pepper
½ teaspoon garlic salt

In a bowl, toss corn, zucchini, red pepper, chiles, and onions. In a jar with tight-fitting lid, combine remaining ingredients; shake well. Pour over salad and stir gently. Chill for several hours or overnight. Serves 8.

Country Classics II (Colorado)

Spicy Southwestern Potato Salad

1 (4-ounce) can green chiles, diced
1 hard cooked egg, finely chopped or mashed
¼ cup dill pickle, chopped
¼ cup onion, finely chopped
1 tablespoon prepared mustard
2 tablespoons mayonnaise
1 teaspoon prepared horseradish
1 teaspoon jalapeño sauce
½ cup diced cheese (optional)
5–6 Colorado potatoes, peeled, cubed, cooked

In a mixing bowl, combine green chiles, chopped egg, dill pickle, onion, mustard, mayonnaise, horseradish, jalapeño sauce, and cheese, if desired. Mix well. Stir in potatoes; mix well. Cover and chill several hours. Makes 6–8 servings.

Colorado Potato Favorite Recipes (Colorado)

Saucy Cowgirl's Deviled Red Potato Salad

3 pounds unpeeled red potatoes
4 hard-boiled eggs
1½ cups mayonnaise
2 tablespoons balsamic vinegar
1 teaspoon chili powder
½ teaspoon salt
¼ teaspoon ground black pepper
¼ teaspoon cayenne pepper
1 cup sliced celery
1 cup diced scallions
2 jalapeño peppers, diced

Cook potatoes until tender but firm. Drain, cool and cut into cubes. Cool, peel, and dice hard-boiled eggs. In a bowl, whisk together mayonnaise, vinegar, chili powder, salt, black pepper, and cayenne pepper. Pour mixture over potatoes and toss. Add eggs, celery, scallions, and jalapeños and toss. Cover and chill at least 2 hours before serving. Serve with cold beer. Serves 3 chili-head wranglers or 6 sissy greenhorns.

Authentic Cowboy Cookery Then & Now (Nevada)

German Potato Salad

4 pounds cooked salad
  potatoes
6 slices bacon, diced
½ cup bacon drippings
½ cup sugar
3 tablespoons flour

2 teaspoon salt
¼ teaspoon pepper
1 cup cider vinegar
1 cup water
4 green onions, sliced

Peel and cut cooked potatoes in thin slices. Fry bacon at 330° until golden brown. Remove from drippings. Blend sugar, flour, salt, and pepper. Stir into ½ cup bacon drippings to make smooth paste. Add vinegar and water. Boil 2–3 minutes. Stir constantly. Combine sauce, potatoes, and onions in skillet and turn skillet to off. Let stand at room temperature 3–4 hours. Sprinkle with crisp bacon just before serving. Makes 10–12 servings.

Traditional Treasures (Nevada)

Avocado, Grapefruit, and Arugula Salad

4 ripe avocados, sliced
1½ grapefruits, sectioned
4 handfuls of arugula,
  cleaned
2 tablespoons extra virgin
  olive oil

2 tablespoons juice from
  fresh grapefruit
Freshly ground black pepper

Toss avocado, grapefruit sections, and arugula with oil and grapefruit juice. Season with pepper to taste and serve on cold plates. Serves 4.

Recipe from Chef James E. Cohen, The Wildflower, The Lodge at Vail
Cooking with Colorado's Greatest Chefs (Colorado)

Sunny Fruit Fiesta

1 whole cantaloupe, halved and seeded	**¼ cup fresh lime juice**
½ whole honeydew melon, halved and seeded	**1 tablespoon orange liqueur (optional)**
¼ cup granulated sugar	**1½ teaspoons lime peel**
2 tablespoons fresh lemon juice	**1 cup fresh strawberries**
	1 cup seedless grapes

Using a melon baller, scoop cantaloupe and honeydew into balls (reserve melon halves). In a large bowl, combine the sugar, lemon juice, lime juice, orange liqueur, and lime peel. Stir well to dissolve sugar. Add the cantaloupe and honeydew balls, strawberries, and grapes. Toss gently to combine. Cover bowl with plastic wrap and refrigerate for at least one hour to blend flavors; stir once or twice.   Spoon into melon half. Serves 6.

What's Cookin' in Melon Country (Colorado)

Indian Paintbrush Fruit Salad

1 (5-ounce) package lemon instant pudding	**1 (8-ounce) can Mandarin oranges, undrained**
6 cups (combined) fresh, sliced fruits of choice	**½ bag miniature marshmallows**
	Chopped nuts
1 (16-ounce) can crushed pineapple, undrained	**1 large container Cool Whip**
	2 bananas

Pour dry pudding mix into a large bowl. Add fruits (such as peaches, strawberries, grapes, apricots, cantaloupe, melon), pineapple, oranges, marshmallows, nuts, and Cool Whip, reserving a portion of the Cool Whip for garnish. Cover and chill salad overnight.

   Just before serving, peel and cut bananas into bite-size pieces, and fold into pudding mixture.   Top with dollops of reserved Cool Whip.

Utah Cook Book (Utah)

Frozen Cranberry Salad

2 (3-ounce) packages cream cheese, softened
2 tablespoons sugar
2 tablespoons mayonnaise
1 can whole or strained cranberry sauce
1 cup well-drained crushed pineapple
½ cup finely chopped pecans (optional)
1 cup cream, whipped

Let cream cheese come to room temperature. Mash with fork; add sugar, mayonnaise, cranberry sauce, pineapple, and nuts. Mix well and add whipped cream. Mix well; pour into a lightly buttered loaf pan and freeze for 6 hours or overnight.

Home Cookin' Creations (Colorado)

Utah's Famous Green Jell-O with Cheese

Mormons, for some unknown reason, have long been known for their consumption of Jell-O, especially green Jell-O. It has become such a tradition in the state, that Utah has named it their official food.

½ cup crushed pineapple
1½ cups water, divided
⅔ cup sugar
1 (3-ounce) package lime Jell-O
1 cup grated cheese
1 cup whipped cream

Mix pineapple, ½ cup water, and sugar. Boil remaining 1 cup water; add lime Jell-O to dissolve. Add pineapple mixture to Jell-O; chill and let set until wobbly. Add grated cheese and whipped cream and mix. Chill until set.

A Mormon Cookbook (Utah)

The people of Salt Lake City, Utah, consume more Jell-O per capita than any other city in the world. In January 2001, the Utah Senate declared green Jell-O the official state snack of Utah. And to celebrate, an annual Jell-O Week was proclaimed.

Shrimp Tomato Aspic

1 (3-ounce) package lemon
  Jell-O
2 cups tomato juice, heated
Pinch of salt, dash pepper,
  and paprika
1 can deveined shrimp

Juice of 1 lemon
1 tablespoon sweet pickle
  juice
1 cup sliced ripe olives
½ cup chopped sweet pickles
½ cup chopped celery

Dissolve Jell-O in hot tomato juice. Add seasonings. Add shrimp and remainder of ingredients. Chill until set. Serves 4–6.

Timbreline's Cookbook (Nevada)

Herbed Vinaigrette Dressing

½ cup olive oil
½ cup water
1½ tablespoons red wine
  vinegar
1½ tablespoons balsamic
 vinegar
½ teaspoon each of cilantro,
  thyme, basil, and salt

¼ teaspoon each of sage and
  ground cumin
1 teaspoon each of honey and
  prepared mustard
½ teaspoon garlic granules, or
  powder
Black pepper to taste

Mix all together in a blender or food processor. Makes about 1 cup.

How to Feed a Vegetarian (Colorado)

Vegetables

FORT COLLINS CVB

Sunlight threads the trees and lights the leaves in beautiful Cache la Poudre River Canyon near Fort Collins, Colorado.

Parmesan Fries

Most kids will love these lowfat fries!

3–4 small baking potatoes
(well scrubbed)
¼ cup grated Parmesan
cheese
½ teaspoon garlic powder

⅛ teaspoon salt
⅛ teaspoon onion powder
1 tablespoon reduced-calorie
margarine, melted

Cut potatoes lengthwise into wedges. Cut into 30 wedges for 3 potatoes or 32 wedges for 4 potatoes. Mix together Parmesan cheese, garlic powder, salt, and onion powder in a large plastic bag. Brush melted margarine onto potatoes. Put 10–11 slices of potato into the bag at a time and shake until potatoes are coated with mixture. Place potatoes on a cookie sheet sprayed with vegetable oil cooking spray. Bake at 400° for 20–25 minutes. Serves 4.

Lowfat, Homestyle Cookbook (Colorado)

Nevada Heat Chili Fries

1 teaspoon chili powder
1 teaspoon cumin powder
1 teaspoon crushed red
pepper flakes

½ teaspoon salt
6 large baking potatoes,
scrubbed (about 3 pounds)

Preheat oven to 500°. In a bowl, combine chili powder, cumin powder, crushed red pepper flakes, and salt. Cut potatoes into sticks. Spray a baking sheet and place potatoes in a single layer. Sprinkle with spices. Bake 10 minutes, then turn over potato slices. Bake another 10–15 minutes, until potatoes are browned and fork-tender. Serves 6.

A Cowboy Cookin' Every Night (Nevada)

Crunchy Potatoes

6–8 medium-size potatoes
1 tablespoon oil
1 package onion soup mix

Butter
Paprika for garnish

Scrub potatoes well. Leave peeling on, slice very thin into 2-quart casserole dish that has been greased with one table-spoon oil. Sprinkle onion soup mix over potatoes, dot with pats of butter, cover and bake in 400° oven until potatoes are soft (about 30 minutes), uncover; sprinkle with paprika and let brown.

The Best of Friends (Colorado)

Silver State Potatoes

2 cups sour cream
1 tablespoon salt
¼ cup milk
¼ cup butter
1 (10¾-ounce) can cream
of chicken soup
½ cup chopped onion

½ cup grated Cheddar cheese
4 medium potatoes, boiled,
peeled, and grated, or hash
browns
1 cup crushed cornflakes
2 tablespoons melted butter

Combine sour cream, salt, milk, butter, soup, onion, and cheese and simmer on low heat until cheese melts. Then add potatoes. Put in 9x13-inch baking dish that has been sprayed with non-stick spray. Combine crushed cornflakes with melted butter and sprinkle on top. Bake in 350° oven for 35–45 minutes.

Our Daily Bread (Nevada)

WIKIPEDIA.ORG

The Comstock Lode was the first major U.S. discovery of silver ore, located under what is now Virginia City, Nevada. After the discovery was made public in 1859, prospectors rushed to the area and scrambled to stake their claims. The excavations were carried to depths of more than 3,200 feet. Since that time, the Comstock Lode has yielded more than $400 million in gold and silver and remains the richest known silver deposit ever discovered in the United States. The mines declined after 1874.

Virginia City Creamy Goat Cheese Mashed Potatoes

3 pounds russet potatoes, peeled, washed, and quartered
¾ stick unsalted butter, softened
1½ cups heavy cream
½ cup crumbled goat cheese
½ teaspoon salt
½ teaspoon black pepper

Bring a large pot of salted water to a boil. Add potatoes to water and return to boil. Cook potatoes until tender, about 15–20 minutes. Drain in a colander. Mash potatoes in a large bowl with a potato masher. Add butter and blend. Add 1 cup cream and blend into potatoes thoroughly. Blend in goat cheese, salt, pepper, and more cream, if necessary, to achieve desired consistency. Serves 8.

A Cowboy Cookin' Every Night (Nevada)

Cattlemen's Club Twice-Baked Potatoes

5 large potatoes, scrubbed and baked
⅓ cup half-and-half
1 cup sour cream
3 tablespoons green onions or chives, minced
4 strips bacon, fried and crumbled
1 cup grated Cheddar cheese
1½–2 teaspoons salt
½ teaspoon pepper
¼ teaspoon garlic salt
1 egg, beaten
⅓ cup butter
½ cup sliced mushrooms, sautéed in butter

Bake potatoes for one hour at 350° or until tender in center. Cut in half lengthwise. Scoop out potato carefully as to not tear skins. Mash potatoes with mixer, add half-and-half and continue to beat until smooth. Add all other ingredients and mix well. Mixture should be somewhat softer than regular mashed potatoes to prevent drying out when baking again. Fill skin shells with mashed potato mixture and arrange on cookie sheet. Top each with extra grated cheese. Bake at 350° for 20 minutes. Great with steaks! Serves 8–10.

Kitchen Keepsakes (Colorado)

Pickaroon Potatoes

A super accompaniment to a grilled steak after a day on the slopes.

6 large potatoes	**½ cup whipping cream,**
2 tablespoons butter	**whipped until stiff**
¼ cup milk	**¼ cup grated Cheddar or**
Salt and pepper to taste	**Parmesan cheese**
1 tablespoon hot	**Paprika**
horseradish	

Peel and wash potatoes and cook in salted boiling water until tender. Drain and mash with the butter and milk. Beat until light and fluffy. Season with salt and pepper, and fold in the horseradish. Pour into a buttered casserole, cover with whipped cream, sprinkle with the cheese and paprika. Bake in a preheated 350° oven until brown on top. Makes 6 servings.

Colorado Cache Cookbook (Colorado)

Prairie Schooners

4 large baked potatoes	**2 tablespoons chopped green**
1 (15-ounce) can Ranch	**pepper**
Style Beans	**2 tablespoons chopped onion**
1 cup sour cream	**1 tablespoon butter or**
1 stick butter, softened	**margarine**
Salt, pepper, and chili	**1 cup grated Cheddar cheese**
powder to taste	

Slice off top ⅓ of baked potato lengthwise. Scoop out potato leaving ¼ inch around potato skin. Mash potato until free of lumps. Drain beans thoroughly, reserving juice. Mash beans. Whip sour cream, butter, mashed beans, salt, pepper, and chili powder. Add to mashed potatoes, adding enough bean juice to moisten. Spoon mixture into potato shells.

Sauté green pepper and onion in margarine. Top each potato with grated cheese, onion, and green pepper. Bake at 425° about 10 minutes or until browned. Serves 4.

Kitchen Keepsakes by Request (Colorado)

Long's Peak Baked Beans

Baked beans have never tasted so good!

½ pound hamburger
5 sliced bacon, chopped
1 small onion, chopped
⅓ cup brown sugar
½ cup ketchup
2 tablespoons prepared
  mustard
¼ teaspoon pepper
⅓ cup sugar
⅓ cup barbecue sauce

2 tablespoons molasses
½ teaspoon salt
½ teaspoon chili powder
1 (46–54-ounce) can pork and
  beans, drained
1 (15-ounce) can black-eyed
  peas, drained
1 (15-ounce) can red kidney
  beans, drained and rinsed

In a skillet, brown hamburger, bacon, and onion. Drain well. Combine remaining ingredients, except beans, and mix well. Mix in beans. Cover and bake at 350° for one hour. Best if left in refrigerator for 3–4 hours before baking.

More Kitchen Keepsakes (Colorado)

Best in the West Beans

1 (16-ounce) can butter
  beans
1 (16-ounce) can pinto beans
1 (16-ounce) can pork and
  beans
½ pound ground beef
10 slices bacon, chopped
½ cup finely chopped onion
⅓ cup brown sugar

⅓ cup sugar
¼ cup ketchup
¼ cup spicy hot BBQ sauce
2 tablespoons Dijon mustard
2 tablespoons dark molasses
½ teaspoon salt
½ teaspoon pepper
½ teaspoon chili powder

Drain butter beans and pinto beans and combine with pork and beans. In large saucepot, brown beef, bacon, and onion; drain. Add beans and remaining ingredients; mix well. Put into large casserole dish and bake, uncovered, for one hour at 350°. Enjoy!

Family Favorites from the Heart (Utah)

Dove Creek "Pinto Bean Capital of the World" Beans

1 pound dried pinto beans
1 large ham bone, or 2
  smoked ham hocks,
  cracked
2 onions, chopped
3 garlic cloves, minced
2 bay leaves
1 teaspoon dried oregano
  leaves, crumbled
1–2 teaspoons ground
  cumin
1–2 tablespoons chili
  powder to taste

Pinch sugar
Pinch crushed red pepper
  flakes
Water to cover
1 (10-ounce) can diced Ro-Tel
  tomatoes with green chiles
1 (16-ounce) can tomatoes
  with juice, broken up
1–2 canned jalapeños,
  chopped, to taste
Salt and pepper
1 (12-ounce) can beer

Rinse beans, discarding any bad ones, and place in large pot. Cover with water and soak overnight or bring water to a boil; boil 2 minutes; remove from heat, cover and let beans soak one hour. Discard water, rinse beans with cold water and drain.

Place beans in pot with all other ingredients. Bring to a boil, reduce heat until liquid barely simmers and simmer, partially covered for 3–4 hours, until beans are very tender. Add water and beer during cooking, as needed, to prevent sticking and scorching. Remove and discard bay leaves. Adjust seasonings while cooking, if necessary. Serves 6–10.

Colorado Foods and More. . . (Colorado)

Pinto beans are the most widely produced bean in the United States and one of the most popular in the Americas. Dove Creek, Colorado, is known as "the Pinto Bean Capital of the World." While pinto beans have been raised in this area for centuries, Dove Creek really only claims to grow the best pinto beans, not the most. One reason that pinto beans grow very well there is that the soil has a very high iron content, and is red in color. And the local folks' faith in the quality and flavor of their crop extends to them turning out products like pinto bean cookies and pinto bean ice cream sauce.

Spicy Green Beans

½ cup soy sauce
¼ cup sesame oil
Crushed red pepper flakes
1 clove garlic, minced
Garlic salt
2 tablespoons black bean
   garlic sauce

1 tablespoon granulated sugar
¼ teaspoon peeled and grated
   fresh ginger
1 pound fresh green beans,
   snipped

Combine all ingredients except beans. Set aside. Boil or blanch green beans. Marinate beans for at least one hour in spicy dressing. Serve at room temperature.

JLO Art of Cooking (Utah)

Stuffed Yellow Summer Squash

Anyone who has grown yellow summer squash in their gardens knows that every once in a while you get busy with your summer fun and turn around twice, and darn those small tender squashes have grown too large and tough to eat. Don't put them in your compost pile; fix this recipe!

2 large yellow squash
8 Ritz Crackers
½ cup grated Cheddar
   cheese
½ small yellow onion, diced
¼ stick butter, diced

1 medium tomato, diced
8 mushrooms, diced
1 tablespoon chopped parsley
Salt and pepper to taste
½ tablespoon minced garlic
¼ stick butter

Boil squash in pot ⅓ full of water until slightly tender, but still very firm. Don't overcook or they will be too hard to handle.

In mixing bowl crumble Ritz Crackers, then add Cheddar cheese, onion, diced butter, tomato, mushrooms, parsley, and seasonings. Preheat oven to 350°. Remove cooked squash from the pot; cool in cold water. When cool, cut squash in half and scrape out seeds, adding seeds to the cracker mixture.

With the ¼ stick butter, butter the bottom of a 9x13-inch pan; place cut squash in pan. Stuff each half of the squash with the mixture. Bake for 30 minutes at 350°. Serves 4.

Recipes & Remembrances (Utah)

Red Peppers and Yellow Squash

2 pounds yellow squash, washed and sliced ¼ inch thick

2 sweet red peppers, washed and cut into pieces about 1x1 inch

2 tomatoes, washed and sliced ¼ inch thick

6 scallions, washed and sliced ¼ inch thick (include tops)

1 clove garlic, peeled and crushed

½ teaspoon crushed dill seed

½ teaspoon crushed coriander seed

1 teaspoon salt

⅛ teaspoon fresh ground black pepper

3 tablespoons butter or margarine

Place all vegetables in a 9x13x2-inch baking pan; sprinkle with seasonings; dot with butter. Toss all together lightly. Cover pan with aluminum foil and let stand at room temperature about 3 hours. Bake at 350° for about one hour.

Southwestern Foods et cetera (Colorado)

Cheese-Topped Zucchini

3 medium zucchini
1 medium onion, diced
Oil
Salt and pepper to taste

Oregano
1 cup tomato sauce
Mozzarella slices
Parmesan cheese

Slice zucchini in halves lengthwise. In large skillet, sauté onion until tender in small amount of oil. Add zucchini halves, cut-side-up; sprinkle with salt and pepper and a little oregano. Pour tomato sauce over zucchini. Cover and cook on medium heat until tender, about 10 minutes. Top zucchini with sliced mozzarella cheese; sprinkle with additional oregano and cook, covered, until cheese melts. Cover with Parmesan cheese and serve.

Favorite Recipes from Utah Farm Bureau Women (Utah)

Italian Zucchini Crescent Pie

4 cups thinly sliced zucchini
1 cup chopped onion
½ cup margarine
½ cup chopped parsley, or
    2 tablespoons dried parsley
    flakes
½ teaspoon salt
½ teaspoon pepper
¼ teaspoon garlic powder

¼ teaspoon basil
¼ teaspoon oregano leaves
2 eggs, beaten
8 ounces shredded mozzarella
    cheese
1 (8-ounce) can refrigerated
    crescent dinner rolls
2 teaspoons mustard

Cook and stir zucchini and onion in margarine for 10 minutes. Stir in parsley, salt, pepper, garlic powder, basil, and oregano leaves. Combine eggs and mozzarella cheese. Stir into zucchini mixture.

Separate an 8-ounce can refrigerated crescent dinner rolls into 8 triangles. Place in ungreased 10-inch pie pan; press over bottom and up sides to form crust. Spread crust with mustard. Pour vegetable mixture into crust. Bake in 375° oven for 20 minutes or until center is set. Cover crust with foil during last 10 minutes of baking to prevent over-browning. Let stand 10 minutes before serving. Serves 6.

Still Cookin' After 70 Years (Nevada)

Tomatoes Baked in Sour Cream

4 tomatoes, sliced
1 red onion, sliced
1 cup sour cream, divided

1 teaspoon sugar
Salt and pepper to taste
Bread crumbs

In casserole dish, make layers alternating stacks of tomato and onion slices, and a dab of sour cream. Keep repeating until casserole dish is full. Sprinkle sugar, salt and pepper on top. Top with remaining sour cream. Sprinkle bread crumbs on top. Bake at 350° for one hour.

Recipes & Remembrances (Utah)

Portobello Mushrooms with Ratatouille and Spinach

1 cup chopped onion
5 teaspoons minced garlic, divided
2 tablespoons extra virgin olive oil, divided
1 (1-pound) eggplant, trimmed, peeled, cut into ½-inch pieces
2 cups ½-inch diced zucchini pieces
1 cup ½-inch diced red bell pepper pieces
2 tablespoons tomato paste
2 teaspoons red wine vinegar
1 teaspoon chopped fresh thyme
Pinch of cayenne pepper
Salt and black pepper to taste
4 (5-inch-diameter) portobello mushrooms, stems removed
¼ cup chopped flat-leaf parsley
1 (10-ounce) package ready-to-use spinach leaves

Preheat oven to 350°. Mix onion, 3 teaspoons garlic, and 1 tablespoon oil in large oven-proof pot. Cover; cook over medium-low heat until onion is very tender, stirring often, about 15 minutes. Stir in eggplant; cover and cook 10 minutes, stirring often. Stir in next 6 ingredients. Season with salt and pepper. Cover; bake until vegetables are very tender, about 30 minutes.

Heat 2 teaspoons oil in large nonstick skillet over medium heat. Add mushrooms, rounded-side-down. Cook until bottoms are golden, about 10 minutes. Turn mushrooms over; cook until just tender, about 6 minutes. Sprinkle with parsley and remaining 2 teaspoons garlic; cook until mushrooms are very tender, about 5 minutes.

Meanwhile, heat remaining 1 teaspoon oil in large nonstick skillet over medium heat. Add spinach; stir until wilted, about 2 minutes. Divide spinach among 4 plates. Top each with 1 mushroom, rounded-side-down.   Fill mushrooms with ratatouille. Yields 4 servings.

Never Trust a Skinny Chef...II (Nevada)

Nutmeg Spinach Soufflé

1 pound fresh spinach
2 tablespoons margarine
2 tablespoons all-purpose
  flour
1 teaspoon salt
1 cup milk

4 eggs, separated
¼ cup chopped onion
⅛ teaspoon nutmeg
¼ teaspoon cream of tartar
3 tablespoons grated
  Parmesan cheese

Wash spinach; cook in small amount of salted water. Drain and press out all excess water; chop spinach. Melt margarine in saucepan; add flour and salt and blend. Gradually add milk and stir until thickened. Gradually add beaten egg yolks. Stir in spinach, onion, and nutmeg. Beat egg whites and cream of tartar until stiff. Fold into spinach mixture. Pour into greased soufflé dish. Sprinkle with Parmesan cheese. Bake at 375° for 50 minutes or until set. Makes 6 servings.

Lion House Entertaining (Utah)

Low Fat Stir-Fried Veggies

½ head red cabbage
1 large onion
½ red or orange bell pepper
1 crown fresh broccoli
1 tablespoon canola oil
Mrs. Dash Spicy Seasoning to
  taste

Garlic powder to taste
Black pepper to taste
2 tablespoons Tamarind sauce
½ pound bean sprouts

Cut all vegetables into bite-size pieces except the bean sprouts. Heat oil in a large skillet or wok. Put in cabbage and onions and cook on medium heat until they are done but cabbage is still crunchy. Add seasonings and then add broccoli. Cook for another few minutes. Add bean sprouts and cook for another 2 minutes, stirring occasionally to be sure it does not stick. Serve and enjoy.

Variation: You may stir-fry a seasoned chicken breast or beef strips separately and add at the end.

The Best of Down-Home Cooking (Nevada)

Skillet Cabbage

2 slices bacon
2 tablespoons brown sugar
2 tablespoons vinegar
¼ teaspoon caraway seeds
  (optional)
2 tablespoons water

Dash of pepper
2 cups coarsely grated
  cabbage
1 cup chopped unpeeled
  apples

In a medium skillet, cook bacon until crisp; drain, reserving one tablespoon grease in skillet. Set bacon aside; crumble. Stir in sugar, vinegar, caraway, water, and pepper; mix well. Stir in cabbage and apples. Cover; cook over low heat, stirring occasionally. For crisp cabbage, cook 15 minutes. For tender cabbage, cook 25 minutes. Stir in bacon. Makes 2 servings.

Easy Recipes for 1, 2 or a Few (Colorado)

Mediterranean Grilled Veggies

1 (8-ounce) package fresh
  mushrooms
1 medium onion, cut into
  wedges

2 small bell peppers (1 red,
  1 green), cut into chunks
2 cups cherry tomatoes

MARINADE:
6 tablespoons extra virgin
  olive oil
2 tablespoons balsamic
  vinegar

1 tablespoon soy sauce
2 garlic cloves, crushed
¼ cup chopped fresh basil

Prepare all the vegetables. Whisk together Marinade ingredients. In a large bowl, toss vegetables in Marinade and marinate for 1 hour. Put veggies, except tomatoes, in a grilling basket or on skewers. Grill, brushing with Marinade and turning several times, for 15 minutes. Add tomatoes and grill 5 minutes longer, or until veggies are as tender as desired.

Cherished Recipes (Utah)

Peperonata

2 tablespoons butter or
margarine
¼ cup olive oil
1 pound onions, sliced
⅛ inch thick (about
4 cups)
2 pounds green and red bell
peppers, peeled,* seeded,
and cut in 1-inch strips
(about 6 cups)

2 pounds tomatoes, peeled,
seeded and coarsely
chopped (about 3 cups)
1 teaspoon red wine vinegar
1 teaspoon salt
Freshly ground pepper

In a heavy 12-inch skillet, melt butter with olive oil over moderate heat. Add onions and cook them, turning frequently, for 10 minutes, or until they are soft and lightly browned. Stir in peppers. Reduce the heat, cover, and cook for 10 minutes.

Add tomatoes, vinegar, salt, and a few grindings of black pepper; cover the pan and cook for another 5 minutes. Then cook the vegetables uncovered over high heat, stirring gently, until almost all the liquid has boiled away. Serve the Peperonata as a hot vegetable dish, preceding or along with the main course, or refrigerate and serve cold as part of an antipasto or as an accompaniment to cold roast meats or fowl.

*To peel peppers easily, place on cookie sheet and broil for about 5 minutes until skins turn black. Put peppers in a paper bag for about 15 minutes. Peel.

Italian Dishes et cetera (Colorado)

Grilled Stuffed Onions

1½ cups herb-seasoned
  stuffing mix
1 cup shredded Cheddar
  cheese
1 teaspoon poultry
  seasoning

⅓ cup butter or margarine,
  melted
⅓ cup hot water
6 medium sweet onions
Vegetable cooking spray
Fresh oregano (optional)

Combine first 5 ingredients, stirring until well blended and set aside. Cut each onion into 3 horizontal slices. Spread 2 table-spoons stuffing mixture between slices and reassemble onions. Place each onion on a 12-inch square piece of heavy-duty aluminum foil coated with cooking spray. Bring opposite corners together and twist to seal. Cook, covered with grill lid, over medium hot coals (350°–400°) 25 minutes or until tender. Garnish with fresh oregano, if desired. Makes 6 servings.

Note: Onions may be baked, unwrapped, in a lightly greased, covered, 7x11x½-inch baking dish at 350° for one hour or until tender.

What's Cookin' in Melon Country (Colorado)

Hot and Spicy Onion Rings

This batter can also be used to make onion blossoms, if you have a blossom cutter.

1 egg
1 cup milk
1 cup flour
1 teaspoon salt
1 teaspoon ground red
  pepper

¼ teaspoon oregano
⅛ teaspoon cumin
Oil for deep-fat frying
2 large onions, sliced thick,
  then separated into rings

Combine egg, milk, flour, and seasonings and mix until the batter is smooth. Heat about 2 inches of oil in the Dutch oven. This will take about 16–20 coals (350°–375°) at bottom heat only. Dip the onion slices into the batter, then fry them in the hot oil, a few at a time. Turn them over to cook both sides, then remove with a slotted spoon and drain on paper towels. Serve with ketchup, ranch dressing, or horseradish sauce. Serves 4–6.

The Beginner's Guide to Dutch Oven Cooking (Utah)

Broccoli with Dill Cheese Sauce

4 cups broccoli flowerets

½ cup water

CHEESE SAUCE:

1 cup low-fat buttermilk
¼ cup grated Parmesan cheese

1 teaspoon Dijon mustard
2 teaspoons cornstarch
1 teaspoon dried dill weed

Place broccoli flowerets and water in a microwave safe dish. Cover dish with plastic wrap and microwave on high power for 8–10 minutes or until tender. Meanwhile, combine buttermilk, Parmesan cheese, Dijon mustard, and cornstarch in a small saucepan. Using a wire whisk, stir constantly until sauce boils. Cook over low heat for 2 minutes. Stir in dill weed and serve over drained broccoli. Yields 4 servings.

Simply Colorado (Colorado)

Oriental Carrots

This is an easy, make-ahead recipe.

1 can tomato soup
½ cup oil
1 cup (scant) sugar
½ cup vinegar
1 teaspoon (scant) salt
¼ teaspoon pepper

1 teaspoon prepared mustard
5 cups sliced cooked carrots
1 medium onion, finely chopped
1 green bell pepper, finely chopped

Combine tomato soup, oil, sugar, vinegar, salt, pepper, and mustard in saucepan. Simmer until sugar is dissolved, stirring constantly. Combine carrots, onion, and green pepper in bowl; mix well. Pour tomato soup mixture over vegetables. Marinate, covered, overnight in refrigerator. May serve cold or hot. Yields 6 servings.

Beyond Oats (Colorado)

Pasta, Rice, Etc.

PHOTO COURTESY OF UTAH STATE PARKS

Oddly shaped stone pillars and knobs (known as goblins or hoodoos) populate Utah's Goblin Valley State Park. Visitors may wonder if they're in Utah or on Mars! Their red, orange, and white colors provide spectacular vistas for park visitors.

Chicken Alfredo

Fast, fabulous, and rich!

6 ounces dried bow tie pasta
2 tablespoons olive oil or
  butter
½ pound chicken tenders or
  boneless, skinless chicken
  breasts cut in strips
2 green onions, chopped
1 tablespoon butter
¾ cup sliced fresh
  mushrooms (optional)

1 tablespoon fresh thyme or 1
  teaspoon dried
½ tablespoon garlic powder
2 cups heavy cream
¾ cup grated Parmesan or
  Romano cheese
½ teaspoon salt
½ teaspoon pepper
⅛ cup toasted pine nuts
  (optional)

Cook pasta according to package directions. Drain and set aside. In a large skillet, heat olive oil or butter over medium heat. Add chicken and stir-fry about 5 minutes or until cooked through. In a separate pan, sauté green onions in 1 tablespoon butter until tender. Add mushrooms (if desired), thyme, and sautéed onions to chicken. Add garlic powder, cream, cheese, salt, and pepper. Simmer about 30 minutes, stirring occasionally, until chicken is cooked and tender. Serve over pasta. Top with pine nuts. Makes 2 servings.

The Essential Mormon Cookbook (Utah)

Dante Blue's Alfredo Blue

16 ounces fettuccine
3 garlic cloves, diced
1 tablespoon olive oil
6 ounces Stiltson blue
   cheese, crumbled
¼ cup grated Parmesan
   cheese
2 cups heavy cream

1½ cups crabmeat, picked
   over
1 tablespoon chopped fresh
   basil
1 tablespoon chopped fresh
   oregano
Salt and black pepper to taste

Cook pasta in boiling water until al dente. Drain and keep hot. Sauté garlic in oil until golden. Reserve garlic and oil. In saucepan over medium heat, combine blue cheese, Parmesan cheese, and cream. Stir until cheeses are melted. Add crabmeat and heat through, about 2–3 minutes. Do not overcook crabmeat. Stir in reserved garlic and olive oil. Season with basil, oregano, salt and pepper. Toss sauce with hot pasta and let stand 5 minutes before serving. Serves 8.

Chef's Note: If you cannot find Stiltson blue cheese, be careful to substitute only high quality blue cheese such as Midnight Blue brand blue cheese from Finlandia. Avoid using creamy blue cheese, as the sauce will turn out relatively bland. Do NOT substitute imitation crab for real crabmeat.

Use Your Noodle! (Nevada)

JEFFREY PANG@WIKIPEDIA.ORG

Nevada has an estimated 314 mountain ranges—more than any other state—all of which have a northeast/southwest orientation. The tallest is the 13,145-foot Boundary Peak. The peak is entirely within the state of Nevada, although it is only about half a mile from the California border. Nevada contains 51 peaks above 9,000 feet. Mountains crisscross the state, and no matter where you travel, these natural Nevada wonders are visible.

Steamboat Alfredo

Try this Alfredo—Steamboat style!

10 ounces medium-size
  shrimp, peeled and
  deveined
10 ounces sea scallops
¼ cup butter
2 tablespoons cream sherry
½ cup heavy cream

1 egg, beaten well
2 cloves garlic, minced
Salt and pepper to taste
Parsley
¾ cup grated Romano and
  Parmesan cheese
1 pound fettuccine, cooked

Sauté seafood in butter 3–6 minutes until scallops turn white. Add sherry and simmer for about one minute. Add cream and bring to a slow boil, stirring constantly. Add egg, garlic, salt, pepper, and a bit of fresh parsley. Stir in cheese until smooth. Add cooked fettuccine and toss well. Garnish with lemon wedges and fresh parsley. Serves 4.

Steamboat Entertains (Colorado)

Basil Shrimp Fettuccine

8 ounces uncooked fettuccine
½ cup chopped onion
¼ cup chopped sweet yellow
  pepper
¼ cup chopped sweet red
  pepper
2 cloves garlic, minced
2 tablespoons olive oil

1 (12-ounce) can evaporated
  milk or half-and-half
¼ cup flour
½ teaspoon salt
1 pound uncooked, peeled, and
  deveined shrimp
2 tablespoons minced fresh
  basil (must be fresh)

Cook pasta; set aside. In a fry pan, cook onion, both peppers, and garlic in oil until tender. In a bowl, mix milk and sifted flour; blend well. Pour over vegetables. Bring to a boil; cook 2 minutes longer. Reduce heat; add salt, shrimp, and basil. Cook about 3 minutes or until shrimp is pink. Pour over pasta. Makes 6 servings.

Family and Friends Favorites (Nevada)

Fettuccine with Bay Scallops and Shrimp

4 tablespoons butter, divided
1 tablespoon olive oil
½ cup chopped shallots
8 ounces uncooked medium
  shrimp, peeled, deveined
8 ounces bay scallops
1 teaspoon chopped fresh
  basil

1 tablespoon chopped fresh dill
¾ cup white wine
1 cup half-and-half
1 pound uncooked spinach
  fettuccine
Salt to taste
½ cup grated Parmesan
  cheese

Melt 2 tablespoons butter with the olive oil in a large skillet. Add shallots and sauté 2–3 minutes or until tender but not browned. Add shrimp and scallops and sauté for 1 minute. Stir in the basil, dill, and wine. Reduce heat and simmer until mixture is reduced by ½. Add half-and-half and cook until mixture thickens, stirring constantly. Remove from heat and keep warm.

Cook fettuccine in boiling salted water in a stockpot until al dente. Drain and toss with remaining 2 tablespoons butter and Parmesan cheese in a serving bowl. Add seafood mixture and toss to mix. Serve with warm sourdough bread. Yields 4–6 servings.

Las Vegas Glitter to Gourmet (Nevada)

Stuffed Manicotti

½ cup chopped onion
1½ pounds hamburger
1 box large shell pasta or
  manicotti shells
2 eggs, slightly beaten
1 cup chopped spinach
4 tablespoons chopped
  parsley
½ teaspoon salt

¼ teaspoon pepper
2 slices French bread, soaked
  in ½ cup milk
1 (26-ounce) jar spaghetti
  sauce
1 cup shredded mozzarella
  cheese
Parmesan cheese

Brown onion and hamburger. Parboil shells about 6 minutes; set aside. Mix all ingredients, except shells, spaghetti sauce, and cheeses. Stuff shells with meat filling. Pour ½ spaghetti sauce in bottom of a 9x13-inch pan. Place stuffed shells, leaving room for shells to expand, and cover with remaining sauce. Sprinkle mozzarella cheese on each shell. Cover and bake for 30 minutes in 350° oven. Uncover and sprinkle with Parmesan cheese. Cook 10 minutes.

A Century of Mormon Cookery, Volume 2 (Utah)

That Old Italian Guy's Fast Pesto Sauce

4 cups fresh basil
4 garlic cloves
¼ stick unsalted butter
¼ cup olive oil
¼ cup toasted pine nuts

¼ cup grated Parmesan
  cheese
⅛ cup grated Romano cheese
¼ teaspoon salt

In a food processor, combine all ingredients for 60–90 seconds. Scrape ingredients down from sides of processor and continue combining until thick and smooth. Makes about 1 cup.

Use Your Noodle! (Nevada)

Penne Pasta with Gabby's Fresh Mushroom-Meat Sauce

A crispy cold tossed salad and a loaf of crusty-warm Italian bread and you've got a wonderful meal—oh, yes, a red beverage of your choice will really make it complete.

12 ounces penne pasta
1 pound extra lean ground beef
½ pound lean ground pork
1 tablespoon olive oil
½ pound fresh mushrooms, sliced
1 small zucchini, thinly sliced
1 small red bell pepper, finely chopped
4–5 pieces of sun-dried tomatoes, thinly sliced
2–3 cloves garlic, pressed or minced

1 quart thick spaghetti sauce (homemade is best)
¼ cup bold dry red wine (Burgundy)
3 tablespoons finely chopped sweet basil, or 1 tablespoon dried
Salt and freshly ground pepper to taste
2 cups shredded mozzarella cheese
1 cup shredded fresh Parmesan cheese

Cook pasta until just barely tender; drain well.

In a large skillet, brown beef and pork in olive oil. Remove meat from pan and add mushrooms, zucchini, bell pepper, dried tomatoes, and garlic to drippings. Sauté this mixture 4–5 minutes over high heat, stirring often. Return meat mixture to pan and stir in the sauce, wine, basil, salt and pepper. Let this mixture come to a simmer, then remove from heat.

Lightly spray a large, shallow baking dish. Layer half of the penne pasta into the dish, then half of the sauce mixture, followed by half of the cheeses. Repeat layers, then bake in a pre-heated 325° oven for 60 minutes. Serves 6–8.

Enjoy! Again and Again (Utah)

Sweet Sausage Bowties

Vegetable oil
1 pound sweet Italian
   sausage, casings removed,
   crumbled
½ teaspoon crushed red
   pepper
½ cup finely chopped onion
3 garlic cloves, minced
2 cups chopped, seeded,
   peeled Roma tomatoes, or
   1 (28-ounce) can tomatoes,
   drained, coarsely chopped

1½ cups heavy cream
½ teaspoon salt
2 teaspoons pesto (optional)
Freshly ground black pepper to
   taste
12 ounces uncooked farfalle
   (bowties)
Salt to taste
3 tablespoons finely chopped
   fresh parsley
¾–1 cup grated Parmesan
   cheese

Heat a small amount of vegetable oil in a heavy skillet over medium heat. Add the sausage and red pepper. Sauté for 7 minutes or until sausage is no longer pink. Add onion and garlic and sauté until onion is tender and sausage is lightly browned. Stir in tomatoes, cream, ½ teaspoon salt, and pesto. Season with black pepper. Simmer for 4 minutes or until mixture is slightly thickened and flavors have blended.

Cook the pasta in boiling salted water in a stockpot until al dente. Drain and add to sausage mixture in the skillet. Cook for 2 minutes, stirring occasionally. Add parsley and Parmesan cheese. Toss to mix well. Yields 6–8 servings.

Las Vegas Glitter to Gourmet (Nevada)

Million Dollar Spaghetti

A good casserole to do ahead; just refrigerate and remove from refrigerator 20 minutes before baking. Good with green salad and French bread.

1 (7-ounce) package thin
  spaghetti
1½ pounds ground beef
1 tablespoon butter
2 (8-ounce) cans tomato
  sauce
Salt and pepper to taste
½ pound cottage cheese

1 (8-ounce) package cream
  cheese, softened
¼ cup sour cream
⅓ cup chopped scallions
1 tablespoon minced green
  pepper
2 tablespoons melted butter

Heat oven to 350°. Cook spaghetti according to directions on package; drain. Sauté beef in 1 tablespoon butter till brown; add tomato sauce, salt and pepper. Remove from heat. Combine cottage cheese, cream cheese, sour cream, scallions, and green pepper.

   In a greased square 2-quart casserole, spread ½ of the spaghetti, cover with cheese mixture. Add remainder of spaghetti and pour melted butter over spaghetti. Spread tomato-meat sauce over the top. Bake for 45 minutes or until hot and bubbly.

Tasteful Treasures (Nevada)

Though common place in the early Nevada mining towns, unregulated gambling was outlawed in 1909 as part of a nation-wide anti-gaming crusade. Due to diminished mining output and the decline of the agricultural sector during the Great Depression, Nevada re-legalized gambling in 1931, with approval from the legislature. It was expected to be a short-term fix. However, re-outlawing gambling has never been seriously considered since the industry has become Nevada's primary source of revenue today.

College Lasagna

1 pound ground beef
½ cup water
1 (32-ounce) jar spaghetti sauce (garden-style is best)
Mushrooms, canned or fresh
1 teaspoon salt
Lasagna noodles (8 ounces)

1 pint cottage cheese
1 (16-ounce) package grated mozzarella cheese (reserve some for top)
1 (8-ounce) package grated Parmesan cheese (reserve some for top)

Brown beef and drain. Add water, spaghetti sauce, mushrooms, and salt. Bring to a boil. In a baking dish, layer this hot sauce, uncooked noodles, cottage cheese, and mozzarella and Parmesan cheeses. Repeat layers, ending with sauce. Top with reserved cheese (both types). Cover with foil and bake in 375° oven for 1 hour. Set dish on a cookie sheet covered in foil to help with cleanup of overflow.

Partyline Cook Book (Nevada)

Make Ahead Macaroni Frankfurter Bake

Very, very good!

6 slices bacon
5 frankfurters, divided
¾ cup sliced celery
½ cup chopped onion
2 tablespoons bacon fat
1 tablespoon flour
½ teaspoon salt

½ teaspoon pepper
1 (10½-ounce) can cream of celery soup
1 can evaporated milk
3 cups hot cooked macaroni
½ cup grated Cheddar cheese

Fry bacon crisp; reserve 2 tablespoons fat. Slice 3 frankfurters. Sauté sliced frankfurters, celery, and onion in bacon fat. Stir in flour, salt, and pepper. Add soup and milk. Cook 10 minutes until slightly thickened, stirring constantly. Crumble bacon; add to sauce. Alternate layers of macaroni and cream sauce mixture in a 1½-quart casserole. Split remaining 2 frankfurters lengthwise. Place on top of casserole. Top with cheese. Bake in moderate oven for 20–25 minutes. Makes 6–8 servings.

Goodies and Guess-Whats (Colorado)

Three Colored Rice

6 tablespoons butter, divided
1 large onion, minced
2 cups Arborio rice
8 cups vegetable stock
Sea salt to taste
4 tablespoons chopped fresh
  parsley

1 tablespoon chopped fresh
  basil
2 tablespoons tomato paste
½ cup freshly grated
  Parmesan cheese

Melt 3 tablespoons butter in a large saucepan, then add onions and sauté until pale yellow. Add rice and mix well. Add stock one cup at a time, stirring until it is absorbed; continue to cook for 5 minutes. Divide rice in 3 equal portions, putting each portion into separate saucepans. Add the parsley and basil to one pan; the tomato paste to another, and nothing to the third. Continue to cook the rice till tender but firm. To the third pan of rice add remaining butter and half the Parmesan cheese. Add remaining cheese to the other 2 rice pans and mix to blend.

To serve, place equal portions of each rice next to each other in rows on the plate.

The Food You Always Wanted to Eat Cookbook (Nevada)

The array of wildlife—which includes numerous birds, desert tortoise, desert bighorn sheep, and wild burros—isn't the only thing that makes Red Rock Canyon unique; the multicolored rock formations contribute to a geologic wonderland composed almost entirely of Aztec Sandstone. It is located about 15 miles west of Las Vegas, Nevada.

Brown Rice Casserole

1 cup brown rice
Boiling water
3 tablespoons chopped onion
3 tablespoons bacon drippings
1 pound ground beef
1 (10¾-ounce) can chicken
  rice soup, condensed

1 (4-ounce) can sliced
mushrooms
½ cup water
⅛ teaspoon each: celery salt,
  onion salt, garlic salt, paprika
  and pepper
1 bay leaf, crumbled

Preheat oven to 325°. Place brown rice in a pot and cover with boiling water; cover the pot and let stand 15 minutes. While rice is sitting, sauté onion in bacon fat until lightly browned, then add ground beef, stirring until brown and crunchy. In a large bowl, combine chicken rice soup, mushrooms, water, and spices. Combine ground beef mixture and rice, then add them to the soup and spices mixture; mix thoroughly. Pour mixture into a buttered or greased casserole dish. Bake, covered, at 325° for 1 hour. Serves 4–6.

God, That's Good! (Nevada)

Mexicali Rice

This is a salsa rice that is a great complement to a Mexican dinner.

3 tablespoons olive oil,
  divided
1 onion, chopped
1 clove garlic, minced
½ cup diced celery
¼ cup diced bell pepper
2 large tomatoes, coarsely
  chopped

2 serrano chiles, seeds and
  stems removed, chopped
2 tablespoons chopped fresh
  cilantro
1 teaspoon fresh lemon juice
½ teaspoon oregano
1 teaspoon salt
3–4 cups cooked rice

Put half the olive oil in a skillet or electric frypan, and sauté the onion and garlic until onion softens. Then add the rest of the ingredients and steam-fry until veggies are bright and still somewhat crisp. Add 3–4 cups cooked rice and the rest of the olive oil. Mix well and serve warm.

Back to the House of Health (Utah)

Ultimate Jambalaya

3 tablespoons unsalted butter
1 pound smoked sausage
  cut in ¼-inch slices
1 pound smoked ham, diced
1 pound boneless, skinless
  chicken breasts cut into
  bite-size pieces
2 bay leaves
2 tablespoons Cajun
  seasoning (low salt)
1 cup chopped onion, divided
1 cup chopped celery, divided

1 cup chopped green bell
  pepper, divided
1½ tablespoons minced garlic
½ cup tomato sauce
1 cup peeled, chopped
  tomatoes
2½ cups chicken stock or
  broth
1½ cups uncooked, long-grain
  rice
1 teaspoon gumbo filé

Remove all the racks from your Ultimate Dutch Oven and spray oven with nonstick vegetable spray. Melt butter in Dutch oven over medium heat (10 or 11 briquettes). Add sausage and ham. Cook until meat starts to brown, stirring frequently and scraping oven bottom well. Add chicken and continue cooking until chicken is brown, stirring frequently and scraping bottom of oven as needed.

Stir in bay leaves, Cajun seasoning, and ½ cup each onion, celery, green pepper, and all the garlic. Stir frequently. Cook until vegetables start to soften. Stir in tomato sauce and cook about one minute, stirring often. Stir in remaining onion, celery, and green pepper, and add tomatoes. Stir in stock and rice, mixing well. Bring to a boil, stirring occasionally.

Reduce heat and simmer, covered, over very low heat (8 or 9 briquettes) until rice is tender but still chewy, about 30 minutes. Stir well, remove bay leaves, add filé, and let stand uncovered 5 minutes before serving.

Ultimate Dutch Oven Cookbook (Utah)

Hoppin' John Squares

½ cup chopped green bell
  pepper
1 tablespoon finely chopped
  onion
2 tablespoons butter
2 tablespoons flour
¾ teaspoon chili powder
¼ teaspoon ground cumin

1¼ cups milk
1 cup shredded Cheddar
  cheese, divided
1 (16-ounce) can black-eyed
  peas, drained
1 cup cooked brown rice
¾ cup diced lean cooked ham
2 large eggs, beaten

Cook pepper and onion in butter till tender; stir in next 3 ingredients. Stir in milk; cook and stir until bubbly. Remove from heat. Stir in ¾ cup of the cheese and remaining ingredients. Turn into a well-greased 8x8x2-inch baking pan. Bake in 350° oven for 30 minutes or till set. Top with remaining cheese. Let stand 5 minutes. Cut into squares to serve. Yields 6 servings.

Still Cookin' After 70 Years (Nevada)

Gourmet Grits Casserole

Grits aren't just for breakfast. This is fabulous for brunch or a side dish with grilled meats.

6 cups water
1½ cups uncooked grits
1 pound longhorn Cheddar
  cheese, shredded
1 (4-ounce) can diced green
  chiles, drained
3 eggs, beaten
¼ cup butter, softened

1 tablespoon savory salt
2–3 cloves garlic, minced
Dash of Tabasco
Dash of Worcestershire
Dash of paprika
Salt and pepper to taste
1 cup crushed cornflakes
¼ cup butter, melted

Cook grits in boiling water according to package directions. Stir in remaining ingredients except cornflakes and melted butter; mix well. Pour into greased 9x13-inch baking dish. Combine cornflakes and butter; sprinkle over casserole. Top with additional paprika, if desired. Bake at 250° 1½–2 hours, or until set. Makes 10–12 servings.

Note: Casserole can be prepared a day ahead, covered and refrigerated. Additional baking time may be needed.

Palates (Colorado)

Spinach-Cream Cheese Enchiladas

This is a really nice dish for entertaining. The sauce can be made a day ahead and the enchiladas can be filled ahead of time. When your guests arrive, pour the sauce over the filled tortillas, top with cheese and bake.

SAUCE:

3 tablespoons oil
3 cloves garlic, minced
2 teaspoons dried Mexican
   oregano
1 tablespoon dried ground
   red chile peppers

3 tablespoons unbleached flour
1 (6-ounce) can tomato paste
4 cups water
1 teaspoon salt or to taste
1 tablespoon apple cider
   vinegar

In oil, sauté garlic over low heat for 3 minutes. Add oregano, dried ground chiles, and flour, and stir until oil is absorbed. Stir in tomato paste, water, salt, and vinegar, and continue stirring until smooth. Bring to a boil; reduce heat and cook over medium heat until thickened.

FILLING:

1 (8-ounce) package cream
   cheese, softened
1 (10-ounce) package frozen
   chopped spinach, thawed
   and squeezed dry
4 scallions, diced

½ cup roasted, peeled, and
   chopped green chile peppers
2 tablespoons lemon juice
12 (8-inch) flour tortillas
½ cup grated Monterey Jack
   cheese

Mix cream cheese, spinach, scallions, green chile peppers, and lemon juice.

Preheat oven to 350°. Grease a 9x13-inch baking pan. Fill each tortilla with 2 tablespoons filling and roll up. Place in baking pan. Reserving one cup sauce for serving at table, pour remaining sauce over filled tortillas. Top with grated cheese. Bake 20 minutes or until sauce is bubbling. Serve with reserved enchilada sauce. Makes 12 enchiladas. Serves 6.

The Durango Cookbook (Colorado)

Crested Butte Chili Cheese Supreme

2 tablespoons vegetable oil
1 medium green pepper, chopped
1 clove garlic, minced
1 (15.5-ounce) can kidney beans, drained
1 (16-ounce) can tomatoes, with juice, coarsely chopped
1 (15-ounce) can tomato sauce
1 tablespoon chili powder, or to taste

1 (15-ounce) carton ricotta cheese
2 cups (8 ounces) shredded Monterey Jack cheese
1 (4-ounce) can chopped green chiles, drained
1 bunch green onions, finely chopped
3 eggs, beaten
1 (8-ounce) bag tortilla chips
2 cups (8 ounces) shredded mild or medium Cheddar cheese

Heat oil in skillet over medium-high heat. Sauté green pepper and garlic until tender. Add kidney beans. Set aside.

In saucepan, combine tomatoes, tomato sauce, and chili powder. Bring to a boil, then reduce heat and simmer, uncovered, for 15 minutes. Add to kidney bean mixture. Combine ricotta and Monterey Jack cheeses, chiles, onions, and eggs.

Spread ¼ of cheese mixture evenly in greased 9x13-inch glass baking dish. Arrange ¼ chips over cheese. Spread ¼ tomato mixture over chips. Repeat layer 3 more times. Cover with foil and bake at 325° for 30–40 minutes. Remove foil and top with Cheddar cheese. Bake 10–15 minutes more. Let stand 5 minutes before serving. Yields 10–12 servings.

West of the Rockies (Colorado)

Mexican Quiche

1 (10-inch) unbaked pie shell
2 tablespoons melted butter
1 (8-ounce) package cream
  cheese, chopped
2 (4-ounce) cans chopped
  green chiles, drained

1 cup shredded Monterey Jack,
  Swiss, or Cheddar cheese
5 eggs
1½ cups whipping cream
½ teaspoon salt
Pepper to taste

Brush pie shell with melted butter and arrange cream cheese in the shell. Chill until the butter sets. Spread drained green chiles on paper towels and pat dry. Sprinkle green chiles and shredded cheese in pie shell. Beat eggs, cream, salt, and pepper in a bowl until smooth. Pour into prepared pie shell. Bake at 425° for 15 minutes. Reduce oven temperature to 350°. Bake for 30 minutes longer or until a knife inserted in center comes out clean. Cool for 5–10 minutes before serving. Yields 6–8 servings.

From Sunrise to Sunset (Nevada)

Rocky Mountain Quiche

Delightful with a fruit cup and muffin.

3 tablespoons vegetable oil
2½ cups coarsely shredded
  Colorado potatoes
1 cup grated Swiss or
  Cheddar cheese
¾ cup cooked and diced
  ham, chicken, or sausage

¼ cup chopped onion
1 cup evaporated milk
2 eggs
½ teaspoon salt
⅛ teaspoon pepper
1 tablespoon parsley flakes

In a 9-inch pie pan, stir together the oil and potatoes. Press evenly into pie crust shape. Bake at 425° for 15 minutes or until just beginning to brown. Remove from oven. Layer on cheese, meat, and onion. In a bowl, beat together milk, eggs, and seasonings. Pour egg mixture onto other ingredients. Sprinkle with parsley flakes. Return to oven and bake at 425° for 30 minutes or until lightly browned and a knife inserted into the center comes out clean. Allow to cool 5 minutes before cutting into wedges to serve. Makes 4–5 servings.

Colorado Potato Favorite Recipes (Colorado)

Company Casserole Quiche

For convenience, assemble a day ahead and refrigerate.

1 pound mushrooms,
  thinly sliced
2 tablespoons butter
8 eggs
1 pint low-fat sour cream
1 pint low-fat cottage cheese
1 cup grated Parmesan
  cheese

½ cup flour
2 teaspoons onion powder
½ teaspoon salt
8 drops Tabasco
1 pound shredded Monterey
  Jack cheese
2 cups cooked, cubed turkey
  or chicken

In a medium skillet, sauté mushrooms in butter until tender; remove and set aside. Combine eggs, sour cream, cottage cheese, Parmesan, flour, and seasonings in a food processor (a blender can also be used, but ingredients will need to be mixed in two batches); blend until smooth. Place reserved mushrooms, shredded cheese, and turkey in 9x13-inch (3-quart) greased baking dish. Pour egg mixture over all; stir lightly to mix. (Cover and refrigerate if you do not wish to bake immediately.)

Bake, uncovered, at 350° 55–65 minutes, or until knife inserted near center comes out clean, and casserole is puffed and golden (refrigerated casseroles may take 10–15 minutes more baking time). Let stand 5 minutes before cutting. Makes 12–16 servings.

Palates (Colorado)

Meats

In Nevada, cowboys still hold a place in modern culture, working on ranches, herding cattle, and riding the trails as they've always done. Shown here is Lamoille Canyon, near Elko, the home of the Western Folklife Center, best known for the National Cowboy Poetry Gathering.

Gourmet Tenderloin with Wine Sauce

The height of luxury, but so easy to prepare.

2 (4-ounce) lobster tails	**½ cup chopped green onions**
1 (6-pound) beef tenderloin	**½ cup dry white wine**
1 tablespoon melted butter	**1 clove garlic, crushed**
1½ teaspoons lemon juice	**¼ pound mushrooms, fluted,**
6 slices bacon, partially	**if desired**
cooked	**Watercress**
½ cup butter	

Place lobster in just enough boiling, salted water to cover; return to boiling. Reduce heat; simmer 5 minutes. Remove lobster meat from tails; cut in half lengthwise. While lobster cooks, butterfly tenderloin by cutting lengthwise through center of meat to within ½ inch of the opposite edge.

Open butterflied tenderloin; place pieces of lobster end-to-end down center of meat. Mix melted butter and lemon juice; drizzle over lobster. Close tenderloin around lobster; tie securely with kitchen twine every inch or so. Roast on a rack in a shallow pan at 425° about 20 minutes for rare beef, or longer to desired doneness. Top with bacon; roast 5 minutes longer, or until bacon is crisp.

Meanwhile, cook green onion in butter in a saucepan over low heat until tender. Blend in wine and garlic; heat, stirring often. Keep warm. Place sliced meat on heated serving platter. Garnish with mushrooms and watercress. Pass wine sauce. Makes 8–10 servings.

Palates (Colorado)

Nevada Ranch Woman's Charcoal Broiled Blue Cheese Steaks

4 ounces blue cheese
1 teaspoon Worcestershire
1 tablespoon heavy cream

6 (8-ounce) sirloin steaks
½ teaspoon black pepper

Crumble blue cheese and blend with Worcestershire and cream.   Broil steaks over charcoal to desired doneness. Spread cheese mixture over steaks and broil 1–2 minutes to melt cheese.   Sprinkle with pepper.   Serve hot.   Serves 6 regular guys or 3 working cowgirls.

Authentic Cowboy Cookery Then & Now (Nevada)

Steak Dinner in a "Pot"

3 medium potatoes, quartered
1 large onion, chopped
1 (10-ounce) can Italian
   green beans, or 1 (10-ounce)
   can seasoned French-style
   green beans
1 (2-ounce) jar pimento,
   chopped and drained
1 pound boneless round
   steak, cut into serving-
   size pieces
¼ cup flour

¼ cup ketchup
1 tablespoon Worcestershire
¼ cup chopped green pepper,
   or 2 teaspoons bell pepper
   pepper flakes
1 teaspoon instant beef
   bouillon
1 teaspoon salt
½ teaspoon dried marjoram
   leaves
¼ teaspoon pepper
¼ cup water

Put potatoes, onion, green beans, and pimento in slow cooker. Dredge meat with flour and arrange over vegetables.   Combine ketchup, Worcestershire, pepper flakes, bouillon, salt, marjoram, pepper, and water.   Pour over all ingredients.   Cover and cook on low 8–10 hours.   Serves 4.

Quick Crockery (Colorado)

Sirloin Tips of Beef

1–1½ pounds sirloin tips
1½ teaspoons salt
1 teaspoon pepper
1 teaspoon garlic powder
Flour (½ cup or so)
2–3 tablespoons shortening
1 cup chopped onions
1 cup chopped celery
1 cup sliced carrots
1 cup cooked tomatoes
Water to cover
Cooked rice or noodles

Dredge meat in seasoned flour. Brown in shortening in 350° oven along with onions. Add celery, carrots, and tomatoes. Cover with water and cook 2 hours or until meat is tender. Serve over rice or noodles. Serves 6.

Dude Food (Utah)

Grilled T-Bone 240

2 (16-ounce) T-bone or
  porterhouse steaks
Salt, to taste
2 tablespoons fresh rosemary,
  minced
2 tablespoons freshly ground
  black pepper
1 tablespoon garlic, minced
½ cup olive oil, divided
2 tablespoons lemon juice

Prepare charcoal grill. Remove steaks from refrigerator to room temperature 2 hours prior to cooking. Rub steaks thoroughly with salt, rosemary, pepper, garlic, and ⅔ of olive oil. Grill steaks over medium-high heat 3–5 minutes per side until desired level of doneness. Remove steaks to a warm serving plate and tent with foil. Let rest 5 minutes. Carve meat from bone and slice in ¼-inch slices, reserving all juices. Squeeze lemon juice into reserved meat juices; season with salt and pepper; pour over sliced steak. Serve on warm plates and garnish with Fire Roasted Onions. Serves 4.

FIRE ROASTED ONIONS:
2 sweet onions (Vidalia,
  Walla-Walla, or Maui)
Remaining olive oil from steak
Salt and pepper

Peel and slice onions; toss with olive oil, salt and pepper, and grill along side of steaks for 2–3 minutes each side.

Recipe by Chef Matthew Franklin—240 Union, Lakewood
Haute Off the Press (Colorado)

Marinated Grilled Flank Steak

Juice of 1 lemon
½ cup soy sauce
¼ cup or more dry red wine
3 tablespoons vegetable oil
2 tablespoons Worcestershire
1 large clove garlic, sliced
Pepper to taste
Chopped green onions or
  chives (optional)
Chopped dill weed (optional)
Celery seed (optional)
1 (1½-pound) flank steak,
  trimmed

Mix all ingredients in the pan in which meat is to be marinated. Marinate flank steak, turning occasionally, for 2–12 hours in the refrigerator. Broil meat over hot coals for 5 minutes per side for rare meat. Slice meat on the diagonal across the grain and serve. Makes 3–4 servings.

Colorado Cache Cookbook (Colorado)

Steak on the Stick

MARINADE:

½ cup soy sauce
2 tablespoons vinegar
1 tablespoon sesame seed oil
2 green onions, finely
  chopped
2 tablespoons brown sugar
1 large clove garlic
Dash of Ac'cent
½ teaspoon prepared mustard

Mix ingredients.

2 pounds flank steak   ½ cup water (if needed)

Marinate steak 2 hours in container with lid. Add water if marinating longer. Cut meat in strips and put on skewers. Barbeque over grill.

Home Cookin' (Colorado)

Pepper Steak

1 pound lean beef steak
   (round or sirloin)
2–3 teaspoons paprika
1 clove garlic, crushed
1 small slice fresh gingerroot
   (optional)
1 tablespoon plus ¼ cup soy
   sauce, divided
2 tablespoons butter
1½ cups beef broth

1 cup sliced onion
1 green pepper, sliced
½ cup sliced celery
½ cup sliced mushrooms
¼ cup water
2 tablespoons cornstarch
1 large fresh tomato, cut in
   wedges
Cooked rice

Slice beef very thin and marinate with mixture of paprika, gar-lic, gingerroot, and 1 tablespoon soy sauce for ½–1 hour. Brown meat in butter in large skillet. Add broth and simmer for 30 minutes. Lightly stir-fry vegetables in small amount of hot oil and add to beef.

Blend ¼ cup soy sauce, water, and cornstarch. Add to meat mixture and simmer until thick and clear. Add fresh tomato wedges. Heat through. Serve over rice.

Favorite Recipes from Utah Farm Bureau Women (Utah)

Corned Beef

1 (3-pound) beef brisket
¼ cup vegetable oil
1 large carrot, chopped
1 large onion, chopped
1 clove garlic, minced
Salt and pepper
1 (1-ounce) package au jus
  mix

2 cups water
2 tablespoons tomato paste
1 bay leaf
¼ teaspoon thyme
1 pound carrots, peeled

Trim excess fat from brisket. Heat oil in Dutch oven. Shallow fry chopped carrot, onion, and garlic in oil. Remove vegetables and add brisket; brown well and season with salt and pepper. Combine au jus mix with water; add to brisket with tomato paste, bay leaf, thyme, and sautéed vegetables. Cover and bake in a 350° oven for 1½ hours. Drain off cooking juices into saucepan. Keep meat hot. Sieve vegetables into sauce; taste and adjust seasonings. Keep hot.

Cut carrots in quarters lengthwise. Cook in boiling, salted water until just done. Carve brisket. Arrange overlapping slices on platter. Cover with hot sauce and garnish with carrots. Makes 4 servings with enough meat left for another meal.

Virginia City Alumni Association Cookbook (Nevada)

The TV Western series *Bonanza* was set on a thousand-square-mile ranch on the shore of Lake Tahoe in Nevada. The nearest town was Virginia City. Film crews shot a good deal of the series on location at the "Ponderosa Ranch." *Bonanza* enjoyed a successful fourteen-year run, from 1959 to 1973. It was also the first Western in television history to be broadcast in color. The show's title "Bonanza" is a term used by miners in regards to a large vein or deposit of ore, and most likely refers to The Comstock Lode, located near the area.

Roast, Dutch Oven Style

1 (4-pound) beef roast
3 onions
4–6 potatoes
3 bell peppers

6 carrots
1 clove garlic
1 (18-ounce) bottle barbecue
    sauce

Prepare pit (see below). Lightly oil a large Dutch oven. Place roast in oven. Peel and quarter onion and potatoes and place in the oven. Seed bell peppers, then cut into quarters and add with whole carrots. Pour entire bottle of barbecue sauce over the top. Place lid firmly on the oven and carefully lower it into the pit. Cook for about 2 hours.

TO PREPARE PIT:

Dig a hole about 2 feet deep and approximately 8 inches bigger around than your Dutch oven. About 2 hours before cooking, heat the hole by burning wood in it. You should use a wood that makes lots of ashes (sagebrush and smaller pine limbs are good). It takes a large fire to heat the ground. After heating the ground, take out the ashes, leaving 3 or 4 inches of ashes in the bottom of the hole. After setting the Dutch oven in the hole, put the ashes back in, surrounding the pan on all sides, and with 3 or 4 inches of ashes on top. Cover the ashes with 1 or 2 inches of dirt to hold the heat in, and you are cooking.

The Great Nevada Cookbook (Nevada)

Dutch Oven Pot Roast with Sour Cream and Mushroom Gravy

3 teaspoons bacon grease or
  vegetable oil
1 (3- to 4-pound) roast beef
1 beef bouillon cube
1 cup boiling water
4 teaspoons ketchup
1 teaspoon Worcestershire
1 small onion, chopped
½ clove garlic, minced
2 teaspoons salt
½ teaspoon pepper
1 teaspoon celery salt
4 teaspoons flour
1 (4-ounce) can mushrooms
1 cup sour cream

In a Dutch oven on top of the stove, put bacon grease or vegetable oil. Brown roast on all sides. Dissolve bouillon cube in boiling water. Add to roast. Combine ketchup, Worcestershire, chopped onion, garlic, salt, pepper, and celery salt. Stir well and add to roast. Put the lid on and cook in the oven at 250° for 2–2½ hours, until meat is tender. Remove from oven.

Take meat from Dutch oven. Blend flour into liquid to make gravy. Add mushrooms and stir in the sour cream. Slice beef and serve with gravy over it. Good eating!

If camping, do it the same way, just don't let the fire get too hot. Also, if cooking a big roast for a lot of people, you will need to increase the ingredients to cover the extra people. Judge for yourself what amount you will need. Cook extra if you have big eaters. They will all want second helpings.

Doin' Dutch Oven: Inside and Out (Utah)

Gabby's No-Peek Prime Ribber

The secret to this preparation is the method of roasting, as you will see.

1 prime rib beef roast, 4–7 ribs long (large or small end; small end has least waste)
Worcestershire to taste
Fresh minced garlic to taste
Sweet Hungarian paprika
Seasoned or freshly ground pepper to taste
Flour to coat the roast

The weight of this roast does not matter, as long as it is between 4 and 7 ribs long. Rub the Worcestershire, garlic, paprika, and pepper over the outside of the entire roast (bone side, too). Dust with flour, then set meat on roasting rack inside a roasting pan.

Bake in a preheated 500° oven for 5 minutes for each pound (you must know the exact weight of the roast) if you want rare meat, 5½ minutes per pound for a more medium to well-done roast. After this roasting period, turn the oven off, but don't you dare open the oven door! If fact, the oven door must not be opened for exactly 2 hours. Now, open it up, place the meat on a warmed platter, and carve away. Serves 6–12.

Oh, this is so good, especially if you have chosen a Certified Angus Beef roast.

Enjoy! Again and Again (Utah)

Taste of the Rockies Casserole

1 pound ground beef
1 tablespoon oil
1 tablespoon chili powder
2 cloves garlic, minced
Salt and pepper to taste
1 large onion, chopped
1 green bell pepper,
  chopped
1 can Ro-Tel tomatoes
  with green chiles

1 (14½-ounce) can whole
  tomatoes
1 (15½-ounce) can kidney or
  pinto beans
¾ cup raw rice
1 (14½-ounce) can beef
  bouillon
¼ cup ripe olives, sliced
1 cup grated Cheddar cheese

Brown meat in oil. Add chili powder, garlic, salt, pepper, onion, and bell pepper. Cook 3 minutes. Add tomatoes with juice, breaking up; then add beans and rice. Turn into greased 2-quart baking dish; pour beef broth over meat and rice mixture and bake, covered, at 350° for 45 minutes. Sprinkle olives and cheese on top, and bake, uncovered, until cheese is melted. Serves 6–8.

Colorado Foods and More. . . (Colorado)

German Cabbage Burgers

1 pound hamburger
⅓ onion, chopped
½ teaspoon salt
Pepper

3 cups shredded cabbage
1 loaf bread dough
Butter, melted

Brown hamburger and onion in skillet. Add salt and pepper; drain grease. Cook cabbage until tender; drain. Roll bread dough ¼-inch thick and cut into 6–8-inch squares. Combine cabbage and hamburger. Spoon onto dough. Fold over and pinch edges together. Bake in 350° oven for 20–25 minutes or until golden brown. Brush top with butter. Good with your favorite mustard.

More Kitchen Keepsakes (Colorado)

Spicy Bean and Beef Pie

1 pound ground beef
2–3 garlic cloves, minced
1 (11½-ounce) can bean
  with bacon soup,
  undiluted
1 (16-ounce) jar thick and
  chunky salsa, divided
¼ cup cornstarch
1 tablespoon chopped fresh
  parsley
1 teaspoon paprika
1 teaspoon salt
¼ teaspoon pepper

1 (15-ounce) can black beans,
  rinsed and drained
1 (16-ounce) can kidney beans,
  rinsed and drained
2 cups shredded Cheddar
  cheese, divided
¾ cup sliced green onions,
  divided
Pastry for (10-inch) double
  crust pie
1 cup sour cream
1 (2¼-ounce) can ripe olives,
  sliced and drained

In a skillet, cook beef and garlic until beef is browned; drain. In a large bowl, combine soup, 1 cup salsa, cornstarch, parsley, paprika, salt and pepper; mix well. Fold in beans, 1¼ cups cheese, ½ cup onions, and beef mixture. Line pie plate with bottom pastry and fill with bean mixture. Top with remaining pastry; seal and flute edges. Cut slits in top crust. Bake at 425° for 30–35 minutes or until lightly browned. Let stand for 5 minutes before cutting. Garnish with sour cream, olives, and remaining salsa, cheese, and onions. Serves 8.

Country Classics II (Colorado)

Aunt Phoebe's Goulash

This is one of my dad's favorite meals. "There's nothing better than a bowl of hot goulash on a cold day."

1 cup cooked elbow noodles
1 pound ground beef
1 onion, diced
1 quart stewed tomatoes
1 quart tomato juice

1 tablespoon Worcestershire
1 tablespoon mustard
Salt and pepper to taste
1 cup grated cheese

Boil noodles in 3 cups water until tender; do not drain. In separate pan, brown ground beef and onion. Stir together tomatoes and juice, Worcestershire, mustard, salt and pepper, and bring to a boil. Add meat and noodles and simmer for 5 minutes. Stir in cheese. Serves 6.

The Cowboy Chuck Wagon Cookbook (Utah)

Sloppy Joe Biscuit Bake

1 medium onion, chopped
2 pounds lean ground beef
2 (1.3-ounce) packages
  Sloppy Joe seasoning mix

2 (6-ounce) cans tomato paste
2 cups water
1 (16-ounce) package prepared
  refrigerator biscuits

Heat a 12-inch Dutch oven over 9 hot coals. Brown onion and ground beef. Add seasoning mix, tomato paste, and water, stirring well, and bring to a boil. Separate individual biscuits and place on top of the meat mixture. Cover with Dutch oven lid and place 15 hot coals on top. Cook, covered, for 15–20 minutes, or until biscuits are browned and cooked through.

Or at home, preheat oven to 350°. In a large skillet, brown onion and ground beef; pour off drippings and add seasoning mix, tomato paste, and water, stirring well; bring to a boil. Transfer mixture to an oven-safe dish if the handle of your skillet is not oven-safe. Separate individual biscuits and place on top of meat mixture. Bake in preheated oven 15 minutes, until biscuits are browned and cooked through. Serves 4–6.

Recipes for Roughing It Easy (Utah)

Deep-Dish Beef Pie

PASTRY:

¾ cup all-purpose flour
½ teaspoon baking powder
3 tablespoons margarine
3 tablespoons cold water

Combine flour and baking powder. Cut in margarine until mixture resembles coarse crumbs. Sprinkle with cold water, one tablespoon at a time, stirring with a fork until mixture holds together. Form into a ball. On a floured surface, roll dough into a circle 1 inch larger than top of casserole.

FILLING:

1 pound lean boneless beef
  for stew, trimmed of fat and
  cut into ½-inch pieces
1 teaspoon cooking oil
1 cup chopped onion
1 cup chopped celery
1 cup sliced carrots
1 cup cubed, peeled turnip
1½ cups tomato juice
¾ teaspoon crushed dried
  thyme or basil
¼ teaspoon salt
⅛ teaspoon pepper
1 cup plus 2 tablespoons
  water, divided
1 tablespoon all-purpose flour
2 cups cut green beans,
  fresh or frozen
1 teaspoon skim milk

Spray a large skillet with nonstick coating. Preheat over medium-high heat. Brown half the meat in skillet. Remove. Add oil. Brown remaining meat. Return all meat to skillet. Stir in onion, celery, carrots, turnip, tomato juice, thyme, salt, pepper, and 1 cup water. Cover and simmer 50–60 minutes or until meat is nearly tender. Combine flour and remaining 2 tablespoons water. Stir into skillet mixture. Cook and stir until thickened and bubbly. Stir in green beans. Spoon into a 1½-quart casserole. Cover with Pastry; flute edges. Brush with milk. Cut vents for steam. Bake in a 400° oven for 30 minutes or until Pastry is lightly browned and meat and vegetables are tender. Serves 6.

Bless This Food (Nevada)

West Coast Wrangler's Camp-out Quickie

1 pound ground beef
1 packet chili mix
1 (15-ounce) can Mexican
  corn, drained

3 (15-ounce) cans chili beans
1 (14½-ounce) can Mexican-
  style tomatoes

Fry ground beef in a large skillet or Dutch oven until browned. Add contents of chili mix packet and the cans of vegetables to beef and heat through. Feeds 2 or 3.

A Cowboy Cookin' Every Night (Nevada)

Hearty Basque-Style Casserole

1 pound extra lean ground
  beef
1 pound extra lean ground
  lamb
1 cup chopped yellow onion
1 (29-ounce) can tomato
  sauce
4 cups chopped green
  cabbage

2 cups chopped purple
  cabbage
1 cup uncooked white rice
½ teaspoon rosemary
½ teaspoon salt
½ teaspoon black pepper
2 (14-ounce) cans low-sodium
  nonfat beef broth

Preheat oven to 350°. Spray a large skillet with nonfat cooking spray and brown beef and lamb. Drain fat. In a large bowl, combine meat, onion, tomato sauce, cabbage, rice, rosemary, salt, and pepper. Pour mixture into a 9x13-inch baking dish; pour broth over mixture and bake, covered, for about 1 hour. Makes 8 servings.

Easy Gourmet for Diabetics (Nevada)

Shepherd's Pie

1 pound cooked beef or lamb	1 tablespoon cooking oil
2 onions, chopped	1 cup gravy
2 carrots, peeled and chopped	2 pounds potatoes, boiled and mashed
3 tablespoons butter, divided	1 egg yolk, beaten

Dice meat. Cook onions and carrots in 1 tablespoon butter and the oil over medium heat until they are tender but not brown. Stir in gravy. (If you do not have gravy, stir the 1 tablespoon flour into onions and carrots in pan and cook slowly for 7 minutes, then add 1 tablespoon tomato paste, and 1 cup bouillon.) Stir and cook until gravy thickens. Stir in diced meat.

With 1 tablespoon butter, grease well a 2-quart shallow oven-proof dish. Spread half the mashed potatoes in the bottom of the dish. Spoon meat and gravy over the potatoes and top with a layer of remaining potatoes. Paint the top of the potatoes with egg yolk. Dot with remaining 2 tablespoons butter. Bake, uncovered, in a 350° oven for 30 minutes. The potatoes should be golden brown on top when the dish is done.

A Gathering of Recipes (Nevada)

Taco Seasoning Mix

¼ cup dried minced onion flakes	1½ teaspoons oregano
4 teaspoons cornstarch	3 teaspoons garlic powder
4 tablespoons chili powder	2 teaspoons instant beef bouillon
3 teaspoons cumin	3 teaspoons cayenne pepper

Mix all together; store in an airtight container in refrigerator. Three tablespoons equals one commercial package.

Easy Recipes for 1, 2 or a Few (Colorado)

Durango Meatballs

1 pound ground pork and
   1 pound ground round,
   ground together
2 cups soft bread crumbs
2 eggs
½ cup finely chopped
   onion

2 tablespoons chopped
   parsley
2 teaspoons salt
2 tablespoons butter
1 (10-ounce) jar apricot
   preserves
½ cup barbecue sauce

Combine meat, bread crumbs, eggs, onion, and seasonings; mix lightly. Shape into medium-size meatballs and brown in butter. Place in a casserole and pour the apricot preserves and barbecue sauce over the meatballs. Bake at 350° for 30 minutes. Makes 4–5 dozen meatballs.

The Durango Cookbook (Colorado)

Meatloaf in an Onion

4 large onions, peeled and
   halved
1 pound lean ground beef
1 egg
¼ cup cracker crumbs

¼ cup tomato sauce
½ teaspoon salt
⅛ teaspoon pepper
½ teaspoon dry mustard

Cut off root at the bottom end of the onion so that removal of the center is easy. Cut onions in half horizontally and remove center part of onion, leaving a ¾-inch thick shell. The removed center of the onion can be diced and combined with ingredients or used later.

   In a 1-gallon plastic zipper bag, combine ground beef, egg, cracker crumbs, tomato sauce, salt, pepper, and dry mustard, and mix by squeezing. Divide meat mixture into 4 portions and roll into balls. Place in the center of the 4 onion halves. Put onions back together. Wrap each onion in foil. Cook over a bed of hot coals for 15–20 minutes per side or in 350° oven for 45–50 minutes, or until ground beef and onions are cooked. Serves 4 as lunch or dinner.

Recipes for Roughing It Easy (Utah)

Western Style Barbecue Sauce for a Crowd

Great for spareribs, beef, or pork.

2 quarts ketchup
2 cups cider vinegar
½ cup dry mustard
½ cup Tabasco
1½ tablespoons black
  pepper
½ cup chili powder
1 cup brown sugar
2 cups tomato juice
¼ teaspoon garlic powder
2 tablespoons salt
30 pounds ribs or rump roasts

Combine all ingredients of sauce. Brown meat in oven at 450° for 20 minutes. Pour in the sauce. Bake covered at 300° for 4–5 hours or until meat begins to fall apart. Serves 50.

Recipes Thru Time (Utah)

Jealous Bourbon BBQ Sauce

1½ onions, chopped
12 cloves garlic, minced
2¼ cups bourbon whiskey
1½ teaspoons black pepper
2 teaspoons salt
6 cups ketchup
1 cup tomato paste
1 cup apple cider vinegar
¼ cup liquid smoke flavoring
¼ cup Worcestershire
1½ cups brown sugar
1½ teaspoons Louisiana hot
  pepper sauce

In a large skillet over medium heat, sauté onions, garlic, and whiskey 5–10 minutes, until onion is translucent. Add black pepper, salt, ketchup, tomato paste, vinegar, liquid smoke, Worcestershire, brown sugar, and hot pepper sauce. Mix well and bring to a boil. Reduce heat and simmer for 20 minutes.

A Cowboy Cookin' Every Night (Nevada)

Braised Beef Short Ribs

5 pounds beef short ribs,
  cut into 1-rib pieces
All-purpose flour, seasoned
  with salt and pepper
¼ cup rendered bacon fat
4 cloves garlic, chopped
3 onions, chopped

6 carrots, sliced
½ teaspoon crumbled dried
  rosemary
Salt and pepper to taste
Mushrooms (optional)
1 cup red wine
3 cups beef broth

Preheat oven to 350°. Dredge ribs in flour, knocking off excess. Heat bacon fat in a 6-quart Dutch oven over moderately high heat until hot but not smoking. Brown the short ribs. Transfer ribs to a large plate. Pour off all but about 2 tablespoons bacon fat remaining in Dutch oven, and in it cook garlic, onions, carrots, and rosemary with salt and pepper to taste over moderate heat, stirring until browned lightly; add mushrooms, if desired. Cook mixture about 6 more minutes.

Deglaze the pot with red wine. Add beef broth to the vegetable mixture and bring to a boil, stirring. Return ribs to the pot and cover. Cook (braise) in the oven until tender, about 2 hours.

The Best of Down-Home Cooking (Nevada)

Barbecued Beef Ribs

4–5 pounds beef ribs
1 teaspoon dry mustard
1 teaspoon onion powder
¼ teaspoon garlic powder
2 tablespoons soy sauce

1 tablespoon vinegar
1 cup ketchup
1 tablespoon Worcestershire
2 tablespoons brown sugar
1 tablespoon molasses

Boil ribs for 40 minutes before baking in Dutch oven. This will reduce fat.

Mix remaining ingredients to make barbecue sauce. Place ribs in oven and bake at 375°, 10–14 coals under, 18–22 on lid for 40 minutes if raw, or 10 if boiled. Brush well with sauce and continue cooking for 15–20 minutes, brushing with sauce every few minutes.

Dutch Oven Delites (Utah)

Silver State Beef Short Ribs

4½ pounds beef short ribs
12 garlic cloves, sliced
1 red onion, sliced

3 quarts water
3 cups good red wine
Salt and pepper to taste

Place ribs, garlic cloves, and onion slices in large pot and cover with water and red wine. Bring to a boil. Reduce heat and simmer uncovered until meat is cooked through, about 50 minutes. Sprinkle with salt and pepper; set aside.

TOMATO CHILE SAUCE:

3 garlic cloves
½ red onion, sliced
3 ripe tomatoes
4–6 mild chiles, stemmed,
  halved, seeded

1–2 ancho chiles, stemmed,
  halved, seeded
2 teaspoons ground cumin
1 teaspoon dried oregano
¼ cup red wine vinegar

Combine all ingredients in a food processor. Blend until chunky. Grill ribs, slathering with about half the Sauce. Serve ribs with remaining Sauce. Serves 4–6.

A Cowboy Cookin' Every Night (Nevada)

Porky Pineapple Spareribs

Great gourmet dish and excellent with Dutch oven potatoes or rice.

1 (20-ounce) can pineapple
  chunks, drained (reserve
  juice)
¼ cup vinegar
½ cup flour
1 teaspoon salt
¼ teaspoon pepper

4 pounds boneless pork
  spareribs
½ cup ketchup
¼ cup molasses
1 large green pepper, chopped
  fine
1 large onion, chopped fine

Warm and oil a 12-inch Dutch oven. Put reserved pineapple juice, vinegar, flour, and seasoning in oven and simmer until bubbling. Put ribs in oven; cover and cook at 350° for 50 minutes. Remove lid and stir ribs to baste with juices. Add ketchup and molasses and cook until ribs are tender, another 10–20 minutes. Add pineapple chunks, green pepper, and onion. Return to heat for 10 minutes to heat through.

Log Cabin Dutch Oven (Utah)

Independence Day Barbecue Spareribs

5 pounds pork spareribs,
  cut into sections
1 cup brown sugar
½ cup chili sauce
½ cup ketchup
¼ cup Worcestershire
¼ cup rum

⅛ cup soy sauce
4 cloves garlic, crushed
1 teaspoon dry mustard
1 teaspoon ground black
  pepper
½ teaspoon cayenne pepper
  (optional)

Preheat oven to 350°. Wrap ribs in double thickness of foil and bake for 45 minutes. Unwrap and drain. Combine brown sugar, chili sauce, ketchup, Worcestershire, rum, soy sauce, garlic, mustard, black pepper, and cayenne, if desired. Pour over ribs. Marinate refrigerated overnight.

   Preheat grill. Grill ribs for 30 minutes, turning once and basting with marinade. Serves 10.

All American Meals Cookbook (Nevada)

Colorado is nicknamed the "Centennial State" because it was admitted to the Union as the 38th state in 1876, the centennial year of the United States Declaration of Independence. Colorado is one of only three U.S. states with no natural borders, the others being neighboring Wyoming and Utah.

Pork Tenderloin à la Crème

A special weekend meal served with a dry white wine, steamed fresh vegetables and crusty French bread.

8 strips bacon
8 sliced pork tenderloin,
  2-inches thick,
  butterflied
¼ cup brandy or cognac
2 teaspoons dry mustard
Salt and freshly ground
  black pepper to taste

¼ cup dry white wine
2–3 tablespoons beef bouillon
  granules
2 cups heavy cream
2–3 tablespoons all-purpose
  flour
¼ pound mushrooms, sliced

Fry bacon until limp. Wrap bacon around outside edge of each butterflied tenderloin, secure with a wooden pick and place in ungreased roasting pan. Using a spoon, drizzle brandy over meat. Sprinkle meat with mustard, salt and pepper. Bake uncovered at 350° for 20–30 minutes. Remove pork. Skim grease from drippings. Add wine and bouillon granules and de-glaze roasting pan over medium heat. Whisk together cream and flour until smooth. Whisk into drippings. Stir and boil until thickened and smooth, about 4 minutes. Return meat to pan, turning to coat both sides. Sprinkle with mushrooms. Bake uncovered at 350° for 15 minutes, or until sauce is thickened. Makes 4–6 servings.

Crème de Colorado (Colorado)

Darned Good Skillet Supper

¼ cup olive oil
2 slices bacon, cut in small
  pieces
3 medium onions, peeled and
  sliced into rings
1 or 2 teaspoons paprika
Salt and coarsely ground
  pepper
8 boneless pork loin chops,
  about ½ inch thick
1½ cups fresh carrots, cut
  in chunks
8 fresh turnips, peeled and
  cut into eighths
16 baby boiling potatoes
  (unpeeled)
2 cloves fresh garlic, minced
  (or ½ teaspoon garlic
  powder)
2 or 3 sprigs fresh thyme (or
  1½ teaspoons dry, crushed)
3 tablespoons chopped fresh
  parsley (or ½ teaspoon dry)
1 generous sprig fresh mint
  (or ½ teaspoon dry)
1 sprig fresh bay leaf (or 1 dry
  leaf, crushed)
1 (14-ounce) can beef broth
½ cup white wine

Add olive oil to hot skillet and cook bacon pieces till clear, not crisp. Remove and set aside. Add onions and cook till soft. Remove and set aside with bacon. Rub paprika, salt and freshly ground pepper on both sides of pork chops. Brown in same skillet. Cook about 5 minutes on each side to medium-well. Remove chops and set aside.

Arrange carrots, turnips, and potatoes in the skillet. Add onions, bacon, and minced garlic. Lay fresh thyme, parsley, mint, and bay leaf over vegetables (or sprinkle dry herbs). Mix beef broth and wine and pour into skillet. Cover with a tightly fitted lid and simmer vegetables until tender, about 35–40 minutes. Uncover and correct seasoning. Arrange the browned chops around the vegetables; cover and reheat chops about 5 minutes longer; remove lid.

For a stunning presentation, place hot skillet supper in the center of the table, accompanied by a tossed salad with vinaigrette dressing.

A Gathering of Recipes (Nevada)

Pork Chops and Potatoes Bake

6 center-cut pork chops,
  ¾–1 inch thick
Worcestershire
Salt and pepper to taste
Garlic salt
Flour
Oil
2 fresh pork sausage links,
  sliced and diced
1 onion, chopped
1 red or green (or mixed)
  bell pepper, chopped

3 stalks celery, chopped
1 garlic clove, minced
1 (4-ounce) can sliced
  mushrooms
¼ cup minced fresh parsley
2 (14½-ounce) cans beef
  broth
4 large Colorado potatoes,
  sliced in rounds, ¼-inch thick
Salt and pepper to taste
Butter

Rub pork chops with small amount of Worcestershire. Season with salt, pepper, and garlic salt. Coat lightly with flour. Fry in hot oil, quickly, browning on both sides. Remove. Pour out excess oil, leaving one tablespoon. Brown sausages in skillet. Add onion, bell pepper, celery, and garlic. Sauté vegetables, stirring to cook evenly, until tender. Add mushrooms and parsley. Add ½ can broth and stir to mix.

In large, flat pan, place sliced potatoes, overlapping, in layer on bottom. Salt and pepper and dot with butter. Top with sausage mixture to cover potatoes. Arrange pork chops on top. Pour one can broth on top. Cover tightly with foil and bake 30 minutes. Uncover, add more broth if necessary, and cook an additional 30 minutes until done. Yields 6 servings.

Colorado Foods and More. . . (Colorado)

Red Mountain Stuffed Pork Chops

¾ cup chopped onions
⅓ cup chopped celery
¼ cup butter
½ loaf bread, broken into
   bread crumbs
½ teaspoon salt
1 tablespoon fresh sage, or
   to taste

1 tablespoon fresh thyme
1 cup chicken broth
5–6 pork chops (have butcher
   cut pockets)
1 can cream of celery soup
½ can water
10 small mushrooms
Minced garlic (optional)

Sauté onions and celery in butter until onions are clear. Put bread crumbs in a large bowl and sprinkle with salt, sage, and thyme. Mix in sautéed vegetables and chicken broth. Mix together and stuff into the pork chops. Place stuffed chops into a well greased 12-inch Dutch oven.

Mix the soup, water, mushrooms, and garlic in a bowl and pour over pork; cover with lid. Put the Dutch oven on hot coals and place more coals on the lid. Bake 90 minutes, turning a quarter turn every 20 minutes. (Or bake in conventional oven at 350° for 20–30 minutes.) Yields 4–6 servings.

West of the Rockies (Colorado)

AFBORCHERT@WIKIPEDIA.ORG

Red Mountain is a set of three peaks in the San Juan Mountains of western Colorado, about five miles south of Ouray, Colorado. The mountain gets its name from the reddish iron ore rocks that cover the surface. In the fall of 1968 the film *True Grit* was filmed in Ouray County, including some scenes in the city of Ouray and the nearby town of Ridgway and, most notably, the interior of the Ouray County Court House.

Bunkhouse Pork Chops in Ranch Sauce

8 pork chops
1½ cups water, divided
2 tablespoons brown sugar
¼ cup chopped onion
1 teaspoon garlic powder
1 tablespoon seasoned salt
¼ cup flour
½ cup sour cream
3 tablespoons ketchup

Place chops in 12-inch Dutch oven. Add 1 cup water, brown sugar, onion, garlic powder, and seasoned salt. Simmer for 1 hour and 30 minutes in 350° oven. Add flour to remaining ½ cup water and mix with sour cream and ketchup. Pour over chops and return to heat. Heat thoroughly without boiling. Chops will be very tender. Use 10 briquettes on bottom and 15 on top, or 12 in Volcano with damper closed halfway (briquettes will last 2 hours).

Log Cabin Dutch Oven (Utah)

Skillet Pork Chops

3 tablespoons flour
5 tablespoons grated
  Parmesan cheese, divided
1½ teaspoons salt
½ teaspoon dill weed
¼ teaspoon pepper
6 or 7 pork chops
1 tablespoon oil
2 medium onions, sliced
⅓ cup water
3 medium zucchini, sliced
½ teaspoon paprika

In a large plastic bag, combine flour and 2 tablespoons Parmesan cheese, salt, dill weed, and pepper. Place pork chops in bag and shake to coat. Shake off excess flour in bag; reserve. Heat oil in a skillet over medium heat; fry and brown pork chops on both sides. Reduce heat; place onion slices on chops. Add water to skillet, cover, and simmer for 15 minutes. Place zucchini slices over onion slices. Mix remaining Parmesan cheese with reserved flour in bag; sprinkle over zucchini, put paprika over that, and simmer for 25 minutes or until chops are nice and tender. Excellent served over rice.

Log Cabin Holidays and Traditions (Utah)

Sweet and Sour Pork

½ teaspoon salt
¼ teaspoon pepper
¼ cup powdered sugar
3 cups cubed pork
1–2 tablespoons oil
¼ cup water
2 tablespoons butter
1 cup finely chopped onion

1 (8½-ounce) can diced
  bamboo shoots, drained
1 (10-ounce) package frozen
  peas
3 tablespoons lemon juice
¼ cup soy sauce
Cooked rice or noodles

In a small bowl, combine salt, pepper, and powdered sugar. Coat pork cubes with mixture. Heat oil in wok. Add pork and stir-fry for about 10 minutes or until evenly browned. Reduce heat and add water. Cover and simmer for 30 minutes or until pork is tender. Push pork up side of wok. Add butter; when melted, add onion and bamboo shoots; stir in pork. Push mixture up on the side of the wok and add frozen peas, lemon juice, and soy sauce; cook for 2 minutes. Mix all together. Serve with rice or noodles.

Log Cabin Presents Lewis and Clark (Utah)

Trailer Treat

Good to cook over the fire while camping.

1 medium onion, chopped
3 tablespoons margarine
1 pound franks, quartered
1 teaspoon salt
1 tablespoon flour
1½ teaspoons chili powder

2 (15-ounce) cans kidney
  beans
1 (16-ounce) can stewed
  tomatoes
1 (12-ounce) can corn kernels,
  drained

Sauté onions in melted margarine. Add franks. Heat until franks are cooked and onions are lightly browned. Blend together salt, flour, and chili powder. Add mixture to onions and franks. Add beans, tomatoes, and corn. Simmer, covered, about 15 minutes.

Variation: May use 1 (15-ounce) can kidney beans, drained, 1 (15-ounce) can baked beans, 1 (10¾-ounce) can tomato soup, 1 (16-ounce) can tomatoes, and 1 (12-ounce) can corn, drained.

Home Cookin' (Colorado)

All American Marmalade Glazed Ham

GLAZE:

1 cup orange marmalade
¼ cup Dijon mustard

2 tablespoons orange juice

Melt marmalade in saucepan. Whisk in mustard and orange juice. Boil until thickened, about 5 minutes. Set aside.

1 (20-pound) smoked bone-in ham
30 whole cloves
1 cup orange juice
2 cups water
4 orange spice-flavored tea bags
1 cup low-sodium chicken broth

4 tablespoons orange marmalade
1 tablespoon Dijon mustard
1 tablespoon cornstarch, dissolved in 1 tablespoon water
Black pepper to taste

Preheat oven to 325°. Score fatty side of ham in a crisscross pattern. Insert a clove into cross sections of score pattern. Place ham on a rack in a roasting pan with orange juice. Bake 3 hours for 45 minutes.

Increase oven temperature to 425°. Baste ham with Glaze and bake until Glaze is set and begins to caramelize, about 20 minutes. Transfer ham to cutting board and let set at least 15 minutes. Reserve pan juices and pour into a saucepan.

In another saucepan, bring water to a boil. Add tea bags and remove from heat. Let steep 10 minutes. Discard tea bags. Add chicken broth and orange marmalade to tea. Bring to a boil; reduce heat. Whisk in mustard and reserved pan juices until blended. Whisk in cornstarch mixture and stir until thickened. Boil until sauce thickens slightly, about 4 minutes. Season with black pepper to taste. Carve ham and serve with sauce. Serves 12.

All American Meals Cookbook (Nevada)

Lamb Stew with Garlic and Pinot Noir

This interpretation of this tummy-warming comfort food has a Lebanese touch. Fresh mint adds an interesting flavor prominent in Lebanese dishes.

½ cup all-purpose flour
Salt and pepper to taste
2 pounds lamb stew meat
  (preferably shoulder)
  trimmed of fat, cut into
  stew-size pieces
3 tablespoons olive oil
1 large head garlic, roasted
  and chopped finely
½ cup chopped yellow onion

¼ cup chopped green pepper
½ cup chopped peeled carrots
½ cup chopped celery
2 cups Pinot Noir (red wine)
½ cup chopped Roma
  tomatoes
2–3 cups lamb stock made
  from bones and trimmings
3 bay leaves
1 tablespoon fresh mint

Combine flour, salt and pepper in a bowl. Add lamb and stir to coat. Set aside. In a large, heavy-bottomed stainless steel pot, heat the olive oil. Add chopped garlic and cook until slightly golden. (Do not allow it to brown or it will add a bitter taste.) Add onion, pepper, carrots, and celery. Cook for 5–10 minutes, stirring, until onion is slightly translucent. Add the lamb and brown on all sides, approximately 10–15 minutes. Add the Pinot Noir. Cook and reduce the liquid by 25 percent. Add the tomatoes, 2 cups lamb stock, bay leaves, pinch of salt and freshly ground pepper. Reduce by another 25 percent.

Lower heat, cover, and simmer over low heat 1–1½ hours. During the last half hour, uncover and let the stew thicken to a nice velvety thick consistency. If it is too thick, add a little more stock. Use your own judgment on the final consistency of this wonderful dish. Add fresh mint just before serving. Serve with polenta. Serves 4.

God, That's Good! (Nevada)

Roasted Leg of Lamb with Raspberry Glaze

1 (5- to 6-pound) leg of lamb
2 cloves garlic, slivered
⅓ cup seedless red raspberry jam (reserve 2 tablespoons for sauce)
3 tablespoons dry white wine
2 teaspoons Dijon mustard
¼ teaspoon rosemary leaves
¼ teaspoon crushed black pepper
1 cup beef broth
1 tablespoon cornstarch

Using the tip of a knife, make small slits evenly over leg of lamb and insert garlic slivers into each. In small bowl, mix together jam, wine, mustard, rosemary leaves, and pepper. Brush lamb with ¼ cup sauce mixture and place fat-side-up in roasting pan. Bake at 350° for 20–25 minutes per pound for medium rare (160° internal temperature). For more well-done meat, add 5 minutes per pound. Pour remaining sauce over lamb during last 40 minutes of cooking time. Remove lamb to warm platter and let stand 15 minutes.

Meanwhile, pour lamb drippings into saucepan. Remove excess grease. Mix broth, cornstarch, and reserved 2 tablespoons red raspberry jam and whisk into drippings. Cook over medium heat, continuing to whisk until sauce thickens. Serve gravy hot with sliced lamb. Makes 6–8 servings.

Favorite Recipes from Utah Farm Bureau Women (Utah)

JAMES RICE @ WIKIPEDIA.ORG

The Bonneville Salt Flats are a 30,000-acre salt (potash) floor ranging from one to six inches thick, and are actually the bed of what was ancient Lake Bonneville. Bonneville Speedway is an area of the Flats near Wendover, Utah, that is marked out for motor sports. It is particularly noted as the venue for numerous land speed records. The salt flats were first used for motor sports in 1912, but didn't become truly popular until the 1930s when Ab Jenkins and Sir Malcolm Campbell competed to set land speed records. The annual Speed Week is held in mid-August.

Garlic and Chili-Rubbed Buffalo Steaks

2 large cloves garlic,
  chopped
1 teaspoon salt
2 tablespoons chili powder
1 teaspoon ground cumin

¾ teaspoon sugar
3½ tablespoons Worcester-
  shire
4 (1-inch thick) buffalo
  rib eye steaks

Combine garlic and salt in a small bowl; mash to a paste. Add chili powder, cumin, and sugar; mix well. Stir in Worcestershire. Arrange steaks on a plate large enough to hold them in one layer. Rub both sides of steaks with chili paste. Transfer to a zip-lock plastic bag and refrigerate for at least 4 hours and up to 2 days.

  Grill steaks on an oiled rack 5 inches over glowing coals, 5 minutes per side for medium rare. Transfer to serving plates and let rest 5 minutes. Makes 4 servings.

Note: Also great on beef steaks and chicken.

Shalom on the Range (Colorado)

Ribs Diablo

8 pounds wild boar spareribs,
  or 10 pounds caribou
  back ribs
1 cup Cabernet Sauvignon
Water
1 Vidalia onion, minced
4 cloves garlic, minced
2 tablespoons butter

1 cup tomato paste
½ cup steak sauce
1 cup honey
1 tablespoon Worcestershire
1 bottle dark beer
1 teaspoon cinnamon
½ teaspoon salt
6 shakes Tabasco or to taste

Boil ribs in wine and enough water to cover 1 hour. Sauté onion and garlic in butter. Add tomato paste, steak sauce, honey, Worcestershire, beer, cinnamon, salt, and Tabasco. Bring to boil; reduce heat and simmer 30 minutes. Drain ribs and bake in 350° oven 30–40 minutes or until brown, basting often with sauce until glazed. Serves 6–8.

Wild Man Gourmet (Nevada)

Elk Enchiladas

2 pounds ground elk
½ cup olive oil
1 (16-ounce) jar picante sauce
1 (7-ounce) can diced green chiles, drained
1 (16-ounce) can pinto beans, drained
½ pound sharp Cheddar cheese, cubed, divided
½ pound pepper Jack cheese, cubed
16–20 corn tortillas
1 cup sour cream
1 cup chopped tomatoes
1 cup sliced olives

Preheat oven to 325°. Brown ground elk in oil in skillet and drain grease. Return meat to skillet and add picante sauce and chiles. Simmer 10 minutes; add beans and ¼ of cheese cubes and simmer until cheese is melted. Fill each tortilla with ¼ cup meat mixture; roll and place in baking dish seam-side-down. Bake 25 minutes; top with remaining cheese cubes. Bake 10–12 minutes or until cheese is melted. Top with sour cream, tomatoes, and olives. Serves 6.

Wild Man Gourmet (Nevada)

Elk Piccata

2 pounds elk steak, cut ½-inch thick, trim all fat
Salt, pepper, flour
3 tablespoons butter
2 tablespoons olive oil
¾ pound fresh mushrooms, sliced
2 cloves garlic, minced
½ cup dry white wine
3 tablespoons fresh lemon juice
3 ounces brandy
4 tablespoons minced parsley
Lemon slices

Sprinkle meat with salt and pepper; pound lightly on both sides. Dust lightly with flour. Heat butter and oil, and brown meat on both sides. Remove meat from skillet. Add mushrooms and garlic to pan and cook 1 minute. Return meat to pan; add wine and lemon juice. Cover and simmer for 25 minutes or until meat is tender. Warm brandy; pour over meat and flame. Remove meat and keep warm on platter. Spoon sauce over meat. Garnish with parsley and lemon slices. Serves 4.

Recipes from Our House (Colorado)

Poultry

The United States Air Force Academy is among the most selective colleges in the United States. The campus covers 18,000 acres on the east side of the Rampart Range of the Rocky Mountains, just north of Colorado Springs, Colorado. The 17-spire Cadet Chapel is a distinguishing feature.

EPICV27, WIKIPEDIA.ORG

Perfectly Roasted Chicken

Simple ingredients give this flawless chicken an intense malty essence that is divine.

1 (3- to 4-pound) chicken, cleaned of fat, skin on, rinsed, and patted dry
Juice of 1 lemon
1½ teaspoons kosher salt (or to taste), divided
1 teaspoon freshly crushed black pepper, divided
1 large clove garlic
1 tablespoon dried sage, or thyme (for fresh sage use 1 teaspoon)
4 tablespoons butter or margarine, softened
Cooking twine
1½ cups Vienna or Marzen-style beer

Rub chicken inside and out with lemon juice. Sprinkle inside with half the salt and pepper. With side of a cleaver, mash garlic and remaining salt to form a paste and mix with sage and butter. Carefully lift skin on each side of the chicken breast and push some of the mixture under. Rub the remaining mixture over the outside.

Truss (using cooking twine, tie the legs together, turn and tie wings together) and place chicken breast side down on well-greased rack in a shallow pan. Pour beer into pan and place in 425° oven for 40 minutes, basting every 10 minutes with beer and pan drippings. Turn breast side up and roast 25 minutes, basting every 8 minutes. Continue roasting and basting until meat thermometer inserted into the thickest part of the thigh registers 160°. The juices should run clear when you puncture the skin at the thigh joint. Remove from pan and place on heated platter. Cover with foil and allow to rest 10 minutes before carving. Serve with pan juices or make into gravy. Or save pan juices to simmer with the carcass for a delicious soup. Serves 4.

Variation: You can use the same recipe and cooking method for a small fresh turkey.

Great American Beer Cookbook (Colorado)

Grilled Chicken with Herbs

2 tablespoons minced fresh
  parsley
2 teaspoons minced rosemary
2 teaspoons minced thyme
1 sage leaf
3 garlic cloves, minced

¼ cup olive oil
½ cup balsamic vinegar
Salt and pepper
1½ pounds boneless, skinless
  chicken breasts

In a blender, combine all ingredients except chicken. Pour marinade over chicken breasts in a bowl. Cover and place in refrigerator and let marinate for at least 2 hours or up to 48 hours. Grill or broil chicken for about 6–7 minutes per side until no trace of pink remains. Makes 6 (4-ounce) servings.

Sharing Our Diabetics Best Recipes (Nevada)

Spicy Gazebo Springs Chicken

1 pound boneless chicken
  breasts, skinned
2 tablespoons corn oil
¼ cup slivered orange peel
1 clove garlic, minced
¾ teaspoon ground ginger
2 tablespoons cornstarch

½ cup dry sherry
1 cup chicken broth
⅓ cup soy sauce
⅓ cup orange marmalade
¾ teaspoon dried crushed
  red pepper

Thinly slice chicken. In a wok or large skillet, heat corn oil over medium-high heat. Add chicken, a few slices at a time. Stir-fry 3 minutes or until browned. Return all chicken to wok. Add orange peel, garlic, and ginger. Stir-fry one minute. Stir together remaining ingredients in a small bowl. Stir into chicken. Stirring constantly, bring to a boil over medium heat and boil several minutes. Serve over rice or pasta. Serves 4.

Steamboat Entertains (Colorado)

Poached Breast of Chicken with Citrus-Garlic Sauce

CITRUS-GARLIC SAUCE:

2½ cups chicken stock
10 garlic cloves, sliced
1 tablespoon chopped fresh
  dill

3 tablespoons orange juice
  concentrate
4 grapefruit segments,
  membranes removed

Place all ingredients in large sauté pan, bring to a boil, reduce heat to low, and simmer for 10 minutes.

POACHED BREAST OF CHICKEN:

4 (4- to 5-ounce) boneless,
  skinless chicken breasts

1 red bell pepper, julienned
  for garnish

Place chicken breasts in sauté pan with sauce; poach, covered, on one side for 4–5 minutes. Turn chicken over and poach, covered, for an additional 3 minutes or until done. Remove chicken breasts and keep warm. Increase heat to high and cook sauce 4 minutes or until it thickens. Strain, reserve sauce. Place chicken on individual plates, top with sauce, and garnish with bell peppers. Serves 4.

Recipe from Chef Stephen Reynolds, C Lazy U Ranch, Granby
Cooking with Colorado's Greatest Chefs (Colorado)

French Country Style Chicken

4 (6-ounce) boneless, skinless
   chicken breasts
Salt and black pepper to taste
1 cup Granny Smith apples,
   unpeeled, cored, sliced
6 scallions, diced
⅔ cup apple cider

1 cube chicken bouillon
1 teaspoon dried sage
½ teaspoon dried ginger
⅔ cup 2% milk
2 teaspoons flour
2 teaspoons Splenda
Parsley as garnish

Spray skillet with nonfat cooking spray. Sauté chicken breasts until browned, about 5 minutes per side. Season to taste with salt and black pepper. Add apples, scallions, apple cider, bouillon, sage, and ginger. Heat to a boil. Reduce heat and simmer, covered, until chicken is tender, 10–12 minutes. Remove chicken and apples to serving platter.

Simmer remaining cider mixture until reduced. Stir in milk, flour, and sugar substitute into skillet. Heat to a boil, stirring constantly, until thickened, about 1 minute. Season to taste with salt and pepper. Pour sauce over chicken and apples. Garnish with parsley and serve hot. Serves 4.

Easy Gourmet for Diabetics (Nevada)

The United States Government has ownership of nearly 30% of its total territory. Much of the federal land is used as military bases, nature parks and reserves, and Native American reservations. Nevada leads the states with 84.5% of its territory owned by the federal government. Utah is third (after Alaska) with 57.4%. More than one-third of Colorado's land area is available for public use. These public lands are managed by various federal and state agencies and local governments.

Chicken Rellenos

6 boneless chicken breast halves (about 1½ pounds)
1½ cups shredded Monterey Jack cheese (6 ounces)
3 tablespoons diced green chiles
3 tablespoons sliced pimentos
30 Ritz crackers, coarsely crushed (about 1½ cups crumbs)
½ teaspoon chili powder
¼ teaspoon ground cumin
2 tablespoons all-purpose flour
1 egg, beaten
3 tablespoons margarine, melted
1 (16-ounce) jar salsa (mild, medium, or hot), or your own homemade

Pound each chicken breast to ¼-inch thickness; top each with ¼ cup cheese. Combine chiles and pimentos; sprinkle one tablespoon chile mixture over cheese. Roll up chicken from short edge; secure with toothpicks. Mix cracker crumbs, chili powder, and cumin. Coat chicken rolls with flour; dip in egg, then roll in crumb mixture. Place chicken rolls in 8x12-inch baking dish. Drizzle margarine over chicken. Bake at 350° for 35–40 minutes or until done. Remove toothpicks; serve with salsa. Makes 6 servings.

Doc's Delights (Colorado)

Chicken Piccata

2 chicken breasts
2 tablespoons flour
¼ teaspoon salt
⅛ teaspoon pepper
2 tablespoons olive oil
¼ small onion, minced
1 clove garlic, minced
½ cup chicken broth, or
  ½ teaspoon bouillon
  dissolved in ½ cup warm
  water

1 tablespoon butter
1 tablespoon sherry
1 tablespoon lemon juice
1 teaspoon capers
1 slice fresh lemon plus ½
  tablespoon chopped parsley
  for garnish

Pound chicken breasts between 2 sheets of plastic wrap until ¼ inch thick. Set aside. Mix together flour, salt and pepper to form seasoned flour. Dip chicken lightly; shake off excess flour. Heat a large dry frying pan over medium heat until a drop of water sizzles. Then add olive oil. Sauté onion and garlic until golden brown. Remove from heat; set aside. In the same frying pan, sauté chicken breasts until golden, turning only once. Remove from heat; set aside. Place in 250° oven to keep warm.

Make sauce by adding chicken broth to the pan. Add onion mixture, butter, sherry, lemon juice, and capers to the same pan. Stir and cook until syrupy and sauce is slightly thick. Add chicken breasts back to pan; simmer for 2–5 minutes until chicken is thoroughly cooked and piping hot. Place chicken breasts on a serving plate. Spoon sauce neatly on the chicken. Garnish with lemon and parsley. You may substitute fresh prawns (shelled and deveined) or thinly sliced pork for chicken. Serve with noodles, steamed broccoli, and garlic bread for a complete meal. Serves 2.

Tasteful Treasures (Nevada)

Colorado Chicken Casserole

4 large chicken breasts
4–6 chicken thighs
1 (10-ounce) can cream of
  mushroom soup
2 (10-ounce) cans cream of
  chicken soup
1 onion, grated

1 (7-ounce) bottle green taco
  sauce
2 (7-ounce) cans chopped
  green chiles
15 corn tortillas, quartered
16 ounces longhorn cheese,
  shredded

Rinse chicken. Place in saucepan with water to cover. Cook until very tender. Drain, reserving broth. Remove skin and bones; discard. Cut chicken into cubes. Mix next 5 ingredients in bowl. Alternate layers of tortillas, chicken, and soup mixture in greased 9x13-inch baking dish until all are used. Top with cheese. Bake at 325° for 1½–2 hours, adding some of reserved broth if mixture becomes dry. Yields 10 servings.

The Flavor of Colorado (Colorado)

Working Barn Stew

A filling, zesty family stew.

2 tablespoons olive oil
4 boneless, skinless chicken
  breast halves, (about
  1 pound), cut into 1-inch
  pieces
1 cup chopped onion
½ medium green bell
  pepper, chopped
½ medium yellow bell
  pepper, chopped
1 teaspoon chopped garlic

2 (14½-ounce) cans stewed
  tomatoes
1 (15-ounce) can pinto beans,
  drained and rinsed
¾ cup medium picante sauce
1 tablespoon chili powder
1 tablespoon ground cumin
½ cup shredded Cheddar
  cheese
6 tablespoons sour cream

In large stockpot, heat olive oil over medium heat. Add chicken, onion, bell peppers, and garlic; cook until chicken is no longer pink. Add tomatoes, beans, picante sauce, chili powder, and cumin. Reduce heat to low and simmer 25 minutes or up to 2 hours. Place in individual serving bowls and top with cheese and sour cream. Makes 6 servings.

Colorado Collage (Colorado)

Conestoga Chicken

12 slices bacon (6 full slices,
  6 quartered)
6 skinless, boneless chicken
  breasts
2 garlic cloves, diced
1 stick butter
1 (16-ounce) can chicken
  broth
2 cups long-grain brown rice

2 cups fresh mushrooms
2 tablespoons sage
½ tablespoon pepper
½ tablespoon onion powder
1 tablespoon Worcestershire
2 cups fresh broccoli florets
2 (10¾-ounce) cans cream of
  mushroom soup

With 12 coals on bottom and 12 coals on top, cook bacon in 12-inch Dutch oven. Remove whole slices; drain grease, leaving quartered bacon in oven.

Pound chicken slightly until thin and workable to roll. Place one slice of bacon on each breast. Roll, securing with toothpick. Add garlic and butter to quartered bacon. Sauté until butter is melted; add chicken rolls, and brown both sides. Remove chicken and set aside.

Add chicken broth, rice, mushrooms, sage, pepper, onion powder, and Worcestershire to oven. Stir lightly to blend together. Place chicken on top of rice. Place broccoli florets around and in between chicken. Place dollops of cream of mushroom soup around oven. Cover and let cook for 30–45 minutes until done.

A Complete Guide to Dutch Oven Cooking (Utah)

Gym Rat's Oven Baked Chicken Strips

2 (8-ounce) boneless, skinless chicken breasts
2 egg whites, beaten
½ cup whole-wheat cracker crumbs
1 teaspoon dried oregano
1 teaspoon dried basil
½ teaspoon dried thyme
1 teaspoon paprika
2 teaspoons grated Parmesan cheese

Cut chicken breasts into strips. Dip strips in egg whites. Combine cracker crumbs, spices, and Parmesan in a plastic bag. Add chicken strips and shake bag to coat with crumb mixture. Put chicken strips on a nonstick baking sheet or baking sheet sprayed with nonfat cooking spray. Bake at 350° for 10–12 minutes until golden and crunchy. Great served with marinara sauce. Makes 4 servings.

The Protein Edge (Nevada)

Munsterrela Chicken Breast

8 boneless, skinless chicken breasts
3 eggs, beaten
2 cups bread crumbs
½ pound fresh, sliced mushrooms
½ pound Muenster cheese, grated
½ pound mozzarella cheese, grated
1 cup chicken broth

Dip chicken breasts in beaten eggs, then roll in bread crumbs. Brown in buttered skillet. Place in a 14-inch Dutch oven; top with mushrooms and grated cheeses. Pour broth over chicken and bake for 45 minutes to 1 hour or until golden brown. Use 10–12 briquettes on bottom and 10–12 on top. Serves 8.

Dutch Oven and Outdoor Cooking, Book Two: Homespun Edition (Utah)

Chicken with Chocolate

You will be surprised at how truly delicious this chicken is. In the Basque region of Navarra, the use of chocolate, especially in game recipes, is popular.

1 (2½- to 3-pound) fryer,
  cut up
¼ cup cooking oil or olive oil
1 large onion, chopped
2 cloves garlic, minced
1 green bell pepper, chopped
  (1–1½ cups)
2 (8-ounce) cans tomato
  sauce

1–2 teaspoons crushed dried
  red pepper
1 teaspoon salt
¼ teaspoon Tabasco
2 cloves garlic, chopped
½ ounce unsweetened baking
  chocolate, finely grated

Soak chicken briefly (10–15 minutes) in cold, salted water. Trim off excess fat. Drain chicken pieces in colander. Pat dry with paper towel, if necessary. Heat oil in frying pan or electric skillet to a moderate 300° heat. Brown chicken pieces in oil. When nicely browned, remove pieces to a Dutch oven or casserole with cover.

In the skillet in which you browned the chicken pieces, sauté onion, garlic, and bell pepper for 10 or 15 minutes on low heat. Add remaining 6 ingredients, mixing well. Simmer about 5 minutes. Spoon sauce over chicken pieces in Dutch oven or casserole. Bake at 350° for one hour. Yields 5–6 servings.

Chorizos in an Iron Skillet (Nevada)

HENRICKSON@WIKIPEDIA.ORG

On average, approximately 300 marriage licenses are issued per day in Las Vegas, which is known as the "Wedding Capital of the World." Las Vegas has over 50 wedding chapels (shown here: Chapel of the Flowers). According to the Nevada Department of Human Resources, almost 90 percent of all people married in Nevada come from other states. The glamour of a Las Vegas wedding attracts many celebrities. Elvis and Priscilla, Frank Sinatra and Mia Farrow, Paul Newman and Joanne Woodward, were all married in Las Vegas.

Smothered Yardbird

1 cup flour
2 teaspoons poultry seasoning
½ teaspoon garlic powder,
  or to taste
½ teaspoon onion powder
1 frying chicken cut into 8
  pieces
½ cup buttermilk
1 cup vegetable shortening
  or oil for frying

2–4 baking potatoes
2 carrots, peeled (optional)
1 onion, sliced thin and
  separated
1 (10¾-ounce) can cream of
  mushroom soup
1 (10¾-ounce) can cream of
  chicken soup
1 soup can water
Salt and pepper to taste

Preheat oven to 300°. Combine flour, poultry seasoning, garlic powder, and onion powder. Dip each chicken piece in buttermilk and coat well with flour mixture. Melt shortening over medium-high heat until hot and water sprinkled in the pan sizzles. Shake extra flour from chicken and fry 3–4 pieces at a time until lightly browned on all sides. Transfer pieces to a large baking pan (a chicken roaster is perfect).

Slice potatoes and carrots about ¼–½ inch thick and fry quickly in the same oil until outsides are crisp, but not cooked all the way through. Remove with slotted spoon and add to chicken in roaster. Pour out all but 2 tablespoons of the oil, add onion, and cook until just soft. Combine soups, water, and seasoning; add to pan and stir until mixed and warm. Pour soup and onion over chicken and vegetables. Bake for 2½–3 hours, until meat is tender and gravy is bubbling.

Note: You may choose to cover the chicken in the oven if it will be unattended for much of the cooking time or if the gravy starts to develop a tough surface. Cover for half of cooking time, or occasionally simply stir the meat down into the gravy.

How to Win a Cowboy's Heart (Utah)

Green Chicken Enchiladas

FILLING:

1 cup grated Cheddar cheese
2 cups grated Monterey Jack cheese
2 cups cubed, cooked chicken
½ medium onion, chopped
½ cup sliced black olives
1½ cups sour cream
2 tablespoons chopped parsley
¾ teaspoon freshly ground pepper

In a large bowl, mix together cheeses, chicken, onion, olives, sour cream, parsley, and pepper, and set aside.

SAUCE:

2 tablespoons butter
2 tablespoons all-purpose flour
½ cup milk
1½ cups chicken broth, divided
1 (10-ounce) package frozen spinach, cooked, drained, and coarsely chopped
⅔ cup sour cream
4 tablespoons chopped green chiles
½ medium onion, chopped
1 clove garlic, minced
¾ teaspoon cumin

In a sauté pan, heat butter over low heat. Add flour and cook for a few minutes, stirring constantly. Stir in milk and add ½ cup chicken broth. Bring to a boil. Boil for one minute, stirring constantly. Add remaining 1 cup chicken broth; cook and stir until hot and thickened; add spinach, sour cream, green chiles, onion, garlic, and cumin.

1 (18-ounce) package flour tortillas
Additional shredded cheese for garnish
Lime and tomato slices for garnish

Dip each tortilla into Sauce, coating both sides. Spoon about ¼ cup Filling onto each tortilla and roll up. Place seam-side-down in an ungreased 9x13-inch baking dish. Pour remaining sauce over enchiladas and bake uncovered at 350° for about 20 minutes or until bubbly. Garnish with shredded cheese and lime and tomato slices. Serve. Serves 6–8.

JLO Art of Cooking (Utah)

Deon's Chicken Pies

Bake these tasty pies and freeze for future eating.

1 (3-ounce) package cream
  cheese, softened
4 tablespoons butter, softened,
  divided
⅛ teaspoon salt
⅛ teaspoon pepper
2 tablespoons finely chopped
  onion
1 tablespoon finely chopped
  celery

1 small bottle pimento, drained
  and chopped
2 tablespoons milk
3 cups diced cooked chicken
2 (8-ounce) cans crescent rolls
1 cup seasoned bread crumbs
⅛ teaspoon garlic powder

Lightly grease a cookie sheet; set aside. Preheat oven to 350°. In a small bowl, combine cream cheese, 2 tablespoons butter, salt, pepper, onion, celery, pimento, and milk; stir with wooden spoon until well blended. Add chicken. Open crescent rolls and separate the dough, keeping 2 triangles together to form a square, for a total of 8 squares. Press the perforations to seal the holes. In the center of each square, place about ½ cup chicken mixture. Pull the 4 corners together and twist top to seal pie.

Melt remaining 2 tablespoons butter. Combine bread crumbs with garlic powder. Brush each pie with butter and sprinkle with crumbs. Place on greased cookie sheet and bake 20 minutes until lightly browned. Serve immediately, or can be kept frozen for up to 2 weeks. To reheat, cook at 325° for 10–15 minutes, or wrap in foil and place on medium coals for 10 minutes. Serves 4.

Vacation Cooking: Good Food! Good Fun! (Utah)

Chicken Pastry Pillows

3 cups cubed, cooked chicken breasts
1 (8-ounce) package cream cheese, softened
½ stick butter, softened
1 cup chopped mushrooms
¼ cup chopped onion
1 package Pepperidge Farm Pastry Sheets

Combine cooked chicken, cream cheese, butter, mushrooms, and onion in a bowl. Thaw pastry sheets according to package instructions. Roll out a bit thinner and cut into 8 rectangles per sheet. Place ¼ cup chicken mixture onto each rectangle (reserving ½ cup for sauce). Fold over and seal with fork. If pastry dries out, wet your fingers and stick together. Prick each pastry pillow with a fork and place on cookie sheet. Bake at 350° for 20–25 minutes. Remove from oven and cover with Mushroom Sauce.

MUSHROOM SAUCE:
1 (10¾-ounce) can cream of mushroom soup
1 cup milk
½ cup water
1 chicken bouillon cube
1 beef bouillon cube
½ cup chicken mixture

Mix all ingredients in saucepan until heated through. You may thicken sauce with flour or cornstarch, if desired.

Making Magic (Utah)

Chicken in a Nest

¼ cup (½ stick) margarine
½ cup chopped onion
½ cup chopped celery
¼ cup unsifted flour
1 teaspoon salt

⅛ teaspoon pepper
1½ cups chicken broth
½ cup heavy cream
3 cups cubed, cooked chicken

Melt margarine in large saucepan. Add onion and celery; sauté over low heat until tender. Stir in flour, salt, and pepper and cook several minutes over low heat. Remove from heat; gradually stir in broth and cream. Cook over low heat, stirring constantly, until mixture comes to a boil. Add chicken. Cook, stirring, until heated through. Serve mixture in Potato Nests.

POTATO NESTS:

1 egg, beaten
3 cups thick mashed
   potatoes

2 tablespoons margarine,
   melted

Add egg to mashed potatoes and mix until blended. Drop mixture by spoonfuls onto greased baking sheets, using ½ cup for each nest. Spread each mound into a 3½-inch circle, shaping sides with spoon. Brush with margarine. Bake at 425° for 15 minutes, or until potatoes are light brown. Makes 6 servings.

Family Favorites from the Heart (Utah)

Carson City, Nevada, one of the lesser populated state capitals in the United States, was named for frontiersman and scout, Christopher Houston "Kit" Carson (December 24, 1809–May 23, 1868), who guided John C. Fremont's mapping expedition across the Nevada Territory in 1843.

Spicy Garlic Chicken Pizza

½ cup sliced green onions, divided
2 garlic cloves, minced
2 tablespoons rice vinegar or white vinegar
2 tablespoons soy sauce
2 tablespoons olive oil, divided
½ teaspoon crushed red pepper, or ¼ teaspoon cayenne pepper
¼ teaspoon black pepper

12 ounces boneless, skinless chicken breasts, cut into ½-inch pieces
1 tablespoon cornstarch
1 (16-ounce) Boboli Italian bread shell
½ cup shredded Monterey Jack cheese
½ cup shredded mozzarella cheese
2 tablespoons pine nuts or sliced almonds

Combine ¼ cup green onions, garlic, vinegar, soy sauce, 1 tablespoon olive oil, red pepper, and black pepper in a bowl and mix well. Add chicken and stir to coat. Let stand for 30 minutes at room temperature. Drain and reserve the marinade. Stir cornstarch into marinade.

Heat remaining 1 tablespoon olive oil in a large skillet and add chicken. Sauté for 3 minutes or until cooked through. Add reserved marinade to skillet. Cook until thick and bubbly, stirring constantly. Spoon chicken mixture evenly onto the bread shell. Sprinkle with Monterey Jack cheese and mozzarella cheese. Bake at 400° for 12 minutes. Top with ¼ cup green onions and pine nuts. Bake for 2 minutes longer. Serve hot. Yields 6 servings.

Las Vegas Glitter to Gourmet (Nevada)

Miners' Turkey Burgers with Black Bean Salsa

3 tablespoons olive oil, divided
½ small red onion, minced
1 carrot, finely chopped
1 stalk celery, finely chopped
1 pound ground turkey
1 slice white bread, crumbled
1 (4-ounce) can chopped mild green chiles, drained
½ teaspoon salt
4 (8-inch) flour tortillas, hamburger buns, or pita breads
1 head Boston lettuce

Heat 1 tablespoon oil in a large skillet over medium heat. Sauté onion, reserving one tablespoon onion. Add 1 tablespoon oil to skillet; add carrot and celery. Sauté until very tender, about 10 minutes. Remove from heat and place in a mixing bowl. Add turkey, bread crumbs, chiles, and salt. Combine well and shape into 4 (¾-inch) thick patties. Heat remaining tablespoon oil in same skillet over medium heat. Cook patties about 10 minutes or until thoroughly cooked and lightly browned on both sides.

To serve, heat tortillas, buns, or pita breads. Top with lettuce leaves and turkey patty. Spoon salsa over patties. Makes 4 servings.

BLACK BEAN SALSA:

2 tablespoons lime juice
¼ teaspoon coarsely ground pepper
1 tablespoon olive oil
½ teaspoon salt
1 large tomato, seeded and diced
1 avocado, diced
1 (15-ounce) can black beans, rinsed and drained
1 (8¾-ounce) can whole kernel corn, drained

Mix lime juice, pepper, oil, and salt. Stir in tomato, avocado, black beans, corn, and reserved onion.

Shalom on the Range (Colorado)

Cranberry Glazed Roast Turkey

Try this recipe with Cornish game hens for a special dinner.

1 (4-pound) turkey roast
1 (16-ounce) can whole or
  jellied cranberry sauce
¼ cup butter or margarine
1 teaspoon Worcestershire

¼ cup orange juice
2 teaspoons orange rind,
  grated
⅛ teaspoon poultry seasoning
2 teaspoons brown sugar

Place turkey roast in slow cooker. Mix together cranberry sauce, butter, Worcestershire, orange juice, orange rind, poultry seasoning, and brown sugar. Pour over turkey. Cover and cook on low 8–10 hours. Baste turkey with cranberry glaze before removing turkey to warm platter to slice. Offer cranberry sauce on the side for those who want extra. Serves 6.

Quick Crockery (Colorado)

Turkey Tetrazzini

½ cup butter or margarine
½ cup flour
4 cups chicken broth
4 egg yolks
4 tablespoons sherry
1 cup light cream
Salt to taste
½ pound mushrooms, sliced,
  sautéed in butter
3 cups diced, cooked turkey

2 (10-ounce) packages
  chopped broccoli, cooked,
  drained
1 (7-ounce) package spaghetti,
  cooked, drained
2 tablespoons grated
  Parmesan cheese
¼ cup slivered, blanched
  almonds

Melt butter; stir in flour. Gradually stir in chicken broth. Cook over low heat, stirring constantly till mixture thickens. Mix egg yolks, sherry, and cream. Gradually beat flour mixture into egg mixture. Reheat until sauce is thickened, but do not boil. Add salt to taste. Fold in mushrooms and turkey. Reheat.

Put layer of cooked broccoli in bottom of shallow serving dish; top with hot, cooked spaghetti and turkey sauce. Sprinkle Parmesan cheese and almonds on top. Put under broiler and brown until cheese is golden. Serve at once. Serves 6.

Timbreline's Cookbook (Nevada)

Baked Chukar

1 cup uncooked white rice
½ cup uncooked brown rice
Salt and pepper
6–8 chukar breasts
1 (1-ounce) envelope dry onion
  soup mix

1 (10¾-ounce) can cream of
  celery soup
2 soup cans water

Put white and brown rice in bottom of a 2-quart casserole. Salt and pepper chukar and place on top of the rice. Sprinkle soup mix over chukar and rice. Cover contents of casserole with cream of celery soup mixed with water. Bake uncovered at 425° for 20 minutes. Then cover casserole and bake at 350° for 1½ hours more. Yields 3–6 servings.

Chorizos in an Iron Skillet (Nevada)

Roasted Duck, Nevada Style

6 slices French bread,
  crumbled
½ cup diced yellow onion
5 cloves garlic, sliced
4 tablespoons butter
4 tablespoons chopped
  cilantro

2 tablespoons diced jalapeño
4 tablespoons chopped
  pine nuts
1 or 2 ducks
1 cup chicken broth
1 cup red wine

Preheat oven to 325°. Combine bread, onion, garlic, butter, cilantro, jalapeño, and pine nuts. Stuff duck(s) with mixture. Rub duck(s) with additional butter. Put in roasting pan; add broth and wine. Bake 4 hours at 325°.

For gravy, add pan juices to a little flour and butter; stir until thick. Serves 1–2 per duck.

Wild Man Gourmet (Nevada)

Seafood

PHOTO COURTESY OF UTAH STATE PARKS

With its sudden storms and expansive spread, the Great Salt Lake in northern Utah is a great test of sailing skills. There are no fish in the Great Salt Lake because of the high salinity. The only aquatic animals able to live in the lake are tiny brine shrimp. However, the adjoining wetlands provide critical habitat for millions of migratory shorebirds and waterfowl.

Grilled Teriyaki Fish

Has fish become humdrum? Try this rather exotic-flavored marinade next time you grill seafood. The combination of soy sauce, porter, and seasonings elevates plain seafood to uncommon heights.

MARINADE:

¼ cup honey, warmed

⅓ cup light soy sauce, or
   3 tablespoons tamari sauce

⅓ cup porter, stout, or
   smoked beer

½ teaspoon liquid smoke
   (optional)

2 tablespoons olive oil or
   other vegetable oil

1 tablespoon dark sesame oil

2 cloves garlic, finely minced
   and crushed

⅛ teaspoon hot red chili
   flakes, ground (optional)

1 teaspoon ground ginger, or
   ½ teaspoon chopped fresh
   ginger

Freshly ground black pepper,
   to taste

1 tablespoon sugar

Whisk together the ingredients and let stand at room temperature one hour.

4 pounds mahi-mahi or other
   firm fish

⅔ cup flour

Brush Marinade over fish and refrigerate for 2 hours before grilling. Sprinkle the fish with flour, and grill, basting often with marinade. Cook fish 10 minutes per inch of thickness. Cook shrimp until they turn pink and scallops until they are no longer translucent. Serves 8.

Note: Large shelled shrimp or sea scallops may be used in place of fish.

Great American Beer Cookbook (Colorado)

Mahi Mahi with Low-Fat Cucumber Sauce

½ cup peeled, seeded, and chopped cucumber
½ cup low-fat plain yogurt
2 tablespoons chopped fresh dill or ½ teaspoon dried
2 tablespoons chopped parsley

2 green onions, white part and first 2 inches of green, chopped
1 teaspoon lemon zest
4 (¼-pound) mahi mahi steaks
1 tablespoon fresh lemon juice

Mix cucumber, yogurt, dill, parsley, green onions, and lemon zest in a bowl and set aside. Arrange mahi mahi on a plate with thickest portions to the outside. Drizzle with lemon juice. Cover with plastic; vent at one corner. Microwave on HIGH for 4–5 minutes until thickest portion is just opaque. Rearrange fish once. If fish is thick, it may need more cooking time. Check frequently, about every 20 seconds, to avoid overcooking. Let stand 5 minutes to finish cooking. Drain. Serve room-temperature yogurt sauce on top of fish.

Recipes from Sunset Garden Club (Nevada)

Cheese-Topped Orange Roughy

An amiable blending of Parmesan cheese and fish—soon to be a favorite.

2 pounds orange roughy (can substitute sole, cod, or snapper)

TOPPING:
⅓ cup light mayonnaise
⅓ cup grated Parmesan cheese
¼ cup sliced green onions

½ teaspoon lemon juice
¼–½ teaspoon garlic powder
Hot sauce to taste

Preheat oven to 350°. Place fish in a shallow glass casserole coated with cooking spray; bake 8 minutes or until fish flakes easily when tested with a fork. Meanwhile, mix topping ingredients. Spread Topping evenly over cooked fish fillets. Broil 6 inches from heat for 5 minutes or until topping is lightly browned. Yields 6 servings.

Simply Colorado (Colorado)

Oven Fried Fish

It's hard to believe, but it's true. With this method there's no pot watching, no turning, and no odor. Try it!

¼ cup milk
2 teaspoons salt
Dash of dried thyme, tarragon, dill, or rosemary (or minced onion, garlic, or Tabasco)
½ cup packaged dried bread crumbs (or crushed corn or wheat flakes)

½ teaspoon paprika
Dash of dry mustard
Dash of chili powder
A little grated cheese
A little snipped parsley
1–2 pounds small fish or fillets or steaks
Salad oil or melted butter

Mix milk and salt with a dash of herbs or seasoning in shallow dish. In a second dish, combine bread crumbs or crushed flakes with paprika and mustard, chili powder, grated cheese, and snipped parsley. Start heating oven to 500°. Now, with one hand, dip each piece of fish into milk, then with other hand roll it in crumbs, arranging side-by-side, in greased shallow baking dish lined with foil. Drizzle a little salad oil or melted butter onto fish. Then bake 12–15 minutes or until golden and easily flakes with fork, but still moist. Serves 6.

A Century of Mormon Cookery, Volume 2 (Utah)

Facts about Utah's Great Salt Lake:
- The largest salt lake in the western hemisphere.
- The largest U.S. lake west of the Mississippi River.
- The 4th largest terminal lake (no outlet) in the world.
- It is a remnant of Lake Bonneville, a prehistoric lake that was 10 times larger than the Great Salt Lake.
- On average, it is about 75 miles long, and 28 miles wide, 35 feet deep, and covers 1,700 square miles. But the lake's size fluctuates substantially due to its shallowness.
- There are eight named islands in the lake that have never been totally submerged during historic time.
- It is typically 3 to 5 times saltier than the ocean.
- It has no fish; the largest aquatic critters are brine shrimp.
- It is one of the largest migratory bird magnets in Western North America.
- The salt industries extract about 2.5 million tons of sodium chloride and other salts and elements from the lake annually.
- No streams empty from the lake, and its high salinity is caused by the accumulation of minerals with no removal and the accompanying water evaporation.

Zane's Catfish BLT's

ZANE'S COCKTAIL SAUCE:

¾ cup mayonnaise
3 tablespoons sweet pickle
  relish
1½ tablespoons bottled
  capers, drained and diced
1 tablespoon Dijon mustard

1 tablespoon fresh lemon juice
1 tablespoon bottled cocktail
  sauce
1 teaspoon lemon zest
⅛ teaspoon cayenne
Salt and pepper to taste

In a bowl, combine all ingredients. Chill covered at least one hour.

FISH BLT'S:

2 large eggs, beaten
½ teaspoon salt
¼ teaspoon cayenne
1 cup all-purpose flour,
  seasoned with salt and
  pepper
1 cup cornmeal
2 pounds catfish fillets, cut
  into 8 (4-ounce) portions

Vegetable oil for deep-frying
8 soft sandwich or sourdough
  rolls, split
1 cup shredded iceberg lettuce
2 ripe tomatoes, sliced thin
½ red onion, sliced thin
16 slices bacon, cooked

Beat eggs with salt and cayenne. Place flour, cornmeal, and eggs in 3 separate shallow dishes. Dredge catfish fillets in flour; shake off excess. Then dip fillets in egg mixture, and finally dredge in cornmeal. Transfer the fish to a plate. In a deep-fryer, heat enough oil to cover fillets to 375°, or in frying pan, heat 1 inch of oil to 375°. Fry the fish in batches for 2–4 minutes on each side, or until it is done inside and crispy golden on the outside. Drain on paper towels.

On each bottom half of roll, layer lettuce, tomatoes, onion, 2 slices of bacon, fish, and Cocktail Sauce. Top with upper half of the roll. Serve with fries or potato chips.

The Hooked Cook (Nevada)

Grilled Trout Fillets with Tomato Butter

This is the fisherman's way to eat fish!

Trout fillets (or any other firm-fleshed white fish fillets)

Lemon pepper
Melted butter

For the best flavor, soak several handfuls of mesquite wood chips in water. Prepare a moderately hot charcoal fire. When the coals are covered with light ash, remove the chips from the water and spread over the coals. Start cooking the fish immediately.

Place one-inch thick fillets, brushed with mixture of lemon pepper and butter, on the grill. Cook for 5–8 minutes on each side, basting often, until fish flakes. Serve immediately with Tomato Butter.

TOMATO BUTTER:

¼ pound unsalted butter
2 tablespoons tomato paste

½ teaspoon salt
¼ teaspoon sugar

Cream all ingredients in a food processor until light and fluffy. Chill, and serve with trout fillets.

More Kitchen Keepsakes (Colorado)

Halibut Supreme

A treasure of the sea.

2 pounds fresh halibut pieces
¼ cup plus 1 tablespoon
  butter, divided
¼ cup flour
2 cups milk
¼ teaspoon salt

¼ teaspoon Worcestershire
3 tablespoons chopped onion
1 cup grated Cheddar cheese
Buttered bread crumbs (1 cup
  crumbs plus 2 tablespoons
  melted butter)

Place halibut in salted boiling water. Simmer, covered, about 20 minutes or until flaky. Drain well and set aside.

In a medium saucepan, make white sauce by melting ¼ cup butter, then stirring in flour until well combined. Add milk, salt, and Worcestershire, stirring constantly over medium heat until the mixture comes to a boil. Continue cooking at a boil for about 2 minutes, until thickened. Remove from heat; set aside.

Sauté onion in 1 tablespoon butter for about 5 minutes, or until tender. Add to white sauce. Layer halibut, cheese, and sauce in greased 2½-quart baking dish, ending with sauce on top. Top with buttered bread crumbs. Bake at 325° for about 30 minutes. Makes 4–6 servings.

The Essential Mormon Cookbook (Utah)

Creamy Baked Halibut Steaks

4 halibut steaks, about
  ¾-inch thick
Salt to taste
Pepper to taste
¾ cup thick sour cream
¼ cup dry bread crumbs

¼ teaspoon garlic salt
1½ teaspoons chopped
  chives, fresh or frozen
⅓ cup grated Parmesan
  cheese
1 teaspoon paprika

Place steaks, close fitting, in a shallow buttered baking dish. Sprinkle with salt and pepper. Mix together sour cream, bread crumbs, garlic salt, and chives, and spread over steaks. Sprinkle with Parmesan cheese and paprika. Bake, uncovered, at 400° for 15–20 minutes, or until fish flakes with a fork. Makes 4 large or 8 small servings.

Lion House Recipes (Utah)

Stuffing for Fish

½ stalk celery
½ dozen mushrooms
1 small onion
4 tablespoons butter
5 cups bread crumbs or
 diced dry bread
Dash of salt

Dash of granulated garlic
Squirt of lemon juice
2 eggs
Water
Crayfish (optional)
Melted butter combined with
 lemon juice

Dice celery, mushrooms, and onion, and lightly fry in butter. Add bread crumbs or bread, salt, granulated garlic, and lemon juice or juice of ½ lemon. Add eggs; mix and add water until you have the consistency of stuffing. You may add crayfish to the stuffing for a really nice accent, if desired.

Fill trout or salmon cavity with stuffing; truss if necessary. Baste fish with melted butter and lemon juice and grill, basting occasionally, till done (be sure to oil grate before placing). Be careful turning fish over.

The Practical Camp Cook (Utah)

Salmon with Cilantro Sauce

Moist, flavorful and easy.

1 (12-ounce) salmon fillet,
 cut into 4 equal-size
 portions
¼ cup lime juice
3 tablespoons chopped fresh
 cilantro

1 tablespoon olive oil
½ teaspoon ground cumin
¼ teaspoon salt
⅛ teaspoon pepper
3–6 drops Tabasco

Preheat oven to 500°. Prepare 4 (12x12-inch) squares aluminum foil, sprayed with nonstick spray. Place a piece of salmon on each foil square. Combine remaining ingredients; drizzle evenly over fish. Tightly seal foil into packets. Place baking sheet in oven 2 minutes to preheat. Put packets on hot baking sheet. Bake 8 minutes, or until fish is opaque and flakes easily with a fork. Makes 4 servings.

Palates (Colorado)

BBQ Salmon with Potatoes and Peppers

¼ pound red-skinned
   potatoes, scrubbed and cut
   into 1-inch cubes
3 tablespoons olive oil
1 red or yellow bell pepper,
   cut into thin strips

1 medium red onion, sliced
1 tablespoon capers
Salt and pepper to taste
2 (8-ounce) skinless salmon
   fillets or steaks, 1 inch thick

Heat oven to 450°. Partially cook the potatoes by boiling or steaming them for 8 minutes; drain and set aside. In a 9- or 10-inch skillet, heat olive oil over medium heat. Add bell pepper and onion. Cook for 5 minutes or until softened. Remove from heat. In an oven-proof dish, combine bell pepper, onion, and potatoes. Add capers, salt and pepper to taste; toss together. Set aside.

SPICE MIXTURE:

2 teaspoons paprika
2 teaspoons brown sugar
Pinch cayenne or red pepper

½ teaspoon salt
½ teaspoon black pepper

Combine all ingredients and sprinkle on a plate. Coat salmon fillets in the spice mixture on both sides, shaking off excess spices. Put salmon on top of potatoes and peppers and place dish in the oven. Roast for 20–25 minutes, or until salmon is firm to the touch. Makes 2 servings.

CASA Cooks (Nevada)

Broiled Herbed Scallops

¼ pound fresh bay scallops
1 green onion, minced
2 tablespoons lemon juice
1 teaspoon vegetable oil

1 teaspoon dried basil
½ teaspoon dried tarragon
Chopped fresh parsley

Put scallops in a bowl. Add remaining ingredients, except the parsley. Toss and marinate at room temperature for 10–15 minutes. Remove scallops from marinade and put on wooden skewers or place in a shallow pan. Broil just until scallops are opaque, being careful not to overcook. Baste with the marinade. Sprinkle on parsley just before serving. Makes 2 servings.

Sharing Our Diabetics Best Recipes (Nevada)

Shrimp Newburg

This is my all-time favorite—easy and deliciously rich. Everyone loves it.

2 tablespoons finely chopped
  onion
Butter
½ teaspoon curry powder
  (to taste)

1 (10¾-ounce) can cream of
  shrimp soup
1 cup sour cream
1 cup cooked shrimp
¼ cup lemon juice

In a 2-quart saucepan, sauté onions in a little butter until transparent. Add curry powder to taste. Stir in canned soup and sour cream, and cook gently over medium heat. Add shrimp and heat through, but do NOT let boil. Add lemon juice to taste. Serves 4–6.

Variation: Cream of shrimp soup is difficult to find. You may substitute cream of chicken soup, then add a drop of red food coloring and slightly more lemon juice. Lemon juice is the key to this recipe's delicious flavor. I also like to cook my own shrimp in seasoned water until barely done. It has more flavor than purchased cooked shrimp.

Recipe by Elaine Jack
Five-Star Recipes from Well-Known Latter Day Saints (Utah)

Shorty's Beer Batter Shrimp Poor Boys

1 cup beer
1 cup cake flour
1 teaspoon salt
1 teaspoon cayenne pepper
1 pound uncooked extra large
  shrimp, peeled, deveined

Canola oil for deep-frying
4 French rolls, split, toasted
1 cup shredded iceberg lettuce
1 ripe tomato, thinly sliced

Combine beer, cake flour, salt, and cayenne pepper. Cover shrimp in batter. Heat oil in deep-fryer to 325°. Fry shrimp until golden. Transfer shrimp to paper towels and drain. Slather rolls with Horseradish Spread. Layer bottom half of rolls with lettuce, tomato, and shrimp. Top with upper half of rolls. Serves 4.

HORSERADISH SPREAD:

1 cup mayonnaise
2 tablespoons fresh lemon
  juice

¼ cup prepared horseradish
2 garlic cloves, minced

Combine well and slather rolls with spread.

The Hooked Cook (Nevada)

Trout are the state fish of Colorado, Nevada, and Utah. Colorado's Greenback cutthroat trout is found east of the Continental Divide in the cold, clear foothill and mountain waters. It is now an endangered species. Nevada's Lahontan Cutthroat Trout, a native trout found in fourteen of the state's seventeen counties, has adapted to habitats ranging from high mountain creeks and alpine lakes to warm, intermittent lowland streams and alkaline lakes where no other trout can live. Utah's Bonneville cutthroat trout is a species native to tributaries of the Great Salt Lake. They are descended from cutthroat trout that once inhabited the Lake Bonneville, but moved upstream due to loss of habitat.

Crusty Shrimp and Crab Salad Sandwiches

1 cup diced cooked shrimp
1 cup shredded crabmeat
¼ cup diced black olives
¼ cup diced celery
⅛ cup minced onion
½ cup chopped hard-boiled eggs
⅔ cup mayonnaise

2 teaspoons lemon juice
½ teaspoon dill
¼ teaspoon salt
8 teaspoons butter, room temperature
8 slices sourdough bread
4 teaspoons chopped fresh parsley or watercress

Combine first 10 ingredients. Chill. Spread butter on slices of sourdough bread. Toast sourdough slices under broiler or in toaster oven. Top 4 of the hot bread slices with chilled shrimp and crab salad. Sprinkle with a teaspoon of parsley or watercress. Top with remaining bread slices. Serve immediately while salad is cold and bread is hot. Serves 4.

The Hooked Cook (Nevada)

Hot Crab Open Faces

7½ ounces flaked crabmeat, fresh or canned
¼ cup mayonnaise
3 ounces cream cheese
1 egg yolk
1 teaspoon finely chopped onion

¼ teaspoon prepared mustard
⅛ teaspoon salt
6 English muffin halves
Hard boiled eggs, tomatoes, or avocados (optional)

Mix the crabmeat, mayonnaise, cream cheese, egg yolk, onion, mustard, and salt together in a bowl. Spread the mixture on the muffin halves. Arrange the halves on a broiler pan and broil 2–3 minutes, until the top is golden brown. Garnish with sliced hard boiled eggs, tomatoes or avocados, depending upon whether it is being served for brunch or lunch. Makes 6 servings.

Recipe from Abriendo Inn, Pueblo
Distinctly Delicious (Colorado)

Deviled Crab

¼ cup butter, melted
3 tablespoons flour
2 tablespoons mustard
1½ teaspoons paprika
⅛ teaspoon nutmeg
⅛ teaspoon cayenne pepper
⅛ teaspoon black pepper
1 cup milk
2 cups flaked crabmeat
3 hard-boiled eggs, chopped
Salt to taste
1 tablespoon lemon juice
8 crab shells
½ cup cracker crumbs
2 tablespoons melted butter
2 tablespoons chopped parsley

Melt butter in saucepan; add next 6 ingredients; mix well. Add milk; mix well. Cook over medium heat until mixture thickens, stirring constantly. Remove from heat. Add crabmeat, eggs, salt, and lemon juice; mix well.

Spoon into crab shells. Sprinkle with mixture of cracker crumbs and 2 tablespoons melted butter. Bake at 350° for 10 minutes or until brown. Garnish with chopped parsley. Yields 8 servings.

The Flavor of Colorado (Colorado)

Crustless Crab Quiche

4 eggs
1½ cups sour cream
½ cup grated Parmesan cheese
½ cup flour
⅛ teaspoon salt
4 drops Tabasco
1 (6½-ounce) can crabmeat, drained
2 cups grated Swiss cheese
1 cup chopped fresh mushrooms
2 shallots, minced
2 tablespoons butter

Preheat oven to 350°. Combine eggs, sour cream, Parmesan cheese, flour, salt, and Tabasco in a large bowl; beat with a whisk until smooth. Stir in crabmeat and Swiss cheese. Sauté mushrooms and shallots in butter until soft and add to mixture. Pour into ungreased 10-inch pie plate. Bake for 45 minutes or until knife inserted near center comes out clean. Cool 5 minutes before serving. Yields 6 servings.

A Pinch of Salt Lake Cookbook

Crab Cobbler

½ cup butter
½ cup chopped green
  pepper
½ cup chopped onion
½ cup flour
1 teaspoon dry mustard
1 teaspoon Ac'cent
1 cup milk

1 cup shredded American
  cheese
1 cup crabmeat
1½ cups drained chopped
  tomatoes
2 teaspoons Worcestershire
½ teaspoon salt

In top of a double boiler, add butter, green pepper, and chopped onion; let cook about 10 minutes. Blend in flour, dry mustard, Ac'cent, milk, and cheese; cook and stir until cheese melts and mixture is very thick. Add crabmeat, tomatoes, Worcestershire, and salt. Pour into a greased 2-quart casserole. Drop topping over crab mixture and bake 20–25 minutes in 450° oven.

CHEESE BISQUICK TOPPING:
¼ cup shredded cheese   ½ cup milk
1 cup Bisquick

Combine all ingredients and drop by teaspoons on top of crab mixture.

NSHSRA High School Rodeo Cookbook (Nevada)

Cakes

There's no place on earth like Nevada's Las Vegas Strip. At night, the Strip comes alive with miles of colored neon and millions of dancing, pulsating lights—giving it the distinction of being just as scenic at night as it is by day. It is a never-in-the-dark neon city.

Orange Carrot Cake

The best and easiest carrot cake you'll ever make or taste.

3 cups flour, divided
2 cups sugar
1 cup shredded coconut
1¼ cups vegetable oil
3 eggs
2 teaspoons vanilla

1 (11-ounce) can Mandarin
  oranges, undrained
2½ teaspoons baking soda
2½ teaspoons cinnamon
1 teaspoon salt
2 cups shredded carrots

Blend 1½ cups flour, sugar, coconut, vegetable oil, eggs, vanilla, and Mandarin oranges in large mixing bowl on high speed for ½ minute. Add remaining 1½ cups flour, baking soda, cinnamon, and salt. Blend on medium speed 45 seconds. Scrape bowl and stir in carrots. Pour into greased 9x13-inch cake pan (or 2 greased and floured 10-inch round pans). Bake in preheated 350° oven for 45–50 minutes (35–45 minutes for 10-inch pans) until tested done. Cool completely. For round pans, let cool 10 minutes before removing to wire racks to finish cooling. Frost with Orange Cream Cheese Frosting.

ORANGE CREAM CHEESE FROSTING:

3 tablespoons butter or
  margarine, softened
1 (8-ounce) package cream
  cheese, softened

1 teaspoon orange extract
2 tablespoons orange juice
  concentrate
2 cups powdered sugar

Cream butter and cream cheese until smooth. Add the rest of the ingredients and blend until smooth. Frosting will not be as stiff as usual. I prefer it this way to get more cream cheese flavor. You may add more powdered sugar for a stiffer frosting. Frosting will harden with refrigeration. I like to garnish this cake with drained Mandarin oranges.

Mystic Mountain Memories (Colorado)

Pioneer Carrot Cake

2 cups flour
2 teaspoons cinnamon
2 teaspoons baking soda
½ teaspoon salt
3 eggs
¾ cup vegetable oil
½ cup buttermilk
¾ cup sugar

2 teaspoons vanilla
1 cup crushed pineapple, drained
2 cups grated carrots
1½ cups flaked coconut (optional)
1 cup chopped nuts

Sift together flour, cinnamon, baking soda, and salt; set aside. Beat eggs; add oil, buttermilk, sugar, and vanilla. Mix well. Add flour mixture to egg mixture. Add pineapple, carrots, coconut, if desired, and nuts. Pour batter into a warmed and greased 12-inch Dutch oven and bake at 350° for about 55 minutes or until you can smell it. A toothpick will come out clean when inserted, and cake will pull away from sides of pan.

CREAM CHEESE FROSTING:

3 cups powdered sugar
12 ounces cream cheese, softened

1 teaspoon milk
1 teaspoon vanilla

Mix well and frost cake when cool.

Log Cabin Dutch Oven (Utah)

Dancing Palomino Spice Cake

3 cups all-purpose flour
4 teaspoons ground ginger
2 teaspoons cinnamon
½ teaspoon ground cloves
½ teaspoon cardamom
2 sticks unsalted butter, softened

1 cup brown sugar
1 cup molasses
1 cup boiling water
2 teaspoons baking soda
2 large eggs, beaten

Preheat oven to 350°. Grease a 9x13-inch pan. Combine flour, ginger, cinnamon, cloves, and cardamom. In a separate bowl, beat together butter and brown sugar until fluffy, about 3 minutes. Whisk together molasses and boiling water in another bowl. Whisk baking soda into hot molasses. Combine dry ingredients and molasses, then fold in butter mixture until blended. Whisk eggs into mixture until smooth. Pour batter into cake pan and bake 55–65 minutes until toothpick inserted in center comes out clean. Cool before removing from pan. Prepare frosting.

CREAM CHEESE FROSTING:

2 (8-ounce) packages cream cheese, softened
1 stick unsalted butter, softened

1 teaspoon orange zest
2 cups powdered sugar

Beat together cream cheese, butter, and orange zest until fluffy. Slowly beat in powdered sugar. Chill frosting before spreading on cooled cake. Serves a couple of cowboys with a sweet tooth or 5 or 6 ranch kids.

Authentic Cowboy Cookery Then & Now (Nevada)

Let Them Eat Cake

2 cups flour
2 cups sugar
1 cup (2 sticks) butter
¼ cup (or more) baking
  cocoa

1 cup water
1 teaspoon baking soda
½ cup buttermilk
2 eggs, beaten
1 teaspoon vanilla extract

Mix flour and sugar in a large bowl. Combine butter, baking cocoa, and water in a saucepan. Bring to a boil. Pour over flour mixture and stir to mix well. Mix baking soda with buttermilk in a small bowl. Stir into cake batter. Stir in eggs and vanilla. Pour batter into a greased 10x15-inch cake pan. Bake at 350° for 30 minutes or until wooden pick inserted near center comes out clean. Cool slightly on a wire rack. Pour warm Creamy Chocolate Frosting over warm cake. Let cool before cutting. Yields 16 servings.

CREAMY CHOCOLATE FROSTING:

½ cup (1 stick) butter
3 tablespoons (or more)
  baking cocoa
5 tablespoons milk

1 (1-pound) package
  powdered sugar
1 teaspoon vanilla extract
½ cup chopped pecans

Heat butter, baking cocoa, and milk in a saucepan until butter melts. Remove from heat. Beat in the powdered sugar, vanilla, and pecans. Let cool slightly. Yields about 3 cups.

Las Vegas Glitter to Gourmet (Nevada)

Upside Down German Chocolate Cake

1 box German chocolate
  cake mix
1 cup flaked coconut
1 cup chopped pecans

1 stick margarine
1 (8-ounce) package cream
  cheese
3½–4 cups powdered sugar

Mix cake mix as directed on box. Sprinkle coconut and pecans on bottom of a greased 9x13-inch pan. Pour batter over coconut and pecans. In saucepan, melt margarine and cream cheese. Then add powdered sugar. Mix. Spread this mixture or drizzle over top of cake. Bake at 350° for 30 minutes or until done.

Doc's Delights (Colorado)

Award-Winning Hot Fudge Cake

½ cup baking cocoa
1 cup brown sugar
2 cups water
1 (10-ounce) package mini
  marshmallows

1 (18¼-ounce) box chocolate
  fudge cake mix
1 cup chopped pecans
Whipped cream or ice cream

Mix cocoa, brown sugar, and water in 12-inch Dutch oven and sprinkle marshmallows evenly on top. Make cake mix according to package instructions. Pour mixture over marshmallows and spread to cover completely. Sprinkle pecans on top. Put on lid. Place about 7 coals on bottom and 15 on top of Dutch oven. Bake for 30 minutes or until done. Serve warm, topped with whipped cream or ice cream.

Note: To make it even richer, try chocolate chips sprinkled on top before cooking.

Dutch Oven and Outdoor Cooking, Y2K Edition (Utah)

Turtle Cake

1 (18¼-ounce) box yellow
  or butter cake mix
1 pound caramels, melted
1 (14-ounce) can sweetened
  condensed milk

1 cup chopped pecans
1 cup chocolate chips

Prepare cake mix according to directions. Pour half of the cake batter in a 12-inch Dutch oven and bake at 350° for 20 minutes. Cake will not be done. Melt caramels and pour over the cake. Pour sweetened condensed milk on as well. Add remaining cake batter and cook for about 10 minutes longer. Top with pecans and chocolate chips. Return the cake to heat and finish baking until cake is done.

Dutch Oven and Outdoor Cooking, Book Two: Homespun Edition (Utah)

Cherry Chocolate Surprise Cake

1 (18¼-ounce) box chocolate
  cake mix
1 (1-pound, 13-ounce) can
  cherry pie filling
1 (8-ounce) package cream
  cheese, softened

1 egg
3 tablespoons sugar
1 teaspoon vanilla
Whipped cream for topping

Prepare cake mix as directed on box. Pour prepared cake batter into a greased 12-inch Dutch oven. Spoon cherry pie filling in clumps over cake batter. In a small mixing bowl, cream together cream cheese, egg, sugar, and vanilla until smooth. Drop by tablespoons over top of cake. Place lid on oven. Bake, using 8–10 briquettes on bottom and 14–15 on top for 1 hour or until you can smell the cake. Serve warm with whipped cream as topping.

Log Cabin Presents Lewis and Clark (Utah)

Peach Dessert Cake

1 cup cake flour
1 teaspoon baking powder
¼ teaspoon salt
½ cup sugar
½ cup shortening

1 teaspoon grated lemon rind
2 eggs, unbeaten
4 ripe peaches, peeled and
  sliced

Sift flour, baking powder, and salt together. Beat ½ cup sugar and shortening until light. Add lemon rind, then eggs, one at a time, beating well. Add flour mixture in fourths, beating after each addition. Spread half the batter in a greased 8x8-inch baking pan. Top with peaches, then remaining batter.

TOPPING:

⅓ cup sugar
½ teaspoon cinnamon

¼ cup chopped walnuts or
  pecans

Combine sugar, cinnamon, and nuts; sprinkle over all. Bake 50 minutes at 350°. Cut into squares and top with whipped cream.

Utah Cook Book (Utah)

Basque Apple Cake

CAKE:

2 cups sugar
3 eggs
1 cup oil
2 teaspoons vanilla
2¼ cups flour

1 teaspoon salt
2 teaspoons cinnamon
1 teaspoon baking soda
4 cups diced apples
½ cup chopped nuts

Mix sugar, eggs, oil, and vanilla. Add flour, salt, cinnamon, and baking soda. Add diced apples and nuts. Bake in greased 9x13-inch pan at 375° for one hour.

FROSTING:

1 (8-ounce) package cream
  cheese, softened
½ cup powdered sugar

2 tablespoons margarine
1 teaspoon vanilla

Combine cream cheese, powdered sugar, margarine, and vanilla until smooth. Frost cooled cake.

Church Family Recipes (Nevada)

Luscious Lemon Cake

1 (18¼-ounce) package
  white cake mix
1 cup water
¼ cup sugar
2 eggs, beaten
2 tablespoons cornstarch
2 tablespoons sugar
Zest of 1 lemon

1 tablespoon butter
3 tablespoons fresh lemon
  juice
1 pint sweetened whipping
  cream, whipped
¼ cup white chocolate
  shavings

Grease and flour 2 (9-inch) cake pans. Set aside. Preheat oven and make cake according to package directions on cake mix. When cake is done, put on cake racks and cool completely. (Cake may be frozen for future use.) While cake is cooling, prepare lemon filling.

Put water, ¼ cup sugar, and beaten eggs in a small saucepan. Mix cornstarch and 2 tablespoons sugar together in a small bowl. Slowly add to mixture in pan. Cook on medium heat, stirring constantly until thickened. When thickened, add lemon zest, butter, and lemon juice. Stir until butter is melted and mixture is well mixed and smooth. Remove from heat and let cool. Cover with plastic wrap while cooling.

When cake is cool, cut each layer in half to make 4 slices. Place a layer on a serving plate and spread with half of cooled lemon filling. Add second layer of cake and spread with whipped cream. Add third layer of cake and spread with remaining half of lemon filling. Top with fourth layer of cake. Frost sides and top of cake with whipped cream. Garnish with white chocolate shavings. Refrigerate until ready to serve. Serves 12–16.

Lion House Desserts (Utah)

Triple Lemon Ripple Cake

FILLING:

1 (8-ounce) package cream
  cheese, softened
⅓ cup sugar

1 egg
2 tablespoons flour
2 tablespoons lemon juice

Beat cream cheese and sugar; beat in egg till fluffy. Add flour. Stir in lemon juice. Set aside.

BATTER:

½ cup butter, softened
1½ cups sugar
3 eggs
3 tablespoons lemon juice

2¼ cups flour
2 teaspoons baking powder
½ teaspoon salt
½ cup milk

Preheat oven to 350°. Spray tube pan with cooking spray. Cream butter and sugar. Beat in eggs till mixture is very light and fluffy. Add lemon juice. Combine dry ingredients and add to creamed mixture alternating with milk.

Pour ½ the Batter into pan. Cover with Filling, then pour in remaining Batter. Gently swirl knife through batter a few times. Bake 50–60 minutes until cake pulls away from sides of pan. Cool in pan 10 minutes. Turn out and cool completely.

GLAZE:

2 tablespoons lemon juice   1½ cups powdered sugar

Stir lemon juice into powdered sugar. Drizzle over cake. Makes 10–12 servings.

Still Cookin' After 70 Years (Nevada)

In 1991, when staff at the Little White Wedding Chapel in Las Vegas, Nevada, noticed that disabled customers had difficulty getting out of their cars and into the chapel, they responded by creating a drive-through ceremony. What began as a simple window today is a "Tunnel of Love" drive-through wedding chapel with a ceiling that features cherubs and starlights.

Pumpkin Sumpthin'

1 cup milk
3 eggs
1 cup sugar
1 teaspoon cinnamon
¼ teaspoon ginger
⅛ teaspoon cloves
½ teaspoon salt

1 (31-ounce) can pumpkin
1 (18¼-ounce) box yellow
  cake mix
1½ sticks margarine, melted
¾ cup chopped nuts
Whipped cream

Combine milk, eggs, sugar, spices, salt, and pumpkin, and mix well. Pour into a greased 9x13-inch baking pan. Sprinkle dry cake mix over top of mixture. Drizzle melted margarine over top. Sprinkle nuts over top. Bake at 350° for one hour or until browned. Serve with whipped cream.

Church Family Recipes (Nevada)

Ugly Duckling Pudding Cake

1 (18¼-ounce) package
  lemon cake mix
1 (3-ounce) package lemon
  instant pudding
1 (16-ounce) can crushed
  pineapple with juice
1 cup flaked coconut

4 large eggs, beaten
½ cup flour
¾ cup water
¼ cup oil
½ cup brown sugar
½ cup chopped nuts

Grease and flour a 10x15-inch pan. Blend the above ingredients and pour into the pan. Bake at 350° for 50 minutes. Cool on rack for 15 minutes and spread Glaze on top.

GLAZE:

½ cup butter
½ cup brown sugar

½ cup evaporated milk
1⅓ cups flaked coconut

Bring butter, sugar, and milk to a boil for 2 minutes. Add coconut and spread on cake. Serves 18. Enjoy!

NSHSRA High School Rodeo Cookbook (Nevada)

Bacardi Rum Cake

1 cup chopped pecans or
  walnuts
1 (18½-ounce) yellow cake
  mix (without pudding)
1 (3.4-ounce) package Jell-O
  instant vanilla pudding mix

4 eggs
¼ cup cold water
½ cup Wesson oil
½ cup Bacardi light or dark
  rum, 80 proof

Preheat oven to 325°. Grease and flour 10-inch tube or 12-cup Bundt pan. Sprinkle nuts over bottom of pan. Mix cake and next 5 ingredients together. Pour batter over nuts. Bake about one hour. Cool for approximately 30 minutes and invert onto serving plate. (Make Glaze while cake is cooling.) Prick all over top of cake with a toothpick. Drizzle and smooth Glaze evenly over top and sides, allowing Glaze to soak into cake. Keep spooning the Glaze over cake until all Glaze has been absorbed.

GLAZE:

¼ pound (1 stick) butter
¼ cup water

1 cup sugar
½ cup Bacardi rum

Melt butter in a medium-size saucepan. Stir in water and sugar. Boil for 5 minutes, stirring constantly. Remove from heat and cool slightly. Stir in rum slowly, so it doesn't splatter. While warm, spoon over cake.

Recipe from St. Mary's Glacier Bed and Breakfast, Idaho Springs
Colorado Bed & Breakfast Cookbook (Colorado)

Sting of the Bee Cake

BIENENSTICH CAKE:

1 cup butter (no substitutes),
  softened
⅔ cup sugar
2 eggs

3 cups sifted flour
3 teaspoons baking powder
1 teaspoon salt
½ cup milk

Cream butter. Gradually add sugar, creaming well. Beat in eggs one at a time; beat until light and fluffy. Add sifted dry ingredients alternately with milk. Spoon batter into a well-greased 9-inch springform pan.

TOPPING:

½ cup butter
1 cup finely chopped almonds,
  blanched or unblanched

½ cup sugar
2 tablespoons milk
2 teaspoons vanilla

Melt butter; blend in chopped almonds, sugar, milk, and vanilla. Bring to a boil. Remove from heat and cool slightly. Spread carefully over batter. Bake at 375° for 50 minutes. Remove from oven and cool. Remove springform pan. Prepare filling.

BUTTER CREAM FILLING:

1 cup butter, softened
2 egg yolks
2 cups powdered sugar

2 teaspoons vanilla
½ cup raspberry jam

To softened butter, add egg yolks, powdered sugar, and vanilla; beat well. Split cake horizontally into 2 layers. Spread bottom layer with Butter Cream Filling. Top with raspberry jam. Very carefully replace top layer of cake. Cut into thin slices and serve. Makes 16–20 servings.

Lion House Recipes (Utah)

Chocolate Pound Cake

½ cup buttermilk
1 tablespoon instant espresso
  or coffee powder, dissolved
  in 1½ tablespoons hot water
1 teaspoon vanilla extract
1⅓ cups sugar
1 cup all-purpose flour
6 tablespoons unsweetened
  Dutch Process cocoa,
  strained after measuring

¼ teaspoon baking powder
¼ teaspoon baking soda
½ teaspoon kosher salt
12 tablespoons sweet butter,
  room temperature
3 large eggs
Powdered sugar for dusting
  (optional)

Preheat oven to 350°. Position rack in lower third of the oven. Prepare a 6-cup decorative tube pan with spray vegetable oil. Combine buttermilk with dissolved coffee and vanilla. Set aside.

In a large mixing bowl, combine sugar, flour, cocoa, baking powder, baking soda, and salt. Mix on medium speed with an electric mixer to blend. Add butter and eggs to the bowl and mix on medium speed just until all the dry ingredients are moistened. Set a timer for 2 minutes and beat on high speed. Add buttermilk mixture and beat on high speed for 2 more minutes. Bake until cake starts to shrink away from sides of pan and toothpick inserted in center comes out clean, about 45–50 minutes. Cool cake on a rack 5–10 minutes. Invert pan to unmold. Cool on a rack. Cake can be prepared to this point, wrapped well, and kept at room temperature where it will remain moist and delicious for 4–5 days; or it may be frozen for up to 3 months. Sieve powdered sugar over cake just before serving, if desired. Yields 10 servings.

Never Trust a Skinny Chef...II (Nevada)

Sock-It-To-Me Cake

STREUSEL FILLING:

2 tablespoons dry cake mix   2 tablespoons cinnamon
2 tablespoons brown sugar   1 cup finely chopped pecans

Combine dry cake mix, brown sugar, and cinnamon in a medium bowl. Stir in pecans and set aside.

BATTER:

1 package Duncan Hines   ⅓ cup oil
   Butter Recipe Cake Mix   ¼ cup water
4 eggs   ¼ cup granulated sugar
1 cup dairy sour cream

Preheat oven to 375°. Combine remaining cake mix, eggs, sour cream, oil, water, and granulated sugar in large bowl. Beat at medium speed with an electric mixer for 2 minutes. Pour ⅔ of Batter into oiled and floured 10-inch tube pan. Sprinkle with Streusel Filling. Spoon remaining Batter evenly over filling and bake 45–55 minutes or until toothpick comes out clean. Cool in pan 25 minutes. Invert onto serving plate. Cool completely.

GLAZE:

1 cup powdered sugar   1–2 teaspoons milk

Combine powdered sugar and milk in small bowl. Stir until smooth. Drizzle over cake.

The Best of Down-Home Cooking (Nevada)

Angel Food Cake

Never fails, even in the classroom.

1½ cups egg whites
¼ teaspoon salt
1 teaspoon cream of tartar
1 cup sifted granulated sugar

1 cup powdered sugar
1 cup sifted cake flour
1 teaspoon vanilla
½ teaspoon almond extract

Set oven at 425° and put 10-inch angel food pan in oven to pre-heat. Beat egg whites, salt, and cream of tartar until stiff. Fold in granulated sugar 2 tablespoons at a time until all is used. Sift together the powdered sugar and cake flour 5 times. Fold it into the egg white mixture 2 tablespoons at a time. Add flavoring. Put in the tube pan and bake 23 minutes. Cool inverted.

Goodies and Guess-Whats (Colorado)

Turtle Cheesecake

CRUST:

1 cup chocolate wafer
   crumbs

4 tablespoons butter, or
   margarine, melted

Combine crumbs and butter. Press onto bottom of 9-inch springform pan.

FILLING:

4 (8-ounce) packages cream
   cheese, softened
1½ cups sugar

1 teaspoon vanilla
4 eggs

Beat cream cheese and sugar until light and fluffy. Add vanilla; then beat in eggs, one at a time. Pour into crust. Bake at 300° for 1 hour 40 minutes. Turn off heat; let cake cool in oven, with door ajar, for one hour. Remove from oven.

TOPPING:

20 caramels
3 tablespoons milk

1 cup chopped pecans

In small saucepan over low heat, melt caramels with milk. Stir until smooth. Pour over cake. Sprinkle with chopped pecans. Chill.

Cheesecakes et cetera (Colorado)

Black Forest Cheesecake

2 cups Oreo cookie crumbs, rolled fine
3 (8-ounce) packages cream cheese, softened
1 cup sugar
3 eggs
¾ teaspoon vanilla
1 teaspoon almond extract
⅓ cup maraschino cherry juice
⅓ cup diced maraschino cherries
1 pint sour cream
3 tablespoons sugar
½ teaspoon vanilla
½ cup chocolate chips

Preheat oven to 300°. Crush Oreo cookies, including frosting centers, to make 2 cups of fine crumbs. Press evenly into bottom of a 10-inch springform pan.

Whip cream cheese in a mixer bowl; gradually add sugar; then add eggs one at a time. Stir in vanilla, almond extract, and maraschino cherry juice. Fold in maraschino cherries. Pour filling into crust. Bake 60 minutes.

Whip sour cream; add sugar and vanilla. Put half of sour cream topping on cheesecake; set remaining half aside. Melt chocolate chips and stir into the remaining sour cream topping. Then swirl this mixture into topping already on cheesecake. Return to oven and bake for 10 more minutes. Cool before removing sides from springform pan. Refrigerate until ready to serve. Makes 10–12 servings.

Lion House Desserts (Utah)

Utah is known more for its red rock than for its forests, but trees cover about a third of the state.

Milk Chocolate Cheesecake

1 cup Oreo cookie crumbs
1 cup butter cookie crumbs
½ cup sweet butter, melted
3 pounds cream cheese, softened
2 cups sugar
6 large eggs
1 cup heavy cream
½ cup all-purpose flour
½ teaspoon kosher salt
1 teaspoon vanilla extract
1 cup melted milk chocolate

2 cups fresh raspberries
Juice of 1 lemon
¼ cup Grand Marnier
Whipped cream in a pastry bag with star tip
Chocolate curls for garnish
Fresh mint sprigs
Powdered sugar in shaker for garnish
Cocoa powder in shaker for garnish

Preheat oven to 350°. Combine crumbs and butter together. Mix well and press into a 10-inch springform pan.

In a food processor, with metal blade, mix cream cheese until smooth. Add sugar and blend. Add eggs, one at a time, to thoroughly incorporate into the cheese mixture. Add the heavy cream, flour, salt, and vanilla and blend until smooth. In a steady stream, pour in the melted chocolate. Pour into prepared pan. Bake for 1 hour and 15 minutes or until cake is set.

Remove from oven and loosen the sides from the pan with a knife. This will prevent cake from splitting down the center. Completely cool the cake before cutting.

Make raspberry sauce by combining the raspberries, lemon juice, and Grand Marnier, and allowing to sit for 2–3 hours. Place a piece of cake on a plate. Spoon raspberry sauce over the top. Garnish with whipped cream, chocolate curls, mint sprigs, powdered sugar, and cocoa powder. Yields 12 servings.

Never Trust a Skinny Chef...II (Nevada)

German Chocolate Cheesecake

Another delicious choice for cheesecake fanatics!

CRUST:

**1 package German chocolate
   cake mix**
½ cup shredded coconut

**⅓ cup butter or margarine,
   softened**
1 egg

Mix crust ingredients until crumbly. Press into ungreased 9x13-inch pan.

FILLING:

16 ounces cream cheese
2 eggs

¾ cup sugar
2 teaspoons vanilla

Beat filling ingredients together until smooth and fluffy. Spread over Crust. Bake at 350° for 25–30 minutes. Cool.

TOPPING:

2 cups sour cream
1 teaspoon vanilla

¼ cup sugar

Combine Topping ingredients and spread over cooled Filling. Refrigerate for several hours before serving. Serves 8–10.

Kitchen Keepsakes by Request (Colorado)

WIKIPEDIA.ORG

Northwest Colorado Springs is home to the Garden of the Gods, a 1,365-acre park where fantastic sandstone formations jut out from the surrounding hills. Entrance to the park is free according to the wish of Charles Elliott Perkins, whose children donated the land to the city in 1909.

Strawberry Glazed Cheesecake

CRUST:

1 cup graham cracker crumbs

2 tablespoons sugar
¼ cup melted butter

Combine crust ingredients. Mix well with pastry blender. Press evenly over bottom and sides of 9-inch pie pan. Bake at 350° for 5 minutes.

FILLING:

1 package cream cheese
2 tablespoons milk, or half-and-half
1 teaspoon lemon juice

1 teaspoon vanilla
¼ teaspoon salt
¼ cup sugar
2 eggs

Beat cream cheese, milk, lemon juice, vanilla, salt, and sugar until smooth and creamy. Add eggs, one at a time, beating well after each addition. Pour into crust. Bake at 350° until Filling is firm, 20–25 minutes.

TOPPING:

1 package frozen strawberries, defrosted
¼ cup sugar

1 tablespoon cornstarch
1 pint fresh strawberries, cleaned and halved

Whiz defrosted strawberries with their juice in blender until smooth, or put strawberries through sieve. Combine sugar and cornstarch in saucepan. Stir in strawberries. Cook over low heat, stirring constantly, until thick and clear. Cool slightly. Arrange strawberry halves on cheesecake. Spoon glaze (cooked strawberries) over strawberry halves. Chill. Serves 8.

What's Cookin' in Melon Country (Colorado)

Awesome Amaretto Cheesecake Loaf

The cookies make the Crust incredible. They are easy to find—they are the small cookies in the red can.

CRUST:

20 amaretti cookies, crushed   3 tablespoons butter, chilled
3 ounces almonds, blanched,
  toasted

Lime a 9x5-inch loaf pan with parchment paper, or use an 8-inch springform pan. Mix amaretti cookie crumbs, almonds, and butter in food processor using on/off turns till crumbly. Pat Crust into bottom and 1 inch up sides of pan.

FILLING:

24 ounces cream cheese,   1 teaspoon chopped candied
  softened   citrus peel
1⅓ cups sugar   ½ teaspoon grated lemon peel
4 eggs, room temperature   ½ cup heavy cream, room
3 tablespoons lemon juice   temperature
2½ tablespoons amaretto   ½ cup sour cream, room
1 teaspoon vanilla   temperature

Preheat oven to 325°. Beat cream cheese with mixer in large bowl on low speed till smooth, about 5 minutes. Gradually beat in sugar. Add eggs, one at a time, beating constantly on low. Add lemon juice, amaretto, vanilla, and fruit peels, and mix well. Beat in heavy cream and sour cream. Pour into prepared Crust. Set pan in larger baking pan and place in oven. Add water to larger pan to come 1 inch up sides of cheesecake pan. Bake till center is almost set, 75–90 minutes (8-inch spring-form pan will be closer to 75 minutes). Remove cheesecake from water bath and cool completely on rack. If using loaf pan, invert cake onto platter. Refrigerate overnight.

Note: I prefer the loaf pan. It is different and easy to work with and easy to freeze. It can be ready to defrost for unexpected company, or when you don't have time to prepare something special.

The Melting Pot (Nevada)

Pumpkin Cheesecake

CRUST:

2 cups crushed cinnamon
   graham crackers
¼ cup sugar

½ teaspoon cinnamon
½ cup butter, melted

Mix all ingredients. Press mixture into bottom and about ¾-inch up the sides of a buttered 9-inch springform pan. Chill for one hour.

FILLING:

3 (8-ounce) packages cream
   cheese
¾ cup sugar
¾ cup brown sugar
5 eggs
¼ cup whipping cream

1 pound plain, solid pack,
   canned pumpkin
1 teaspoon cinnamon
½ teaspoon ground cloves
½ teaspoon nutmeg

Cream first 3 ingredients. Add eggs, one at a time, beating well after each addition. Add all remaining ingredients and beat 3–5 minutes at medium speed, scraping sides of bowl. Pour filling into chilled crust. Place pan on an edged baking sheet (cake will drip) and bake at 350° for 1½–1¾ hours. Cool on rack until cake settles. Cover lightly and refrigerate for 6 hours.

Steamboat Entertains (Colorado)

DENVER METRO CONVENTION AND VISITORS BUREAU

Measuring 955 feet from deck to the river below, the Royal Gorge Bridge held the record of highest bridge in the world from 1929 to 2001. It is still the highest bridge in North America. The bridge was not originally constructed for transportation purposes, but was built as a tourist attraction, and continues to be one of Colorado's most-visited tourist attractions.

Best-Ever Thumb Print Cookies

1 cup butter	2 egg whites, slightly beaten
½ cup brown sugar	Finely chopped nuts
2 egg yolks	Butter Cream Frosting
1 teaspoon vanilla	Crabapple jelly or
2 cups flour	maraschino cherries
½ teaspoon salt	

Cream butter and brown sugar. Add yolks and vanilla, mix well. Stir in flour and salt. Roll into 1-inch balls. Dip each ball into egg whites then roll in chopped nuts. Place on ungreased cookie sheet. Bake 5 minutes at 375°. Make thumb print in center of each cookie. Bake 8 minutes longer. At Christmas, these are pretty filled with green Butter Cream Frosting and topped with a spoonful of crabapple jelly or a maraschino cherry.

BUTTER CREAM FROSTING:

⅓ cup butter	1½ teaspoons vanilla
3 cups powdered sugar	2–3 tablespoons milk

Cream butter and sugar, stir in vanilla and add enough milk to make frosting smooth and spreading consistency. Makes 30–36 cookies.

Kitchen Keepsakes (Colorado)

Denver is the capital and the most populous city of Colorado. It is nicknamed the "Mile-High City" because its elevation is one mile, or 5,280 feet above sea level. Denver has the largest city park system in the nation with 205 parks in the city limits and 20,000 acres of parks in the nearby mountains.

Unforgettables

This is a sugar cookie you'll want to remember.

2 cups butter, softened
2 cups sugar
6 eggs
7 cups flour
2 teaspoons baking soda

4 teaspoons cream of tartar
1 tablespoon vanilla extract
4 teaspoons almond extract

Cream the butter and sugar in a mixing bowl until light and fluffy. Beat in eggs. Add flour, baking soda, and cream of tartar and mix well. Mix in the flavorings. Roll half the dough at a time on a floured cloth. Cut into circles and place on a cookie sheet. Bake at 350° for 10–12 minutes or until light brown. Cool on cookie sheet for several minutes. Remove to wire rack to cool completely. Frost with Cream Cheese Frosting. Decorate with sprinkles or as desired. Yields 7 dozen.

CREAM CHEESE FROSTING:

1 (8-ounce) package cream
   cheese, softened
2 tablespoons butter, softened

1 (16-ounce) package
   powdered sugar
2 teaspoons vanilla extract

Beat cream cheese and butter in a mixer bowl until fluffy. Add powdered sugar and vanilla and mix well. Add a small amount of cream or milk, if needed, to make of spreading consistency. Tint as desired with food coloring. Yields enough to frost 7 dozen cookies.

From Sunrise to Sunset (Nevada)

Chocolate-Covered Cherry Cookies

COOKIE DOUGH:

½ cup butter, softened
1 cup sugar
1 egg
1½ teaspoons vanilla
1½ cups flour

½ cup cocoa
¼ teaspoon salt
¼ teaspoon baking soda
Maraschino cherries, drained,
  reserve juice

Cream butter, sugar, egg, and vanilla. Add remaining ingredients, except cherries. Blend. Dough will be stiff. Shape dough into 48 (1-inch) balls. Place balls 2 inches apart on ungreased cookie sheet (or spray with nonstick spray). Push ½ cherry into each ball. When all cookies are molded, prepare Frosting and use immediately.

FROSTING:

1 cup semisweet chocolate
½ cup sweetened condensed
  milk

¼ teaspoon salt
1½ teaspoons reserved cherry
  juice

Melt chocolate with milk, stirring constantly. Remove from heat. Add remaining ingredients. Stir until smooth. Spread ½ teaspoon Frosting over each cherry. Bake at 350° for 8–10 minutes. Yields 4 dozen cookies.

Recipes from the Heart (Nevada)

Melt-Aways

COOKIE:

1 cup butter, softened   ⅓ cup powdered sugar
¾ cup sifted cornstarch   1 cup flour

Beat butter until very soft. Add cornstarch, sugar, and flour. Mix very well. Drop ½- to 1-inch balls onto ungreased cookie sheet. Bake at 350° for 10–12 minutes or until set and very lightly browned. Cool on wire rack in single layer, never stacked or overlapped.

FROSTING:

3 ounces cream cheese,   1 cup powdered sugar
  softened   2 drops milk
1 teaspoon vanilla   2 drops food coloring

Combine all ingredients and beat until smooth. Drop a dab on top of each Cookie.

JLO Art of Cooking (Utah)

Pioneer Molasses Cookies

(Gingersnaps)

The pioneers used molasses because sugar was expensive and rarely available.

¾ cup butter   2 teaspoons baking soda
1 cup sugar   ½ teaspoon salt
1 egg   2 teaspoons ground ginger
¼ cup dark molasses   ¾ teaspoon ground cinnamon
2 cups flour   ¼ teaspoon ground cloves

Cream butter and sugar. Beat until fluffy, and add egg and molasses. Stir together flour, baking soda, salt, ginger, cinnamon, and cloves, and blend into beaten ingredients. Form dough into balls, and roll in granulated sugar. Place on non-greased baking sheet, and bake at 350° for 10 minutes or until cookies have flattened and have cracks on top. Makes 5 dozen.

Recipes Thru Time (Utah)

Wagon Wheel Cookies

FILLING:

1 cup water	2 cups chopped dates
1 cup sugar	1 cup chopped nuts
1½ tablespoons lemon juice	

Cook Filling ingredients, except nuts, at medium heat, stirring until mixture thickens. Set Filling mixture aside to cool. When Filling mixture is cool, add nuts.

DOUGH:

1 cup shortening	1 teaspoon baking soda
2 cups brown sugar	1 teaspoon vanilla
3 eggs, well beaten	½ teaspoon salt
4 cups sifted flour	

Beat together shortening, brown sugar, and eggs. Add flour, baking soda, vanilla, and salt. Mix until well blended. Divide Dough in half. Wrap each half in plastic wrap and chill for at least 30 minutes.

Roll each section of Dough into a rectangle. Spread with Filling and roll from long side. Wrap in plastic wrap and return to refrigerator for one hour.

Remove wrap and cut into ¼-inch slices. Place on greased cookie pan and bake at 350° for 10–12 minutes.

Recipes Thru Time (Utah)

BARNEY McKEE

The Valley of Fire, not far from Las Vegas, has fascinating petroglyphs of animals and fish and birds and symbols. Editor Gwen McKee wonders: "Is there an early cookbook here?"

Porter House Oatmeal Cranberry Cookies

Reach for one of these delicious cookies whenever you need a pick-me-up!

1 cup butter (2 sticks), softened
1 cup firmly packed brown sugar
2 eggs
2 cups flour
1½ teaspoons baking soda

2 cups oatmeal (old fashioned or quick)
1½ cups dried cranberries
1½ cups white chocolate chips
½ cup chopped walnuts (optional)

Beat together the butter and brown sugar. Add eggs and mix until combined. Stir in the flour, baking soda, and oatmeal. Add the cranberries, chips, and nuts. Use a cookie scoop for evenly-sized cookies, or drop by rounded tablespoons onto lightly greased baking sheet. Bake in preheated oven at 375° for 10–12 minutes. Let stand for about 2 minutes; remove to wire rack to cool completely. Makes about 7–8 dozen cookies.

Recipe from Porter House Bed and Breakfast, Windsor
Colorado Bed & Breakfast Cookbook (Colorado)

English Toffee Cookies

1 cup brown sugar
1 cup butter, softened
1 egg
2 cups flour

1 teaspoon vanilla
1 large Hershey's bar
Chopped slivered almonds

Cream sugar and butter. Stir in remainder of ingredients until blended and pat into 10x15-inch jellyroll pan. Bake at 350° 15–25 minutes until barely brown. Remove from oven. Break up Hershey's bar and put pieces on hot cookies and spread around as the chocolate melts. Sprinkle with almonds.

A Century of Mormon Cookery, Volume 2 (Utah)

Almond Shortbread

2 cups flour
1 cup sugar
1 cup butter, softened
1 egg, separated

¼ teaspoon almond extract
1 tablespoon water
½ cup chopped almonds

Heat oven to 350°. In a large mixer bowl, combine flour, sugar, butter, egg yolk, and almond extract. Beat at low speed, scraping bowl often, until particles are fine, 2–3 minutes. Press in bottom of greased 10x15x1-inch jellyroll pan.

In small bowl, beat egg white and water until frothy; brush on dough. Sprinkle almonds over top. Bake for 15 minutes or until browned. Cool completely before cutting into bars.

Twentieth Century Club Cook Book (Nevada)

Coconut Chews

¾ cup shortening
  (half butter or
  margarine), softened
¾ cup powdered sugar
1½ cups all-purpose flour
2 eggs

2 tablespoons flour
½ teaspoon baking powder
½ teaspoon salt
½ teaspoon vanilla
½ cup walnuts, chopped
½ cup flaked coconut

Heat oven to 350°. Cream shortening and powdered sugar. Blend in 1½ cups flour. Press evenly in bottom of ungreased 9x13x2-inch baking pan. Bake 12–15 minutes. Mix remaining ingredients; spread over hot baked layer and bake 20 minutes longer. While warm, spread with icing. Cool. Cut into bars. Makes 32 cookies.

ORANGE-LEMON ICING:

1½ cups powdered sugar
2 tablespoons butter or
  margarine, melted

3 tablespoons orange juice
3 teaspoon lemon juice

Mix until smooth and of spreading consistency.

Cookie Exchange (Colorado)

Jumbo Double Chocolate Chip Cookies

This is my favorite of our jumbos. My willpower is vulnerable whenever these chocolate temptations are nearby—especially ones that are warm out of the oven.

½ pound (2 sticks) unsalted
   butter, softened
1 cup sugar
¾ cup firmly packed brown
   sugar
2 eggs
1 teaspoon vanilla extract
½ teaspoon instant espresso
   coffee powder

2 cups all-purpose flour
⅔ cup cocoa powder
1 teaspoon baking soda
1 teaspoon salt
¾ cup white chocolate
   morsels
½ cup semisweet chocolate
   morsels

Preheat oven to 325°. In a large bowl, using an electric mixer, cream the butter, sugar, and brown sugar until light and fluffy. Add the eggs, vanilla, and espresso powder. Mix well and scrape the sides and bottom of the bowl. Sift together the flour, cocoa powder, baking soda, and salt. Mix into the creamed butter, scraping again. Stir in the white and semi-sweet chocolate morsels.

   Line 3 large baking sheets with parchment paper or oil them lightly with canola oil. Scoop the cookie dough into 12 large (⅓ cup) mounds, arranging them 4 to a sheet at least 3 inches apart. Bake until cookies are flat, 20–25 minutes. Makes 12 jumbo or 24 smaller cookies.

Chocolate Snowball (Utah)

The Best of All
Chocolate Chip Cookies

1 cup solid shortening
½ cup butter or margarine,
  softened
1⅓ cups sugar
1 cup brown sugar
4 eggs
1 tablespoon vanilla
1 teaspoon lemon juice

2 teaspoons baking soda
1½ teaspoons salt
1 teaspoon cinnamon
½ cup rolled oats
3 cups flour
2 (12-ounce) packages
  semisweet chocolate chips
2 cups chopped walnuts

In large bowl, beat shortening, butter, and sugars until light and fluffy (about 5 minutes). Add eggs, one at a time, beating well after each addition. Beat in vanilla and lemon juice.

In another bowl, stir together baking soda, salt, cinnamon, oats, and flour. Beat into creamed mixture until well combined; stir in chocolate chips and nuts.

For each cookie, drop a scant ¼ cup dough on a lightly greased baking sheet, spacing cookies about 3 inches apart. Bake in a 350° oven for 16–18 minutes or until golden brown. Transfer to racks and let cool. Makes about 3 dozen large cookies.

A Century of Mormon Cookery, Volume 1 (Utah)

Chocolate Chunk/ White Chocolate Chip Cookies

¾ cup brown sugar
¾ cup butter or margarine
2 eggs
1 teaspoon vanilla
2½ cups flour

1 teaspoon baking soda
6 ounces chocolate chunks
5 ounces Hershey's vanilla
  chips
¼ cup chopped walnuts

Preheat oven to 375°–400°. Soften brown sugar and butter in microwave for 1 minute on HIGH. Add eggs and vanilla. Mix well. Add flour and baking soda to sugar/egg mixture. When well mixed, add chocolate chunks, vanilla chips, and walnuts. Place by well-rounded teaspoonfuls on ungreased insulated cookie sheet. Bake for 10–12 minutes or until slightly brown on top. Makes approximately 2 dozen cookies.

Recipe from Holden House, Colorado Springs
Colorado Columbine Delicacies (Colorado)

Crazy Chocolate Caramel Cookies

1 (18¼-ounce) package
  chocolate cake mix
½ cup oil

2 eggs, slightly beaten
Rolo candies

Heat oven to 350°. In large bowl, combine cake mix, oil, and eggs. Blend well. Place a Rolo candy in the center of a piece of cookie dough. Roll the dough in a ball around the Rolo. Place on ungreased cookie sheet 2 inches apart. Bake 8–10 minutes. Cool 1 minute and remove from cookie sheet. Makes 4 dozen cookies.

Making Magic (Utah)

Speedy Little Devils

1 stick margarine, melted
1 Duncan Hines Deluxe II Devils Food cake mix
¾ cup creamy peanut butter
1 (7½-ounce) jar marshmallow crème

Combine melted margarine and dry cake mix. Reserve 1½ cups of this topping for top crust. Pat remaining crumb mixture into ungreased 9x13x2-inch pan. Top that layer with combined peanut butter and marshmallow crème; spread evenly. Crumble remaining mixture over that. Bake 20 minutes at 350°. Cool. Cut into 3 dozen bars.

Colorado Cookie Collection (Colorado)

Magic Cookie Bars

½ cup margarine, melted
1½ cups graham cracker crumbs
1 cup chopped walnuts
1 (6-ounce) package semi-sweet chocolate morsels
1⅓ cups flaked coconut
1 (15-ounce) can condensed milk

Pour melted butter in the bottom of a 9x13-inch Pyrex dish. Sprinkle crumbs evenly over melted butter; sprinkle chopped nuts over crumbs. Scatter chocolate morsels over nuts. Sprinkle coconut over morsels, then pour sweetened condensed milk over coconut. Bake in a moderate (350°) oven for 25 minutes. Cool in pan 15 minutes, then cut into 24 bars.

Historical Boulder City Cookbook (Nevada)

Chocolate Scotcheroos

Easy delicious dessert!

1 cup sugar	**6 cups Rice Krispies**
1 cup light Karo syrup	**1 cup butterscotch chips**
1 cup peanut butter	**1 cup chocolate chips**

Dissolve sugar and Karo syrup over low heat until hot. Add peanut butter; melt. Stir until blended. Stir Rice Krispies into melted mixture. Spread into greased 9x13-inch pan. Pat. Cool.

Melt chips together over low heat. Spread over Krispies mixture. Cool. Cut into squares. Yields 24–36 bars.

Still Cookin' After 70 Years (Nevada)

Lemon Bars

CRUST:

2 cups flour	**½ cup powdered sugar**
1 cup butter	**½ teaspoon salt**

Cream together ingredients; pat into dripper pan (or cookie sheet) that has been greased and floured. Bake for 20 minutes at 350°.

TOPPING:

4 eggs, slightly beaten	**1 tablespoon lemon juice**
2 cups sugar	**Grated rind of 1 lemon**
½ teaspoon baking powder	**Powdered sugar**
4 tablespoons flour	

Mix together all but powdered sugar; pour over hot Crust. Bake for 20 minutes at 350°. Remove from oven; sprinkle with powdered sugar.

Ladies' Literary Club Cookbook (Utah)

Date Bars

1 cup sugar	1 cup chopped pecans or
1 cup flour	walnuts
2 teaspoons baking powder	1 cup chopped dates
2 extra large eggs	Powdered sugar
1 teaspoon vanilla	

Mix sugar, flour, and baking powder together. Add lightly beaten eggs. Add vanilla, chopped nuts, and chopped dates. Bake in ungreased baking dish in 350° oven for 40 minutes, or until toothpick comes out clean. Cover generously with powdered sugar and cut into 2-inch squares.

Historical Boulder City Cookbook (Nevada)

Danish Apple Bars

CRUST:

2½ cups flour	1 cup shortening
½ teaspoon baking powder	1 egg, separated
1 teaspoon salt	Milk
1 tablespoon sugar	½ teaspoon vanilla

FILLING:

1 cup cornflakes, crushed	1 cup sugar
4–5 apples, peeled and	1 teaspoon cinnamon
sliced	Egg white

GLAZE:

1 cup powdered sugar	½ teaspoon vanilla
1 teaspoon hot water	

Mix dry ingredients for Crust. Cut in shortening as for pie crust. Mix egg yolk plus milk, to equal ⅔ cup liquid; add vanilla. Combine with dry ingredients. Divide dough in half. Roll out to fit a 12x15-inch pan. Over top of dough, sprinkle cornflakes and a layer of apples. Sprinkle with sugar and cinnamon. Roll out rest of dough and put on top; moisten edges and seal well. Beat egg white, brush on top. Bake at 400° for 10 minutes. Reduce heat to 350° and bake 35–40 minutes. Mix Glaze ingredients. Drizzle over the top of warm bars. Makes 12–15.

Country Classics (Colorado)

Creamy Almond Puff Bars

1 cup butter, divided
2 cups flour, stirred and
  measured, divided
1 cup plus 2 tablespoons
  water, divided

1 teaspoon almond extract
3 large eggs
Almond Cream Cheese Frosting
Sliced almonds

Cut 1 stick butter into 1 cup flour, as for pastry. Add 2 tablespoons water; mix with fork until ball forms. Divide. On large ungreased jellyroll pan, pat each portion into a strip 3x12-inches, spacing strips about 3 inches apart.

In a saucepan, bring 1 cup water and other stick of butter to a boil. When butter is melted, stir in remaining flour all at once, and stir vigorously until mixture pulls away from sides of pan to gather into a smooth ball. Remove from heat. Add almond extract. Add eggs, one at a time, beating each into the dough until well incorporated and smooth. Divide dough in half and spread each half onto one pastry strip. Bake at 350° for one hour or until golden brown. Cool. Spread with frosting and top with sliced almonds. Slice diagonally.

ALMOND CREAM CHEESE FROSTING:

4 ounces cream cheese,
  softened
½ cup butter, softened

2½ cups powdered sugar
½ teaspoon almond extract

In large bowl, cream the cheese and butter until smooth. Gradually beat in the sugar and almond extract. Beat until of spreading consistency, adding a little evaporated milk, if necessary.

Only the Best (Utah)

Fudgy Brownies

1½ cups butter (3 sticks),
  softened
2⅔ cups sugar
1 tablespoon vanilla
4 eggs

2 cups flour
1 cup baking cocoa
½ teaspoon salt
1 cup chopped nuts (optional)

Grease 2 round cake pans. Heat oven to 350°. Cream butter, sugar, vanilla, and eggs in one bowl. In another bowl, combine flour, baking cocoa, salt, and nuts. Mix together. Batter may be stiff, and that's okay. Spread it out in the round cake pans. Bake until set, 30 minutes or so. Don't overbake, as they will continue to bake a little while as they are cooling.

Bless This Food (Nevada)

Pecan Pie Surprise Bars

1 package Pillsbury Plus
  yellow or butter cake mix,
  divided
⅓ cup margarine or butter,
  softened
4 eggs, divided

1½ cups dark corn syrup
½ cup brown sugar, packed
  firmly
1 teaspoon vanilla
3 eggs
1 cup pecans, chopped

Heat oven to 350°. Grease 9x13-inch pan. Reserve ⅔ cup of dry cake mix for filling. In large bowl, combine remaining dry cake mix, margarine, and 1 egg at low speed until well blended. Press in bottom of greased pan. Bake at 350° for 15–20 minutes or until light golden brown. In large bowl, combine reserved ⅔ cup dry cake mix, corn syrup, brown sugar, vanilla, and remaining 3 eggs at low speed until moistened. Beat one minute at medium speed or until well blended. Pour filling mixture over warm base. Sprinkle with pecans. Bake an additional 30–35 minutes or until filling is set. Cool completely. Cut into bars. Store in refrigerator. Makes 36 bars.

What's Cookin' in Melon Country (Colorado)

Marbleized Brownies

1 (8-ounce) bar German
  sweet chocolate
¾ cup margarine, softened,
  divided
6 eggs, divided
2 cups sugar, divided
1 cup plus 2 tablespoons
  flour, divided

½ teaspoon salt
1 teaspoon baking powder
3 teaspoons vanilla, divided
½ teaspoon almond extract
1 cup chopped nuts
6 ounces cream cheese,
  softened

Melt chocolate and 6 tablespoons margarine over low heat. Cool slightly. In bowl, beat 4 eggs until light colored; add 1½ cups sugar and beat well. Add 1 cup flour, salt, and baking powder. Blend in chocolate mixture, 1½ teaspoons vanilla, almond extract, and nuts.

In another bowl, combine cream cheese and remaining 4 tablespoons softened margarine; cream until smooth. Gradually add remaining ½ cup sugar; blend in 2 eggs, 2 table-spoons flour, and 1½ teaspoons vanilla. Lightly butter a 12-inch Dutch oven. Spread ½ of chocolate mixture in bottom. Spoon white batter over evenly. Spoon remainder of chocolate batter on top. Zigzag knife through batter to give marbleized effect. Bake at 350° for 40 minutes (6–8 coals on bottom, 12–16 coals on top).

Dutch Oven Gold (Utah)

WIKIPEDIA.ORG

Throughout the Colorado State Capitol in Denver is the rare and price-less Colorado Rose Onyx, commonly called Beulah Red Marble. Cutting, polishing, and installing the marble in the Capitol took six years, from 1894 to 1900. It is said the only known supply (near Beulah, Colorado) was completely used up in the capitol, but some sources claim enough of the marble was made available for the old McClelland Library and the Pueblo County Courthouse to have fireplace trims of it.

Genoa Candy Dance Fudge

24 ounces marshmallows
  (1½ bags)
6 cups (54 ounces) semi-
  sweet chocolate chips
3 cups chopped walnuts
  (optional)

3 (12-ounce) cans evaporated
  milk
6 sticks (1½ pounds)
  margarine
15 cups sugar
6 tablespoons corn syrup

Combine marshmallows, chocolate chips, and nuts in large bowl and set aside. Combine milk, margarine, sugar, and corn syrup in large saucepan and bring to a boil, stirring constantly. Cook to soft-ball stage (213°). Remove from heat. Pour over marshmallow-chocolate chip mixture and beat with spoon until it loses its gloss. Pour into tray, which has been lined with buttered butcher paper. Let set overnight.

In morning, grab butcher paper at both ends and lift carefully. Set on counter and cut into 1-inch squares. This is a creamy fudge. Makes 15 pounds.

Note: If it begins to dry out, place a piece of bread alongside and cover tightly. It will soften overnight.

The Great Nevada Food Festival Cookbook (Nevada)

Butterfinger Balls

1 pound powdered sugar
½ cup butter, softened
1 cup creamy peanut butter
3 cups rice crispies

4 squares sweet chocolate
Chopped nuts or crushed rice
  crispies

Mix sugar, butter, peanut butter, and rice crispies in a bowl and chill for one hour.

Remove from refrigerator and shape into 1-inch balls. Melt chocolate in a saucepan over low heat. Roll balls in it, then in nuts or crushed rice crispies. Store in cool place or refrigerator, covered.

Log Cabin Holidays and Traditions (Utah)

Miracle Caramel Corn

This is made in a brown paper grocery bag.

**2 gallons popped corn
  (1 cup unpopped)**
1 stick butter
2 cups brown sugar

½ cup white corn syrup
1 tablespoon water
Pinch baking soda

In large double-strength grocery bag (or 2 bags, one inside the other), place popped corn. Bag should be about ⅓ full. Roll down edges of bag to the inside about 2 inches. Melt butter in saucepan. Add brown sugar, corn syrup, and water. Mix and place on medium heat. Stir constantly and bring to a hard boil. Add pinch of soda, remove immediately from heat, and pour syrup over popped corn in bag. Close bag at top, carefully shake, then knead the bag with both hands, over and over until the corn is well coated with syrup. The bag will get soggy, but if sturdy, should last.

Like magic, the corn will be thoroughly coated. Form into balls or leave in clusters. Serve immediately or place in containers for storage. May be frozen for several weeks, if desired.

A Century of Mormon Cookery, Volume 2 (Utah)

DAVID MCCONEGHY @WIKIPEDIA.ORG

During the summer of 1848, a flock of California gulls descended upon, and for two weeks, ate the Rocky Mountain crickets that were destroying the crops of the early Latter-day Saints in the Salt Lake Valley. The Seagull Monument located on Temple Square in Salt Lake City, Utah, stands as a memorial to the gulls. Designed and created by Mahonri M. Young, a grandson of Brigham Young, the monument was dedicated on October 1, 1913. The California gull was selected as the state bird of Utah by the legislature in 1955.

Forgotten Kisses

Turning the oven off is the key to success with this recipe.

4 egg whites	**Dash of liquid peppermint**
¼ teaspoon salt	**flavoring**
1 teaspoon cream of tartar	**Few drops food coloring**
1½ cups granulated sugar	**(optional)**
1 teaspoon vanilla	**½ cup mini chocolate chips**

Heat oven to 350°. The oven needs to be heated for at least 15 minutes before the kisses are placed in it. Grease a cookie sheet very well.

Beat egg whites, salt, and cream of tartar together until almost stiff. Gradually add sugar, alternating with vanilla, peppermint, and coloring, beating until stiff. Fold in the chocolate chips.

Using 2 teaspoons, place bite-size drops on the prepared cookie sheet. These will not change size while baking. Place sheet in center of preheated oven and turn the oven off. Forget the kisses. (Overnight is good.) These can be frozen.

God, That's Good! (Nevada)

Great Salt Lake Taffy

Grandma used to say, "Cook it on a dry day, use a heavy pan, do not stir while cooking, don't undercook, and butter your hands."

1½ cups white vinegar	**1 tablespoon butter or**
3 cups white sugar	**margarine**
¼ teaspoon baking soda	

Combine vinegar and sugar in a heavy pan until sugar is dissolved. Cook over medium heat to soft-crack stage (between 270° and 290° on candy thermometer). Do not undercook. Remove from heat and add soda and butter. Pour onto greased platter to cool. When cool enough to handle, grease or butter hands, and pull until white. Cut into pieces and wrap in wax paper.

Recipes Thru Time (Utah)

Pies and Other Desserts

The 400- to 1,000-foot sandstone buttes, mesas, and pillars located in Monument Valley Navajo Tribal Park on the Utah/Arizona border were created as material eroded from the ancestral Rocky Mountains and was deposited and cemented into sandstone. Monument Valley has been featured in countless commercials and films, including John Wayne's Stagecoach.

Coconut Banana Cream Pie

PIE CRUST:

1⅓ cups flaked coconut   3 tablespoons margarine,
⅔ cup rolled oats   melted

Mix well all ingredients in a 9-inch pie pan. Press into bottom and sides of pan. Bake at 300° for 15 minutes, or until golden.

FILLING:

3 cups milk   2 tablespoons margarine
⅓ cup cornstarch   1½ teaspoons vanilla
3 eggs, separated   2 large bananas
¾ cup sugar, divided

In large saucepan, mix milk, cornstarch, yolks, ½ cup sugar, and margarine. Cook over medium heat, stirring constantly until it boils and thickens. Boil one minute. Stir in vanilla. Slice bananas into pie shell. Pour custard on top. Beat egg whites until stiff peaks form. Gradually stir in remaining ¼ cup sugar. Spread meringue over filling, being sure to seal edges. Bake in preheated 400° oven 10 minutes, or until meringue is golden. Cool on wire rack. Makes 8 servings.

Easy Recipes for 1, 2 or a Few (Colorado)

Dixie's Buttermilk Pie

1 (9-inch) unbaked pie shell   ½ cup butter, melted
1½ cups sugar   1 cup buttermilk
3 tablespoons flour   2 teaspoons vanilla
2 eggs, well beaten   1 teaspoon lemon extract

Combine sugar and flour; stir in eggs. Add melted butter and buttermilk; mix well. Stir in vanilla and lemon extract. Pour into chilled pie shell and bake at 425° for 10 minutes. Reduce heat to 350° and bake 35 additional minutes. Serves 8.

Kitchen Keepsakes (Colorado)

Margarita Pie

1 cup crushed graham
  crackers
3 tablespoons powdered
  sugar
⅓ cup plus ¼ cup frozen
  margarita mix, thawed,
  divided

2 cups lime sherbet
2 cups vanilla ice cream,
  softened
Fresh strawberries
Whipped cream

Mix cracker crumbs, sugar, and ¼ cup margarita mix. Press against the bottom and an inch up the side of a 10-inch Dutch oven. Mix sherbet and ⅓ cup margarita mix together. Mix in softened ice cream and spread evenly. Follow directions for Frozen Desserts below.

Cut strawberries in half and put on top of dessert just before serving; top each piece with whipped cream. Make this after breakfast and bury it until after dinner for a great surprise.

FROZEN DESSERTS:

You can make any frozen dessert in your Dutch oven easily—simply follow the recipe and make in the Dutch oven as you would at home in a regular dish. To freeze the dessert, dig a pit in the ground. Put a clean garbage bag in the hole and pour ice in the bottom of the bag and set your Dutch oven on top of the ice. Top with more ice and twist the bag closed and cover with dirt. Leave until you're ready to eat! Don't forget where you buried dessert; if necessary, mark you buried treasure! This doesn't take a lot of ice; one bag should be plenty; just experiment with it and see what works best for you.

Dutch Oven and Outdoor Cooking, Y2K Edition (Utah)

Lion House Pie Dough

¼ cup butter
⅓ cup lard
¼ cup margarine
⅓ cup shortening
1 tablespoon sugar
½ teaspoon baking powder
1 teaspoon salt

1 tablespoon nonfat dry milk
  (powdered)
1½ cups pastry flour
1½ cups bread flour
½ cup cold water (may need
  1 tablespoon more water)

In a mixer, cream together butter, lard, margarine, and shortening. In a bowl, mix sugar, baking powder, salt, and dry milk powder together. Then add to the creamed butter mixture and mix briefly. Add pastry flour and beat until it is blended. Add bread flour and mix slightly. Pour water in and beat again only until water is incorporated.

Divide dough into 2 or 3 balls. Roll out on floured board. Line pie pan with dough and cut off excess dough. For baked pie shells, flute edges. Prick holes in bottom with fork and bake at 425° for 12–15 minutes or until light golden brown. For fruit pies and other pies that bake in the crust, fill pie shell and follow instructions for particular pie recipe you are using. Yields 2–3 pie shells.

Note: All-purpose flour can be used instead of the combination of bread and pastry flour. The crust can also be made using the traditional pie crust method: by hand-cutting fats into the dry ingredients.

Lion House Desserts (Utah)

The Lion House is one of Salt Lake City's most famous and enduring landmarks. A truly elegant mansion, the Lion House is decorated with countless antiques. Built in 1856 by Brigham Young, the home derives its name from the stone statue of the reclining lion over the front entrance. Once home to Young and his family, today the Lion House is an open social center. It features a restaurant on the street level called The Lion House Pantry.

BOB J. GALINDO, WIKIPEDIA.ORG

Pack Creek Campground Shoo Fly Pie

½ teaspoon baking soda
¾ cup boiling water
1 egg yolk
½ cup molasses
½ cup brown sugar
⅛ teaspoon ground ginger
½ teaspoon cinnamon

¾ cup flour
⅛ teaspoon nutmeg
⅛ teaspoon ground cloves
¼ teaspoon salt
2 tablespoons butter or
  shortening
1 (9-inch) pie pastry

Dissolve baking soda in boiling water, then add egg yolk and molasses. Set aside. Stir sugar, ginger, cinnamon, flour, nutmeg, cloves, and salt together, and mix well. Cut in butter or shortening until mixture looks like coarse crumbs. Pour molasses into pie shell. Sprinkle crumbs evenly over top. Do not stir. Bake at 450° for 15 minutes, then reduce heat to 350° and bake 20 minutes longer. Cool, then serve.

Recipes & Remembrances (Utah)

Un-Apple Pie

4–5 cups peeled, seeded,
  and sliced zucchini
Water
1 cup sugar
¼ cup brown sugar
1 teaspoon cinnamon
¼ teaspoon nutmeg

¼ teaspoon allspice
1½ teaspoons cream of tartar
2 tablespoons flour or
  cornstarch
Pinch of salt
2 (9-inch) unbaked pie shells

Cover zucchini slices with water and boil 2 minutes. Drain and set aside to cool. Mix all other ingredients together and stir gently through zucchini. Pour into pie shell and cover with top crust. Bake at 400° for 10 minutes, then lower heat to 350° for 20 minutes or until brown.

How to Enjoy Zucchini (Utah)

No Crust Pecan Pie

3 jumbo egg whites
1 cup sugar
1 cup chopped pecans

12 unsalted soda crackers
1 teaspoon vanilla
Whipped cream

Beat egg whites; beat in sugar until stiff. Add nuts. Crumble soda crackers and fold into mixture; add vanilla. Put into buttered 9-inch pie dish. Bake in 350° oven for 35 minutes or until done. When cold, top with whipped cream.

Our Daily Bread (Nevada)

Peanut Butter Pie

5 cups vanilla ice cream,
  softened
⅓ cup plus 2 tablespoons
  creamy peanut butter,
  divided
1 graham cracker crust,
  baked
½ cup light corn syrup,
  divided

3 packages unsweetened
  liquid chocolate
1½ cups sugar
1 cup evaporated milk
Pinch of salt
1 teaspoon vanilla
Whipped topping, thawed
Chopped nuts

Combine ice cream and ⅓ cup peanut butter. Mix until smooth and pour into graham crust. Cover with wax paper and freeze. Combine remaining peanut butter and ¼ cup corn syrup; blend well and spread on top of frozen pie. Return to freezer. Combine in a saucepan remaining ¼ cup corn syrup, unsweetened chocolate, sugar, milk, salt, and vanilla. Cook, stirring constantly about 5 minutes, or until thickened to make fudgy sauce. When ready to serve pie, defrost slightly and spoon some whipped topping, hot fudge sauce, and a sprinkle of nuts on each serving.

Kitchen Chatter (Nevada)

Famous Kelly Pumpkin Pie

3 eggs, slightly beaten
1 (16-ounce) can solid-pack
  pumpkin
¾ cup sugar
½ teaspoon salt
1 teaspoon ground cinnamon

¼ teaspoon ground cloves
½ teaspoon ground ginger
1 (5-ounce) can evaporated
  milk
1 (9-inch) deep-dish pie shell
Whipped cream or topping

Combine ingredients except whipped cream in the order given, mixing well after each addition. Pour filling into deep-dish pie shell and bake in center of the oven for 70 minutes at 375°. Pie will test done if knife is inserted in the center and comes out clean. Cool. Top with whipped cream or topping.

Log Cabin Holidays and Traditions (Utah)

Rollin' Pin Strawberry Pie

This was the favorite pie at the Rollin' Pin Bakery and Restaurant. It is unlike any strawberry pie you will eat!

3 egg whites
½ teaspoon baking powder
¾ cup sugar
10 soda crackers, crushed
  fine

½ cup pecans, chopped
2–3 pints fresh strawberries,
  sliced
Frozen whipped topping,
  thawed

Spray a 9-inch pie pan with non-stick cooking spray. Beat egg whites and baking powder until stiff. Add sugar and continue beating until very stiff. Fold in crackers and pecans. Pour into pie pan. Bake at 300° for 50 minutes. Remove from oven; with fork, press crust down. Cool completely. Fill with strawberries. (Add no sugar to strawberries.) Press strawberries down to compact them. Cover with whipped topping. Chill at least 2 hours. Serves 6–8.

Country Classics (Colorado)

Soda Cracker Pie with Berries

14 soda crackers
3 egg whites
1 cup sugar
1½ teaspoons vanilla extract
2 teaspoons praline liqueur
  (optional)

½ cup chopped pecans
½ teaspoon baking powder
1 cup heavy cream
3 tablespoons sugar
1 cup fresh raspberries,
  washed and drained

Crush crackers into fine crumbs. Beat egg whites until stiff and fold in sugar. Add vanilla and liqueur. Fold in cracker crumbs, pecans, and baking powder. Bake in a buttered 9-inch glass pie plate. Bake at medium heat or 70% power in microwave oven for 5 minutes. Turn dish and bake another 2 minutes. Turn again and bake 1½ minutes. Pie shell should start to pull away from the sides of the pan. Cool completely.

Whip cream and sweeten. Stir in berries. Spoon into the cooled pie shell. Let stand in refrigerator at least 4 hours before serving. Yields 6 servings.

Note: May substitute boysenberries or strawberries for the raspberries.

Easy Cookin' in Nevada (Nevada)

A tailor named Jacob Davis from Reno, Nevada, is credited with inventing what is known today as blue jeans. One of Davis' customers kept ripping the pockets of the pants that Davis made for him. As a way to strengthen the man's trousers, Davis put metal rivets at the points of strain, such as on the pocket corners. Since Davis regularly purchased bolts of fabric from a dry goods store in San Francisco operated by Levi Strauss, he offered Strauss a half interest in the invention if Strauss would come up with $68 for the patent. Strauss took him up on his offer, and the two men received a patent on May 20, 1873. When the patent expired 20 years later, dozens of garment manufacturers began to imitate the riveted clothing, which has become the most popular clothing product in the world.

Blackberry and Apple Pie

1½ pounds large cooking
  apples
2 tablespoons melted butter
4 ounces sugar, divided
2 pounds fresh blackberries
  (or frozen blackberries,
  thawed)

Pastry for 1 crust pie
1 egg yolk, mixed with
  1 tablespoon sugar
Whipped cream for garnish

Peel, core, and slice apples. In a heavy sauté pan, melt butter and cook apples over medium heat. Sprinkle with 2 table-spoons sugar and stir well. The apples should not fall apart. Combine remaining sugar with the blackberries; taste and add more sugar if necessary.

Spread blackberries in a 2-inch-deep pie dish. Spoon apples over top. Cover whole surface of pie with crust, sealing the edges (to edge of pie dish). Brush top with egg yolk-sugar mix-ture. Bake for 20–25 minutes in a 400° oven or until the crust is golden brown. Cool pie at room temperature and serve with whipped cream.

A Gathering of Recipes (Nevada)

Apple Crisp

3 cups peeled and sliced
  apples
½ cup granulated sugar
1 tablespoon plus ¾ cup
  flour, divided
¼ teaspoon salt
Cinnamon as desired
¾ cup oatmeal

¾ cup well-packed brown
  sugar
¼ teaspoon baking soda
¼ teaspoon baking powder
⅓ cup butter, softened
Raisins and chopped nuts
  (optional)

In a greased baking dish, combine sliced apples, granulated sugar, 1 tablespoon flour, and salt. Sprinkle with cinnamon as desired. Mix oatmeal, remaining ¾ cup flour, brown sugar, baking soda, and baking powder; cut in butter. Sprinkle mixture over apples. Add raisins and nuts, if desired. Bake at 400° for 30 minutes until browned and apples are tender.

Dude Food (Utah)

Pike's Peak Spiked Apple Crisp

5 cups peeled and sliced
  apples (Pippin, Jonathan,
  or Winesap)
½ teaspoon cinnamon sugar
1 teaspoon grated lemon
  rind
1 teaspoon grated orange
  rind
1 jigger Grand Marnier

1 jigger Amaretto de Saronno
¾ cup granulated sugar
¼ cup light brown sugar,
  packed
¾ cup sifted flour
¼ teaspoon salt
½ cup butter or margarine
Cream, whipped cream or
  ice cream for topping

Arrange apple slices in greased 2-quart round casserole. Sprinkle cinnamon, lemon and orange rinds and both liqueurs on top of apples. In a separate bowl, mix sugars, flour, salt, and butter with a pastry blender until crumbly. Spread mixture over top of apples. Bake uncovered at 350° until apples are tender and top is lightly browned, approximately one hour. Serve warm with cream, whipped cream, or vanilla or cinnamon ice cream. Makes 8 servings.

Colorado Cache Cookbook (Colorado)

DAVID SHANKBONE, WIKIPEDIA.ORG

Pikes Peak is a mountain in the Front Range of the Rocky Mountains, 37 miles west of Colorado Springs, Colorado. Katharine Lee Bates was moved to write the words to the famous song "America the Beautiful" in July, 1893, after having traveled to the top of Pikes Peak on a carriage ride.

Mixed Berry Crisp

Berries in season are always best. When not in season, use frozen.

CRISP TOPPING:

1 cup all-purpose flour

1 cup finely chopped walnuts

1 cup brown sugar

1 cup oatmeal

½ cup (1 stick) butter or
    margarine, melted

In a medium bowl or 1-quart plastic zipper bag, add flour, walnuts, brown sugar, oatmeal, and butter or margarine, and mix. This can be prepared at home and added to the Berry Crisp outdoors. Excellent on cooked fruit or added to coffee cake before baking.

1 (10-ounce) bag frozen
    raspberries, thawed

1 (10-ounce) bag frozen
    blueberries, thawed

1 (10-ounce) bag frozen
    boysenberries or blackberries,
    thawed

¾ cup sugar

In a bowl combine berries and sugar; set aside. Heat a 12-inch Dutch oven over 9 hot coals. Cover with Dutch oven lid and place 15 hot coals on the top. Preheat 10 minutes. Pour the berry mixture into the Dutch oven. Sprinkle Crisp Topping evenly onto berries. Bake, covered, for 30–35 minutes. At home in oven, follow same directions, but cook in a baking dish at 350° for 30–35 minutes, or until golden brown. Serve warm or cold. Serves 6–8.

Recipes for Roughing It Easy (Utah)

Christmas Nut Crunch

½ cup butter, melted
2 cups graham cracker
  crumbs
2 (3.5-ounce) packages
  vanilla instant pudding
2 cups milk
1 quart butter pecan or
  pralines and cream ice
  cream, softened

1 (8-ounce) container Cool
  Whip
2 candy bars, crushed (Heath,
  Krackel, or anything
  crunchy)

In a bowl, combine melted butter and crumbs. Mold in the bottom of a 9x13-inch cake pan or 2 pie tins. In large bowl, beat pudding mixes and milk. Blend well and fold in the ice cream. Fold in Cool Whip, then pour into crust. Sprinkle with crushed candy bars. Freeze for one hour or more and serve when ready. Makes 16–20 servings.

Variation: You may substitute crushed candy bars with chopped nuts, crushed frosted flakes, or use your imagination.

Log Cabin Holidays and Traditions (Utah)

Rhubarb Crunch

CRUMB CRUST/TOPPING:
1 cup sifted flour
¾ cup uncooked rolled oats
1 cup brown sugar

½ cup butter, melted
1 teaspoon cinnamon

Combine ingredients until crumbly. Press half of crumbs into 9-inch greased pan, reserving half for top.

FRUIT MIXTURE:
4 cups sliced rhubarb
1 cup sugar
2 tablespoons cornstarch

1 cup water
1 teaspoon vanilla

Place sliced rhubarb in crust. In a small saucepan, combine sugar, cornstarch, water, and vanilla. Cook, stirring until thick and clear. Pour over rhubarb. Cover with reserved crumbs. Bake at 350° for 1 hour.

The Ruby Valley Friendship Club Cookbook II (Nevada)

Strawberry Tiramisu

Guaranteed rave reviews from guests.

¾ pound (1½ cups) mascarpone cheese, room temperature

3 tablespoons powdered sugar

3 tablespoons orange-flavored liqueur, divided

1½ cups heavy cream

1 pint strawberries, rinsed and hulled

¼ cup granulated sugar

¼ cup orange juice

24 sponge ladyfingers

In medium bowl, whisk mascarpone cheese, powdered sugar, and 1 tablespoon of the orange liqueur until well blended. In large chilled bowl with electric mixer at medium speed, beat heavy cream until soft peaks form; gently fold whipped cream into mascarpone mixture until blended. In blender or food processor, blend together remaining liqueur, strawberries, sugar, and orange juice to a smooth purée. Pour strawberry mixture into shallow bowl.

Dip 12 ladyfingers in strawberry mixture to coat; arrange in a 9-inch square glass dish, side-by-side, in 2 rows touching. Spread ½ of the strawberry mixture evenly over rows. Spread ½ of the cream mixture on top. Repeat with remaining ladyfingers; arrange over cream layer. Spread with remaining strawberry mixture. Spread with remaining cream, smoothing top with spatula. Cover and refrigerate at least 8 hours or overnight.

To serve, cut into 9 squares. Place on dessert plates and dust each with cocoa powder; top with a sliced fanned strawberry.

Note: If mascarpone cheese is unavailable, purée in blender or food processor 2 tablespoons of the heavy cream with 1¼ cups ricotta cheese, 3 tablespoons softened cream cheese, and 1 teaspoon fresh lemon juice until smooth.

Recipes from Our House (Colorado)

Toffee Crunch Trifle

Dynamite dessert looks and tastes spectacular, and is easy to make.

1 (18-ounce) chocolate cake
  mix
Eggs, oil and water (as
  directed on cake mix)
½ cup Kahlúa
1 (16-ounce) jar chocolate or
  fudge sauce

3 Skor or Heath candy bars,
  broken into bite-size
  pieces
1 (12-ounce) carton frozen
  whipped topping, thawed

Prepare cake according to package directions, baking in a 9x13-inch pan. Cool. Poke holes all over top of cake with a large fork. Pour Kahlúa slowly over cake, allowing it to soak in. Cover tightly with plastic wrap; refrigerate at least 3 hours or overnight.

Assemble the day you want to serve (trifle gets watery assembled too far ahead) in a 3-quart trifle or straight sided, see-through bowl. Layer ingredients beginning with about a 1-inch layer of cake, ¼ fudge sauce, 1 candy bar, and ¼ whipped topping. Repeat layers 2 more times, reserving the last candy bar and ¼ of fudge sauce to decorate top of trifle. Drizzle fudge sauce over top layer of whipped topping and sprinkle with candy pieces. Refrigerate until ready to serve. Makes 10–12 servings.

Note: A 3-quart trifle dish (about 7 inches in diameter and 5 inches deep) will only use about half of cake. Freeze remaining cake in a plastic bag for later use. If you have a larger container or make 2 trifles at the same time, double the fudge sauce, candy, and whipped topping.

Palates (Colorado)

Blueberry Whiskey Sabayon

Sabayon is a mousse-like dessert sauce, the French name for the fluffy Italian zabaglione made with sweet Marsala wine. Sabayon has three primary ingredients; egg yolks, sugar, and alcohol. For a sabayon to accompany chocolate nut torte, omit the blueberries and the first sugar and substitute dark rum for the whiskey. Or prepare sabayon with white wine or champagne, to use as a topping for fresh fruit.

½ cup blueberries, fresh or frozen

2 tablespoons plus 2 tablespoons sugar

2 egg yolks

2 tablespoons bourbon whiskey

½ cup heavy cream, whipped

Cook the blueberries with 2 tablespoons of the sugar in a stainless steel (noncorrosive) saucepan over low heat, stirring until sugar dissolves. Continue cooking until the berries are very soft and have released most of their juice, 5–8 minutes.

Place the cooked blueberries and juice, the egg yolks, the remaining 2 tablespoons of sugar, and the whiskey in the top of a double boiler. Place over gently boiling water; the upper pan should not touch the water. Cook, whisking often, until the custard has thickened and reaches 160° on an instant-read thermometer, about 10 minutes.

Prepare an ice bath: Fill a large bowl with ice and nest the bowl of cooked blueberry mixture in it. Whisk the mixture until it is cold. You can refrigerate this sabayon base, covered, for up to 6 days. Before serving, fold in the whipped cream. Makes about 1½ cups.

Chocolate Snowball (Utah)

Cold Grand Marnier Soufflé

2 envelopes unflavored gelatin	2 cups sugar, divided
¾ cup orange juice, divided	¼ cup Grand Marnier
6 eggs, separated	¼ cup lemon juice
Grated rind of 2 oranges	Salt to taste
and 1 lemon	2½ cups whipping cream

Cut a piece of wax paper long enough to serve as collar of souf-flé dish. Fold paper into halves, oil inside, and tie around dish. Soften gelatin in ½ cup orange juice in small bowl. Place in hot water; stir until gelatin dissolves. Combine remaining orange juice with egg yolks, orange rind, lemon rind, 1¼ cups sugar, liqueur, lemon juice, and salt in heavy saucepan; mix well. Cook until sugar dissolves and mixture coats spoon; remove from heat. Beat in gelatin mixture. Cool over ice or in refrigerator just until mixture is syrupy.

Beat egg whites in mixer bowl until soft peaks form. Add remaining ¾ cup sugar gradually, beating until stiff peaks form. Reserve a small amount of whipped cream for topping. Fold remaining whipped cream and beaten egg whites into gelatin mixture. Spoon into prepared dish. Chill overnight or until firm.

Remove collar carefully. Pipe reserved whipped cream into rosettes on top; garnish with candied violets. Yields 12 servings.

Best Bets (Nevada)

Amaretto Bread Pudding

1 loaf French bread	1½ cups sugar
1 quart half-and-half or milk	2 tablespoons almond extract
2 tablespoons butter	¾ cup golden raisins
3 eggs	¾ cup sliced almonds

Break up bread and cover with half-and-half. Cover and let stand one hour. Preheat oven to 325°. Grease 9x13x2-inch dish with the butter. Beat eggs, sugar, and almond extract. Stir into bread mixture. Gently fold in raisins and almonds. Spread evenly in dish. Place on middle rack and bake 50 minutes. Remove and cool.

AMARETTO SAUCE:

8 tablespoons unsalted butter	1 egg, beaten
1 cup powdered sugar	4 tablespoons amaretto liqueur

Using double boiler, stir together butter and sugar until very hot. Remove from heat. Whisk the egg well into butter and sugar mixture. Add liqueur. To serve, cut pudding into 12–15 pieces. Spoon sauce over and serve immediately.

The bread pudding freezes well. The sauce will keep in the refrigerator for several weeks.

Recipes from Our House (Colorado)

Our Grandma Adelaide's Old-Fashioned Plum Pudding

2 cups soft bread crumbs
1 cup flour
1 teaspoon baking soda
½ teaspoon salt
2 teaspoons ground cinnamon
½ teaspoon ground cloves
4 ounces chopped suet
1 cup sugar

2 eggs
⅓ cup orange juice
1 cup milk
1 cup dark seedless raisins
1 cup currants
1 cup chopped nuts
1 cup candied fruit

Mix all ingredients thoroughly. Put in well-greased plum pudding pan or mold and steam for 5–6 hours.

SAUCE:

1 cup sugar
2 tablespoons cornstarch
¼ teaspoon salt

2 cups boiling water
¼ cup butter
½ cup dark rum

Mix sugar, cornstarch, and salt. Add boiling water. Then slowly add butter to mixture. Stir well. Add rum; serve hot over plum pudding.

Historical Boulder City Cookbook (Nevada)

Gold mining in Nevada is a major industry, and one of the largest sources of gold in the world. Nevada currently produces 80% of all the gold mined in the United States. Although Nevada was known much more for silver in the 1800s, many of the early silver-mining districts also produced considerable quantities of gold.

Peaches with Sour Cream and Strawberries

8 ripe peaches
Brandy
Lemon juice
2 cups sour cream
1 pint hulled strawberries

Superfine granulated sugar
2 tablespoons Grand Marnier,
  rum, or brandy
Macaroon crumbs

Skin peaches; halve and pit them. Sprinkle with brandy and lemon juice. Chill well. Fold sour cream into strawberries, add sugar (not too much) and Grand Marnier.

To serve, arrange peach halves in large bowl, or in individual champagne glasses. Spoon strawberry cream mixture over top and sprinkle with finely crushed macaroon crumbs. Serves 8.

The Colorado Cookbook (Colorado)

Strawberries Divine

1 (8-ounce) package cream
  cheese, softened
3 tablespoons powdered
  sugar
2 tablespoons orange juice

1 quart fresh strawberries,
  washed and dried (do not
  remove stem)
Strawberry or mint leaves for
  garnish

Beat cream cheese until fluffy. Add powdered sugar and orange juice. Fill a cake decorator tube with mixture. From the point, slit each berry into quarters (do not cut through the bottom of the berry). Pipe cream cheese mixture into each berry. Arrange on a serving tray and garnish with strawberry or mint leaves.

A Pinch of Salt Lake (Utah)

Chocolate Divine Dessert

Paradise found!

½ cup slivered almonds
12 ounces semisweet
  chocolate chips
3 tablespoons sugar
3 large egg yolks,
  beaten

3 large egg whites, stiffly
  beaten
2 cups heavy cream, whipped
1 teaspoon pure vanilla
  extract
1 (8-ounce) angel food cake

Place almonds on ungreased cookie sheet and bake at 350° until light golden brown. Watch carefully so almonds do not burn! Cool and set aside.

In top of double boiler over hot water, melt chocolate chips with sugar. Cool. Mix in beaten egg yolks. Gradually fold in stiffly beaten egg whites. Fold in whipped cream and vanilla. Tear up angel food cake into ½-inch pieces. Put half of cake pieces on bottom of buttered 10-inch springform pan. Cover with half of chocolate mixture. Layer remaining cake and chocolate. Refrigerate at least 24 hours. Remove springform rim. Top with toasted almonds. May be made up to 3 days in advance. Makes 10–12 servings.

Crème de Colorado (Colorado)

Sopapillas

4 cups flour   **3 tablespoons shortening**
3 teaspoons baking powder   **Water**
1 teaspoon salt

Sift flour, baking powder, and salt. Cut in shortening, adding enough water to make a stiff dough. Roll out dough until it is ¼-inch thick. Cut into 3-inch squares and deep-fry until golden brown. Serve warm with honey. Yields 4 dozen.

From an Adobe Oven to a Microwave Range (Colorado)

Caramel Dumplings

SYRUP:

1 cup sugar   **2 tablespoons butter**
2½ cups boiling water   **1 teaspoon vanilla**

Caramelize ½ cup sugar until golden brown in a heavy pan. Add boiling water. Stir until lumps are dissolved. Add rest of sugar, butter, and vanilla. Pour into a 9x9-inch baking pan.

BATTER:

½ cup sugar, divided   **1 teaspoon salt**
2 tablespoons butter   **1 teaspoon baking powder**
1½ cups flour   **½ cup milk**

Mix sugar with butter. Then mix in flour, salt, baking powder and milk. Mix well. Drop by tablespoons into hot Syrup. Bake in 425° oven for 20 minutes.

Colorado Boys Ranch Auxiliary Cookbook (Colorado)

Angel Feathers

GRAHAM CRACKER CRUST:

**16 graham crackers, rolled
 fine**

**4 tablespoons brown sugar
Melted butter**

Mix crushed crackers with brown sugar and enough butter to make it hold together. Line an 8-inch-square pan with this mixture. Pour in custard. May reserve a small amount of the graham cracker mixture to garnish the top of this dessert.

**⅓ cup sugar
½ cup milk
2 eggs, separated
1 teaspoon vanilla**

**1 tablespoon (1 envelope)
 gelatin, soaked in ½ cup
 cold water
½ pint cream, whipped**

Make a custard of sugar, milk, and 2 egg yolks in a double boiler. When smooth, remove from heat and add vanilla and soaked gelatin. Cool; add whipped cream and 2 egg whites, beaten stiff. Place this mixture in a Graham Cracker Crust. Sets in an hour. Cut in squares to serve.

The Ruby Valley Friendship Club Cookbook I (Nevada)

Contributing Cookbooks

PHOTO © NEVADA COMMISSION ON TOURISM

Virginia City, Nevada, is one of the largest federally designated Historical Districts in America, and is maintained in its original condition. "C" Street, the main business district, is lined with buildings constructed in the late 1800s, now housing specialty shops, rather than the boisterous saloons of yesteryear.

Listed below are the cookbooks that have contributed recipes to this book, along with copyright, author, publisher, city, and state.

All American Meals Cookbook ©2004 The JB Ranch Staff, JB Publications, Stagecoach, NV

Always in Season ©1999 Junior League of Salt Lake City, Inc., UT

Aspen Potpourri ©1968 by Mary Eshbaugh Hayes, Aspen, CO

Authentic Cowboy Cookery Then & Now ©2004 by Carol Bardelli & F.E. "Lizzie" Hill, JB Publications, Stagecoach, NV

Back to the House of Health ©1999 by Shelley Redford Young, Woodland Publishing, Orem, UT

Backyard Dutch Oven ©2002 by Bill LeVere, Backyard Dutch Oven, Ogden, UT

The Beginner's Guide to Dutch Oven Cooking ©2000 by Marla Rawlings, Horizon Publishers and Dist. Inc., Bountiful, UT

Best Bets ©1993 Nathan Adelson Hospice, Las Vegas, NV

The Best of Down-Home Cooking ©2003 The Holy Trinity AME Church Courtesy Club, North Las Vegas, NV

The Best of Friends, Fort Morgan Museum, Fort Morgan, CO

Beyond Oats, Arabian Horse Trust, Westminister, CO

Bless This Food, First Baptist Church, Indian Springs, NV

CASA Cooks, CASA Foundation, Las Vegas, NV

A Century of Mormon Cookery, Vol. I & II ©2002 by Hermine B. Horman, Horizon Publishers and Dist. Inc., Bountiful, UT

Championship Dutch Oven Cookbook, by Val and Marie Cowley, Logan, UT

Cherished Recipes, by Karen Smith, Layton, UT

Chocolate Snowball ©1999 by Letty Halloran Flatt, The Globe Pequot Press, Guilford, CT

Christine's Kitchen, by Christine and Regas Halandras, Meeker, CO

Church Family Recipes, Carson Valley United Methodist Church, Gardnerville, NV

Colorado Bed & Breakfast Cookbook ©1996 3D Press, Inc., Denver, CO

Colorado Boys Ranch Auxiliary Cookbook, La Junta, CO

Colorado Cache Cookbook ©1978 The Junior League of Denver, CO

Colorado Collage ©1995 The Junior League of Denver, CO

Colorado Columbine Delicacies ©1994 by Tracy M. Winters and Phyllis Y. Winters, Greensburg, IN

Colorado Cookie Collection ©1990 by Cyndi Duncan and Goergie Patrick, C&G Publishing, Inc. Greeley, CO

Colorado Foods and More ... ©1990 by Judy Barbour, Bandera, TX

Colorado Potato Favorite Recipes ©1995 Colorado Potato Administrative Committee, Hilliard, OH

A Complete Guide to Dutch Oven Cooking, by Ken and Cheryl Allred, Riverton, UT

Cookie Exchange ©1990 by Cyndi Duncan and Georgie Patrick, C&G Publishing, Inc. Greeley, CO

Cooking with Colorado's Greatest Chefs ©1995 by Marilynn A. Booth, Westcliffe Publishers, Englewood, CO

Country Classics I & II ©1995 by Ginger Mitchell and Patsy Tompkins, Karval, CO

The Cowboy Chuck Wagon Cookbook ©2003 by Kelsey Dollar, Apricot Press, American Fork, UT

A Cowboy Cookin' Every Night ©2004 JB Publications, Stagecoach, NV

Creme de Colorado ©1997 The Junior League of Denver, Inc. CO

Distinctly Delicious ©1997 by David Richardson & Javana M. Richardson, StarsEnd Creations, Greenwood Village, CO

Doc's Delights, Keefe Memorial Hospital, Cheyenne Wells, CO

Doin' Dutch Oven: Inside and Out ©1990 by Robert L. Ririe, Horizon Publishers and Dist. Inc., Bountiful, UT

Dude Food, by Jeannette Wilcox, Price, UT

The Durango Cookbook, by Jan Fleming, Durango, CO

Dutch Oven and Outdoor Cooking, Y2K Edition ©2001 by Robyn Heirtzler and Larry and Jeanie Walker, WH Publishing, American Fork, UT

Dutch Oven and Outdoor Cooking, Book Two; Homespun Edition ©1999 by Larry and Jeanie Walker, WH Publishing, American Fork, UT

Dutch Oven Delites ©1995 by Val and Marie Cowley, Logan, UT

Dutch Oven Gold ©1990 by Val and Marie Cowley, Logan, UT

Dutch Oven Secrets ©1995 by Lynn Hopkins, Horizon Publishers, and Dist. Inc., Bountiful, UT

Easy Cookin' in Nevada ©1984 by June Broili, Anthony Press, Reno, NV

Easy Gourmet for Diabetics ©2004 JB Publications, Stagecoach, NV

Easy Recipes for 1, 2 or a Few ©1994 by Anna Aughenbaugh, Starlite Publications, Fort Collins, CO

Enjoy! Again and Again ©1997 by Fred Wix (The Gabby Gourmet), Lady Lake, FL

The Essential Mormon Cookbook ©2004 by Julie Badger Jensen, Deseret Book Co., Salt Lake City, UT

Family and Friends Favorites, by B. Knight, Las Vegas, NV

Family Favorites from the Heart, by Cheryl C. Huff, Springville, UT

Favorite Recipes from Utah Farm Bureau Women, Utah Farm Bureau Women's Committee, Sandy, UT

Favorite Utah Pioneer Recipes ©2000 by Marla Rawlings, Horizon Publishers and Dist. Inc., Bountiful, UT

Feeding the Flock, Meadow Fellowship Foursquare Church, Las Vegas, NV

Five-Star Recipes from Well-Known Latter Day Saints ©2002 by Elaine Cannon, Eagle Gate, Salt Lake City, UT

The Flavor of Colorado ©1992 Colorado State Grange, Superior, CO

Four Square Meals a Day, Women's Ministries, Lamar, CO

From an Adobe Oven to a Microwave Range ©1980 Junior League of Pueblo, CO

From Sunrise to Sunset ©1997 Sunrise Children's Foundation, Las Vegas, NV

The Fruit of the Spirit, First Baptist Church of Reno, NV

A Gathering of Recipes, Western Folklife Center, Elko, NV

God, That's Good!, St. Peter's Episcopal Church, Carson City, NV

Good Morning, Goldie!, by Goldie Veitch, Meeker, CO

Great American Beer Cookbook ©1993 by Candy Schermerhorn, Brewers Publications, Boulder, CO

The Great Nevada Cookbook ©1993 Nevada Magazine, Carson City, NV

The Great Nevada Food Festival Cookbook ©1997 Nevada Magazine, Carson City, NV

Haute Off the Press ©1994 by Pat Miller and Bob Starekow, Dillon, CO

Historical Boulder City Cookbook, Boulder City Museum and Historical Assn., Boulder, City, NV

Home Cooking, Truckee Meadows Habitat for Humanity, Reno, NV

Home Cookin' Creations, First Baptist Church, Delta, CO

Home Cookin', NPS Denver Employees' Assn. Denver, CO

The Hooked Cook ©2004 JB Publications, Stagecoach, NV

How to Feed a Vegetarian ©1996 by Suzanne D'Avalon, Colorado Springs, CO

How to Enjoy Zucchini ©1983 by Josie Carlsen, Carlsen Printing, Ogden, UT

How to Win a Cowboy's Heart ©1995 by Kathy Lynn Wills, Gibbs Smith, Pub., Layton, UT

Italian Dishes et cetera ©1991 by Shirley Michaels, Loveland, CO

JLO Art of Cooking ©2003 Junior League of Ogden, Design Solutions, Ogden, UT

Kitchen Chatter, by Pat Duran, Henderson, NV

Kitchen Keepsakes ©1983 by Bonnie Welch and Deanna White, Kiowa, CO

Kitchen Keepsakes by Request ©1993 by Bonnie Welch and Deanna White, Kiowa, CO

Ladies' Literary Club Cookbook, Salt Lake City, UT

Lake Tahoe Cooks! ©2002 Parents' Clubs of Zephyr Cove Elementary School, Kingsbury Middle School, and George Whittell High School, Zephyr Cove, NV

Las Vegas Glitter to Gourmet ©2001 Junior League of Las Vegas, NV

Lighter Tastes of Aspen ©1994 by Jill Sheeley, Aspen, CO

Lion House Desserts ©2000 Hotel Temple Square Corp., Deseret Book Co., Salt Lake City, UT

Lion House Entertaining ©2003 Hotel Temple Square Corp., Deseret Book Co., Salt Lake City, UT

Lion House Recipes ©1980 Hotel Temple Square Corp., Deseret Book. Co. Salt Lake City, UT

Lion House Weddings ©2003 Hotel Temple Square Corp., Deseret Book Co., Salt Lake City, UT

Log Cabin Campfire Cookn' ©2001 by Colleen Sloan, Sandy, UT

Log Cabin Dutch Oven ©1993 by Colleen Sloan, Sandy, UT

Log Cabin Holidays and Traditions ©1999 by Colleen Sloan, Sandy, UT

Log Cabin Presents Lewis and Clark ©2003 by Colleen Sloan, Sandy, UT

Lowfat, Homestyle Cookbook ©1995 by Christina Korenkiewicz, Bailey, CO

Making Magic ©2003 University of Utah, Virginia Tanner Dance Programs and Children's Dance Theatre, Salt Lake City, UT

The Melting Pot ©2003 Moms in Business Network, Henderson, NV

More Goodies and Guess-Whats, by Helen Christiansen, Walsh, CO

More Kitchen Keepsakes ©1986 by Bonnie Welch and Deanna White, Kiowa, CO

A Mormon Cookbook ©2002 by Erin A. Delfoe, Apricot Press, American Fork, UT

Mountain Cooking and Adventure, Montrose Chamber of Commerce, Montrose, CO

Mystic Mountain Memories ©1990 by Josie and Jerry Minerich, C&G Publishing, Inc., Greeley, CO

Never Trust a Skinny Chef...II ©1999 by Les Kincaid, Las Vegas, NV

No Green Gelatin Here!, Women's Alliance-First Unitarian Church of Salt Lake City, UT

Nothin' but Muffins ©1991 by Cyndi Duncan and Georgie Patrick, C&G Publishing, Inc., Greeley, CO

NSHSRA High School Rodeo Cookbook, Nevada State High School Rodeo Association, Battle Mountain, NV

101 Things To Do With a Slow Cooker ©2003 by Stephanie Ashcraft and Janet Eyring, Gibbs Smith, Publisher, Layton, UT

Only the Best, by Gayle Holdman, Highland, UT

Our Daily Bread, Old St. Paul's Episcopal Church, Virginia City, NV

Palates ©1995 Colorado Springs Fine Arts Center, Colorado Springs, CO

Partyline Cook Book ©1995 Jackson Mountain Homemakers, Dale De Long, Winnemucca, NV

A Pinch of Salt Lake Cookbook ©1989 Junior League of Salt Lake City, Inc. UT

Pleasures from the Good Earth, Common Thread, Inc., Sandy, UT

The Protein Edge ©2004 JB Publications, Stagecoach, NV

Pure Gold—Colorado Treasures ©1992 by Tracy M. Winters and Phyllis Y. Winters, Winters Publishing, Greensburg, IN

Quick Crockery ©1997 by Cyndi Duncan and Georgie Patrick, C&G Publishing, Inc., Greeley, CO

Recipes & Remembrances, Moab Area Chamber of Commerce, Moab, UT

Recipes for Roughing It Easy ©2001 by Dian Thomas, Holladay, UT

Recipes from Our House, Assistance League of Denver, CO

Recipes from the Heart, St. Mark Lutheran Church and Preschool, Elko, NV

Recipes from Sunset Garden Club, by Diane McIntyre, Henderson, NV

Recipes Thru Time, Tooele County Daughters of Utah Pioneers, Transcript Bulletin, Stansbury Park, UT

Roughing It Easy at Girls Camp ©2003 by Dian Thomas, Deseret Book Co., Salt Lake City, UT

Ruby Valley Friendship Club Cookbook I & II, Ruby Valley Friendship Club, Ruby Valley, NV

Savor the Memories ©2002 by Marguerite M. Henderson, Salt Lake City, UT

Sharing Our Best/Muleshoe Ranch, by La Vaughn Linnens, Mancos, CO

Sharing Our Best, St. Mary Magdalene Episcopal Church, Boulder, CO

Sharing Our Diabetics Best Recipes, St. Rose D.A.T.E., Henderson, NV

Simply Colorado ©1989 Colorado Dietetic Assn., Denver, CO

Smoothies & Ice Treats, by Lindsay Barnes and Amy Shawgo, Back to Basics Products, Inc., Draper, UT

Soup for Our Souls, St. Paul's Episcopal Church, Sparks, NV

Southwestern Foods et cetera ©1989 by Shirley Michaels, Loveland, CO

Steamboat Entertains ©1991 Steamboat Springs Winter Sports Club, Steamboat Springs, CO

Still Cookin' After 70 Years, Grace Community Church, Boulder City, NV

Taking Culinary Liberties, Liberty High School Library, Colorado Springs, CO

Tasteful Treasures, Reno First United Methodist Church, Reno, NV

30 Days to a Healthier Family ©2003 by Peggy Hughes, Deseret Book Co., Salt Lake City, UT

Timbreline's Cookbook, Ammon Ra Temple #56 Timbreline Group, Daughters of Nile, Reno, NV

Traditional Treasures, Sun City Aquacize Club, Las Vegas, NV

Twentieth Century Club Cook Book, Twentieth Century Club, Reno, NV

Ultimate Dutch Oven Cookbook ©2003 by Denene Torgenson, Camp Chef, Salina, UT

Use Your Noodle! ©2004 by Carol Bardelli, Nikki Diavolo, and Dante "Blue" Azzurro, JB Publications, Stagecoach, NV

Utah Cook Book ©1999 by Bruce and Bobbi Fischer, Golden West Publishers, Phoenix, AZ

Vacation Cooking: Good Food! Good Fun! ©1989 by Ruth Atkinson Kendrick and Florence Harris Boss, Horizon Publishers and Dist. Inc., Bountiful, UT

Virginia City Alumni Association Cookbook, Historic Fourth Ward School Museum, Virginia City, NV

West of the Rockies ©1994 Junior Service League of Grand Junction, CO

What's Cookin' in Melon Country, Rocky Ford Chamber of Commerce, Rocky, Ford, CO

Wild Man Gourmet ©2004 JB Publications, Stagecoach, NV

A Little Bit About
Dutch Oven Cooking

OVEN SIZES AND QUANTITIES

8-inch	**2 quarts**	(vegetables, baked beans)
10-inch	**4 quarts**	(baked bread, rolls, small cobblers)
12-inch	**6 quarts**	(most common size used for main dishes)
14-inch	**8 quarts**	(main dishes and cobblers; when cooking for large groups)

COALS NEEDED FOR VARIOUS HEAT-DEGREE

12–15 coals 300°	**16–20 coals 400°**
13–17 coals 325°	**17–22 coals 425°**
14–18 coals 350°	**18–23 coals 450°**
15–19 coals 375°	**19–24 coals 475°**

Coals are ready to use when they are mostly gray in color. If longer cooking time is called for, you will need to start an additional batch of briquettes about the end of the first hour to add as needed. Your oven will function better if you get it as level as possible.

Make sure your lid is set on securely to make a good seal. The heavy lid will act as a pressure cooker when set on correctly. Rotate your oven and lid 90° about every 10–15 minutes while cooking. This will rotate the hot spots and prevent over-cooking the food in one area.

Roasting: Use equal heat on top and underneath.

Stewing or Simmering: Use a 4/1 ratio.

Frying or boiling: All the heat goes underneath.

Baking: Use a 1/3 ratio, one being the number of coals on the bottom and 3 the number on top. When fixing a fire for baking of cobblers, upside down cake, cake, cookies, pies, etc., most of the heat must be on top so you will use a checkerboard pattern on the bottom of only 6–8 briquettes and 18–24 on top in a circle pattern.

Index

DENVER METRO CONVENTION AND VISITORS BUREAU

Nestled in the Rocky Mountain Foothills fifteen miles west of Denver, Colorado, Red Rocks is a geologically formed, open-air amphitheatre unlike any other in the world. The amphitheatre consists of two, three-hundred-foot monoliths (Ship Rock and Creation Rock) that provide acoustic perfection for any performance.

Frostings and Icings:
  Almond Cream Cheese Frosting 239
  Butter Cream Frosting 226
  Chocolate-Covered Cherry Cookies
    Frosting 228
  Cream Cheese Frosting 205, 206,
    227
  Creamy Chocolate Frosting 207
  Melt-Aways Frosting 229
  Orange Cream Cheese Frosting 204
Frozen Cranberry Salad 101
Fruit: *see also specific fruits*
  India Slaw Salad 91
  Indian Paintbrush Fruit Salad 100
  Sunny Fruit Fiesta 100
  Wagon Wheel Cookies 230
Fudgy Brownies 240

Gabby's No-Peek Prime Ribber 146
Garlic and Chili-Rubbed Buffalo Steaks
  167
Gayle's Chicken Tortilla Soup 72
Genoa Candy Dance Fudge 242
German Cabbage Burgers 147
German Chocolate Cheesecake 221
German Potato Salad 99
Glen Canyon Dip 17
Gourmet Grits Casserole 132
Gourmet Tenderloin with Wine Sauce
  138
Great Salt Lake Taffy 244
Green Chicken Enchiladas 181
Green Chili and Bean Soup 66
Grilled Chicken with Herbs 171
Grilled Stuffed Onions 117
Grilled T-Bone 240 140
Grilled Teriyaki Fish 190
Grilled Trout Fillets with Tomato Butter
  194
Grits Casserole, Gourmet 132
Gym Rat's Oven Baked Chicken Strips
  178

Halibut Supreme 195
Ham:
  All American Marmalade Glazed Ham
    164
  Dove Creek "Pinto Bean Capital of
    the World" Beans 109
  Ham Quiche Biscuit Cups 48
  Ham Spread 18

Hearty Potato-Ham Chowder 79
Hoppin' John Squares 132
Split Pea Soup with Ham 74
Ultimate Jambalaya 131
Hearty Basque Style Casserole 151
Hearty Potato-Ham Chowder 79
Herbed Vinaigrette Dressing 102
Here's to the USA Crostini 20
Homemade Chicken Noodle Soup over
  Mashed Potatoes 73
Hoppin' John Squares 132
Hot & Spicy Ribbon Chips 20
Hot and Spicy Onion Rings 117
Hot Artichoke Dip 16
Hot Crab Open Faces 200
Hot Mushroom Turnovers 22

Independence Day Barbecue Spare Ribs
  157
India Slaw Salad 91
Indian Paintbrush Fruit Salad 100
Italian Hero Loaf 64
Italian Zucchini Crescent Pie 112

Jealous Bourbon BBQ Sauce 154
Johnny Cakes 51
Jumbo Double Chocolate Chip Cookies
  233

Khemosabi Quiche 56

Lamb Stew with Garlic and Pinot Noir
  165
Lemon Bars 237
Lemon Garlic Shrimp 26
Let Freedom Ring Buttermilk Drop
  Biscuits 35
Let Them Eat Cake 207
Light and Healthy Bean Soup 66
Lion House Pie Dough 248
Lobster/Gourmet Tenderloin with Wine
  Sauce 138
Long's Peak Baked Beans 108
Low Fat Stir-Fried Veggies 114
Luscious Lemon Cake 211

Magic Cookie Bars 236
Mahi Mahi with Low-Fat Cucumber
  Sauce 191

INDEX

The recipes included in the REGIONAL COOKBOOK SERIES
have been collected from the

BEST OF THE BEST STATE COOKBOOK SERIES

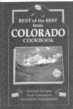

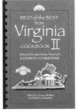

Best of the Best from the Mountain West Cookbook
Selected Recipes from the Favorite Cookbooks of Colorado, Utah, and Nevada

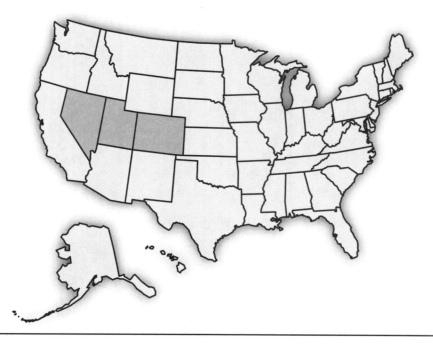

Best of the Best Regional Cookbook Series
(7x10 • layflat paperbound • 288 pages)

1. Deep South
Louisiana, Mississippi, Alabama

2. East Coast
Delaware, New Jersey, Washington DC, Virginia, North Carolina

3. Plains
Idaho, Montana, Wyoming, North Dakota, South Dakota, Nebraska, Kansas

4. Southeast
South Carolina, Georgia, Florida

5. Midwest
Iowa, Illinois, Indiana, Ohio

6. Pacific Rim
Washington, Oregon, California, Alaska, Hawaii

7. Mid-South
Tennessee, Kentucky, West Virginia

8. Southwest
Texas, New Mexico, Arizona

9. Great Lakes
Michigan, Minnesota, Wisconsin

10. Mid-America
Missouri, Arkansas, Oklahoma

11. Mountain West
Colorado, Utah, Nevada

12. Northeast
New York, Pennsylvania, Massachusetts, Connecticut, Vermont, New Hampshire, Rhode Island, Maine